AZTLÁN

AZTLÁN

Essays on the Chicano Homeland

Rudolfo A. Anaya
Francisco A. Lomelí

University of New Mexico Press
Albuquerque

ISBN 0-8263-1261-6
Library of Congress Catalog Card No. 89-083-942

Cover design *"Las Garzas de Aztlán"* by Delilah.

El Norte Publications is the publishing arm of Academia, a non-profit
corporation whose goal is to preserve and disseminate the culture and
art of New Mexico.

Table of Contents

Acknowledgments

"ABC: Aztlán, the Borderlands, and Chicago" was originally published in *Missions in Conflict: Essays on U.S.-Mexican Relations and Chicano Culture*. Von Bardeleben, Renate et al. Tübingen, West Germany: Gunter Narr Verlag, 1986, pp. 13-23. It appears here by permission of the author.

"Return to Aztlán: The Chicano Rediscovers His Indian Past" was previously published in *The Chicanos, As We See Ourselves*. Arnulfo Trejo, editor. Tucson, Arizona: University of Arizona Press, 1979.

"Aztlán: Mito y conciencia histórica del chicano" appeared originally in *El Oficio*, núm. 6 (Septiembre, 1987), pp. 45-59. Secretaría de Educación y Bienestar Social: Dirección de Asuntos Culturales, Mexicali, Baja California, México.

"Aztlán, Cíbola, and Frontier New Spain" was first published in *Campo Libre* 1 (Summer, 1981: pp. 193-211) then as chapter 1 of *The Lost Land/The Chicano Image of the Southwest*, pp. 7-22. Copyright 1984 by the University of New Mexico Press, Albuquerque, New Mexico.

"The Homeland, Aztlán/El Otro México" was published in *Borderlands/La Frontera: The New Mestiza*, 1987, Spinster/Aunt Lute Book Company, P.O. Box 410687, San Francisco, CA 94141.

"Myth, Identity and Struggle in Three Chicano Novels: Aztlán... Anaya, Méndez and Acosta" was previously published in *Missions in Conflict: Essays on U.S.-Mexican Relations and Chicano Culture*. Von Bardeleben, Renate et al. Tübingen, West Germany, Gunter Narr Verlag, 1986.

"In Search of Aztlán" appeared in *The Denver Quarterly*, 16, No. 3 (Fall, 1981), pp. 16-22. Reprinted in *Aztlán y México: Perfiles literarios e históricos*, Luis Leal. Binghamton, NY: Bilingual Press, pp. 21-28.

i

Introduction

The concept of homeland occupies a central position in the thought and development of most cultures. In some, as in Native American cultures of the Southwest, the place of origin is crucial to spiritual orientation. For other groups of people, such as the Hispanic community of this country, defining the origins of a homeland was a necessity for survival.

Knowledge of the homeland provides an important element of identity. The Mexican American community in this country in the 1960s lived at the margin of the society, and thus at the margin of history. If it was to exist as a viable Hispanic community within the confines of the country, it had to define and assert its identity, and so the Chicanos reappropriated Aztlán as their homeland. The concept became the rallying cry of the Chicano Movement and a turning point in the Hispanic reaffirmation known as a contemporary renaissance period.

For Chicanos the concept of Aztlán signalled a unifying point of cohesion through which they could define the foundations for an identity. Aztlán brought together a culture that had been somewhat disjointed and dispersed, allowing it, for the first time, a framework within which to understand itself. During the decade from 1965-1975, Chicanos not only demonstrated in the streets to increase their opportunities and status, they also struggled to define a sense of a mythic past and history in order to recapture what official history had omitted. Aztlán became a collective symbol by which to recover the past that had been wrestled away from the inhabitants of Aztlán through the multiple conquests of the area. It should be kept in mind that by reappropriating Aztlán the Chicano did not choose to live in the past; rather, the community chose to find its tap root of identity in its history so that it could more confidently create the future.

The conquests of Aztlán, first by the Spaniards and then by Anglo Americans, have transformed the social fabrics of the region, but its mythic dimension never vanished. There lies its power and fascination. Chicano scholarship has grappled with the concept of Aztlán over the past quarter century, and it has vigorously analyzed the many assumptions which exist concerning Aztlán's historical/anthropological/symbolic nature. Nevertheless, the legend which embodies Aztlán caught the Chicano community's fancy with such persuasion that few bothered to examine its pluralistic meanings and its intrinsically mysterious constitution.

Where did the legend of Aztlán originate and what are its artistic, social, and political ramifications? That is the central question we hope to answer through this collection of studies. We do not intend to provide definitive resolutions about Aztlán; rather, the intent is to contribute to the discussion and examination of a concept that has attracted much commitment in terms of political discourse and literary substance. The result, we hope, is the attainment of a clearer delineation of cultural identity by defining a modern mythopoetics that is relevant to Chicanos.

Aztlán offers a variety of meanings for Chicanos. The term "Aztlán" helped establish the context for the acceptance and promotion of a single umbrella term under which we could fit the various labels we call ourselves. For some, Aztlán may appear to be an anachronism from the pages of Aztec or Náhuatl mythology that was lost in the annals of Native American history. The revival of it by Hispanicized mestizos attests to the role of myth in a culture where facts do not outweigh faith, beliefs, or the power of oral tradition. The legend of Aztlán never died; it was only dormant in the collective unconscious. For people of Mexican descent, Aztlán exists at the level of symbol and archetype. It is a symbol which speaks of origins and ancestors, and it is a symbol of what we imagine ourselves to be. It embodies a human perspective of time and place.

All cultures have followed a similar path in defining themselves, ours is no different. The circumstances and the details may be unique, but the process is universal. For those who yearn to know the origins of their history in this continent, Aztlán is anthropologically sound and historically reliable.

For all groups or nations myth offers a core of common meaning and generally accepted values. The element of identity is but a fragment of the totality that permits the experiencing of origins as a comfort zone which enhances our development. Aztlán localizes this process in a particular milieu in relation to a complex network of historical events and happenings. In other words, through Aztlán we come to better understand psychological time (identity), regional makeup (place), and evolution (historical time). Without any one of these ingredients, we would be contemporary displaced nomads, suffering the diaspora in our own land, and at the mercy of other social forces. Aztlán allows us to come full circle with our communal background as well as to maintain ourselves as fully integrated individuals.

This collection of articles aims to expand on the previous singular treatment of the subject. The interface is through a variety of perspectives and methodologies but the central focus is to give shape to the topic of homeland as a viable way to delineate a culture's trajectory and existence. By bringing together such a wide spectrum of views and approaches, we hope to contribute to the understanding of Aztlán as a uniquely mythological concept that has relevance in our present day. The approaches of the scholars in this collection range from historical and anthropological explorations to comparative cultural analyses, and from symbolic treatments in literary works to interpretations of myth as the backdrop of beliefs that are accepted as truth. No longer can Aztlán be viewed as an isolated case study; its social ramifications go beyond the individual to encompass our collective history.

El Plan Espiritual de Aztlán

In the spirit of a new people that is conscious not only of its proud historical heritage but also of the brutal "gringo" invasion of our territories, *we*, the Chicano inhabitants and civilizers of the northern land of Aztlán from whence came our forefathers, reclaiming the land of their birth and consecrating the determination of our people of the sun, *declare* that the call of our blood is our power, our responsibility, and our inevitable destiny.

We are free and sovereign to determine those tasks which are justly called for by our house, our land, the sweat of our brows, and by our hearts. Aztlán belongs to those who plant the seeds, water the fields, and gather the crops and not to the foreign Europeans. We do not recognize capricious frontiers on the bronze continents.

Brotherhood unites us, and love for our brothers makes us a people whose time has come and who struggles against the foreigner "gabacho" who exploits our riches and destroys our culture. With our heart in our hands and our hands in the soil, we declare the independence of our mestizo nation. We are a bronze people with a bronze culture. Before the world, before all of North America, before all our brothers in the bronze continent, we are a nation, we are a union of free pueblos, we are *Aztlán*.

Program

El Plan Espiritual de Aztlán sets the theme that the Chicanos (La Raza de Bronze) must use their nationalism as the key or common denominator for mass mobilization and organization. Once we are committed to the idea and philosophy of El Plan de Aztlán, we can only conclude that social, economic, cultural and political independence is the only road to total liberation from oppression, exploitation, and racism. Our struggle then must be for the control of our barrios, campos, pueblos, lands, our economy, our culture, and our political life. El Plan commits all levels of Chicano society—the barrio, the campo, the ranchero, the writer, the teacher, the worker, the professional—to La Causa.

Nationalism

Nationalism as the key to organization transcends all religious, political, class, and economic factions or boundaries. Nationalism is the common denominator that all members of La Raza can agree upon.

Organizational Goals

1. UNITY in the thinking of our people concerning the barrios, the pueblo, the campo, the land, the poor, the middle class, the professional—all committed to the liberation of La Raza.

2. ECONOMY: economic control of our lives and our communities can only come about by driving the exploiter out of our communities, our pueblos, and our lands and by controlling and developing our own talents, sweat, and resources. Cultural background and values which ignore materialism and embrace humanism will contribute to the act of cooperative buying and the distribution of resources and production to sustain an economic base for healthy growth and development. Lands rightfully ours will be fought for and defended. Land and realty ownership will be acquired by the community for the people's welfare. Economic ties of responsibility must be secured by nationalism and the Chicano defense units.

3. EDUCATION must be relative to our people, i.e., history, culture, bilingual education, contributions, etc. Community control of our schools, our teachers, our administrators, our counselors, and our programs.

4. INSTITUTIONS shall serve our people by providing the service necessary for a full life and their welfare on the basis of restitution, not hand-outs or beggar's crumbs. Restitution for past economic slavery, political exploitation, ethnic and cultural psychological destruction and denial of civil and human rights. Institutions in our community which do not serve the people have no place in the community. The institutions belong to the, people.

5. SELF-DEFENSE of the community must rely on the combined strength of the people. The front line defense will come from the barrios, the campos, the pueblos, and the ranchitos. Their involvement as protectors of their people will be given respect and dignity. They in turn offer their responsibility and their lives for their people. Those who place themselves in the front ranks for their people do so out of love and carnalismo. Those institutions which are fattened by our brothers to provide employment and political pork barrels for the gringo will do so only as acts of liberation and for La Causa. For the very young there will no longer be acts of juvenile delinquency, but revolutionary acts.

6. CULTURAL values of our people strengthen our identity and the moral backbone of the movement. Our culture unites and educates the family of La Raza towards liberation with one heart and one mind. We must insure that our writers, poets, musicians, and artists produce literature and art that is appealing to our people and relates to our revolutionary culture. Our cultural values of life, family, and home will serve as a powerful weapon to defeat the gringo dollar value system and encourage the process of love and brotherhood.

7. POLITICAL LIBERATION can only come through independent action on our part, since the two-party system is the same animal with two heads that feed from the same trough. Where we are a majority, we will con-

trol; where we are a minority, we will represent a pressure group; nationally, we will represent one party: La Familia de la Raza!

Action

1. Awareness and distribution of El Plan Espiritual de Aztlán. Presented at every meeting, demonstration, confrontation, courthouse, institution, administration, church, school, tree, building, car, and every place of human existence.

2. September 16, on the birthdate of Mexican Independence, a national walk-out by all Chicanos of all colleges and schools to be sustained until the complete revision of the educational system: its policy makers, administration, its curriculum, and its personnel to meet the needs of our community.

3. Self-defense against the occupying forces of the oppressors at every school, every available man, woman, and child.

4. Community nationalization and organization of all Chicanos: El Plan Espiritual de Aztlán.

5. Economic program to drive the exploiter out of our community and a welding together of our people's combined resources to control their own production through cooperative effort.

6. Creation of an independent local, regional, and national political party.

A nation autonomous and free—culturally, socially, economically, and politically—will make its own decisions on the usage of our lands, the taxation of our goods, the utilization of our bodies for war, the determination of justice (reward and punishment), and the profit of our sweat.

El Plan de Aztlán is the plan of liberation!

The *Plan de Aztlán*, which was written at the First Chicano National Conference in Denver, Colorado in 1969, is the ideological framework and concrete political program of the Chicano Movement because of its emphasis on nationalism and the goal of self-determination.

Source: *Documents of the Chicano Struggle,* Pathfinder Press, Inc. 1971.

In Search Of Aztlán

Luis Leal

Translated by Gladys Leal

One of the functions of the critic is to discover and analyze literary symbols with the object of broadening the perception that one has of a certain social or national group, or of humanity in general. In the case of Chicano literature, a literature that has emerged as a consequence of the fight for social and human rights, most of the symbols have been taken from the surrounding social environment.

For that reason Chicano literary symbolism cannot be separated from Chicano cultural background. In order to study this symbolism, it is necessary to see it in context with the social ideas that predominate in Chicano contemporary thought. Therefore, we must consult the large bibliography that already exists regarding the social, racial, linguistic, and educational problems which the Chicano has confronted since 1848. The social and literary symbols, as we shall see, are the same. Their origin is found in the socio-political struggle, from where they have passed on to literature.

The symbols which have served to give unity to the Chicano movement and which appear in literature are many: Aztlán, the black eagle of the farm workers, the Virgin of Guadalupe, *la huelga*, the expression¡*Viva la Raza!*, and the characteristic handshake, the latter, of course, being outside of the literary field. The greatest part of these symbols, which give form to the concept of *chicanismo*, are of recent origin; they were born with the political and social movement which was initiated with the strike in Delano in 1965. But they have their roots in Mexico's historic past. The Virgin of Guadalupe was one of the symbols that helped to create Mexican nationality and political independence, her image having been hoisted by Father Miguel Hidalgo in 1810. The eagle of the farmworkers has an older origin, the foundation of Tenochtitlán by the Aztecs in 1325, where the people from Aztlán found on an island an eagle sitting on a nopal devouring a serpent. César Chávez, the creator of this Chicano symbol, has said:

> I wanted desperately to get some color into the movement, to give people something they could identify with, like a flag. I was reading some books about how various leaders discovered what colors contrasted and stood out the best. The Egyptians had found that a red field with a white circle and a black emblem in the center crashed into your eyes like nothing else. I wanted to use the Aztec eagle in the center, as on the Mexican flag. So I told my cousin Manuel, "Draw an Aztec Eagle." Manuel had a little trouble with it, so we modified the eagle to make it easier for people to draw (*Ramparts Magazine*, July, 1966).

According to accepted definitions, the symbol is a sensory image which represents a concept or an emotion that cannot be expressed in its totality by any other method. The symbol expresses, with that sensory image, the significance of the spiritual. The image that we see reveals to us or makes us aware of the existence of something beyond the material. In other words, the sensory image, or symbol, is associated with a concept or an emotion (the symbolized thing). Therefore, it is necessary to interpret the symbol (the thing expressed) in terms of what is not expressed. Since the symbol can be social and not necessarily archetypal or mythical, it often has significance only for the group that has produced it; and also, frequently, only for the artist who has created it.

As a visual symbol, and not literary, the black eagle in the white circle over a red background symbolized for the Chicano the triumph over economic injustice by means of the farm workers' union, whose aim is to obtain a better standard of living, and also cultural identity. For those who are not Chicanos, the symbol loses its significance. Nevertheless, since the colors–red, black, and white–have a universal symbolic meaning the image has a broad emotional significance, but not necessarily the same for all as the one that the Chicano understands. At the same time the use of the eagle from the Mexican flag, and of the colors red and white, has a symbolic meaning for the Mexicano, since it reminds him of the national flag. The eagle, Aztlán, the Quinto Sol, and other Chicano symbols of Mexican origin form a part of a mythic system, a characteristic often attributed to the symbol.

Aztlán, which we propose to examine in this study, is as much symbol as it is myth. As a symbol, it conveys the image of the cave (or sometimes a hill) representative of the origin of man; and as a myth, it symbolized the existence of a paradisiacal region where injustice, evil, sickness, old age, poverty, and misery do not exist. As a Chicano symbol, Aztlán has two meanings: first, it represents the geographic region known as the Southwestern part of the United States, composed of the territory that Mexico ceded in 1848 with the Treaty of Guadalupe Hidalgo; second, and more important, Aztlán symbolized the spiritual union of the Chicanos, something that is carried within the heart, no matter where they may live or where they may find themselves.

As a region in mythical geography, Aztlán has a long history. According to the Nahuatl myth, the Aztecs were the last remaining tribe of seven, and they were advised by their god Huitzilopochtli to leave Aztlán in search of the promised land, which they would know by an eagle sitting on a nopal devouring a serpent. Later the Aztecs (whose name is derived from Aztlán) remembered the region of their origin as an earthly paradise. Already in the fifteenth century Moctezuma Ilhuicamina (ruler from 1440 to 1469) sent his priests in search of Aztlán. The historian Fray Diego Durán, in his *Historia de las Indias de Nueva España e Islas de Tierra Firme*, a work finished in 1581, says that Moctezuma I, desiring to know where their ancestors had lived, what form those seven caves had, and the relation between their history and their memory of it, sent for Cuauhcóatl, the royal historian, who told him:

"O mighty lord, I, your unworthy servant, can answer you.

Our forebears dwelt in that blissful, happy place called Aztlán, which means 'Whiteness.' In that place there is a great hill in the midst of the waters, and it is called Colhuacan because its summit is twisted; this is the Twisted Hill. On its slopes were caves or grottos where our fathers and grandfathers lived for many years. There they lived in leisure, when they were called Mexitin and Azteca. There they had at their disposal great flocks of ducks of different kinds, herons, water fowl, and cranes. Our ancestors loved the song and melody of the little birds with red and yellow heads. They also possessed many kinds of large beautiful fish. They had the freshness of groves of trees along the edge of the waters. They had springs surrounded by willows, evergreens and alders, all of them tall and comely. Our ancestors went about in canoes and made floating gardens upon which they sowed maize, chili, tomatoes, amaranth, beans and all kinds of seeds which we now eat and which were brought here from there.

"However, after they came to the mainland and abandoned that delightful place, everything turned against them. The weeds began to bite, the stones became sharp, the fields were filled with thistles and spines. They encountered brambles and thorns that were difficult to pass through. There was no place to sit, there was no place to rest; everything became filled with vipers, snakes, poisonous little animals, jaguars and wildcats and other ferocious beasts. And this is what our ancestors forsook. I have found it painted in our ancient books. And this, O powerful king, is the answer I can give you to what you ask of me." [*The Aztecs*, (1964), p. 134. Trans. Doris Heyden]

Moctezuma Ilhuicamina called for all of his sorcerers and magicians and sent them in search of Aztlán and of Coatlicue, the mother of Huitzilopochtli. The sorcerers in Coatepec, a province of Tula, transformed themselves through the art of magic into birds, tigers, lions, jackals, and wildcats, and in this way arrived at that lagoon in the middle of which is the hill of Culhuacan. They again took the form of humans and asked for Coatlicue, "and the place which their ancestors left, which was called Chicomostoc (seven caves)."

The emissaries were taken in canoes to the island of Aztlán, where the hill is. "They say," relates Durán, "that the top half of the hill is made up of a very fine sand." There they found Coatlicue, who demonstrated to them that in Aztlán men never become old. She tells them:

"Stop so that you can see how men never become old in this country! Do you see my old servant? Watch him climb down the hill! By the time he reaches you he will be a young man."

The old man descended and as he ran he became younger and younger. When he reached the Aztec wizards, he appeared to be about twenty years old. Said he, "Behold, my sons, the virtue of this hill; the old man who seeks youth can climb to the point on the hill that he wishes and there he will acquire the age that he seeks." [Trans. Doris Heyden, p. 138.]

The emissaries again transformed themselves into animals in order to make the return trip, which many of them did not succeed in completing because of having been eaten by wild beasts on the way.

That is the Aztlán of the Aztec myth, the Aztlán that, like the mythical Atlantis, has never been pinpointed in geography. The seach for it, like that for the Fountain of Youth, has never ceased. Cecilio Robelo, the Mexican historian of Nahuatl mythology, tells us, "It is generally believed that Aztlán was located to the north of the Gulf of California." But not even that conjecture is accepted, since later he adds, "The inexorable question, then, of the place where the Mexica came from, still remains." And the inexorable question still stands, in spite of the efforts of erudite historians, whether they be Mexican, European, or American, such as Clavijero, Humboldt, Prescott, Orozco y Berra, Eustaquio Buelna, Chavero, Fernando Ramirez, Lapham, Wickersham, or Seler. There was even a book published in 1933 entitled *Aztalán*, trying to prove that Aztlán can be found in the lakes of Wisconsin. Others have said that it was in Florida; others believe that it was in New Mexico; and still others in California. It was even said that Aztlán was to be found in China. The historian of Santa Barbara, Russell A. Ruiz, in a pamphlet published during the summer of 1969 which treats of the passing of the expedition of Portalá through the region, tells us that when the Governor arrived on the 20th of August, 1769, at what is today Goleta, he baptized the land with the name Pueblos de la Isla, which Father Crespí, who accompanied him, called Santa Margarita de Cortona, and to which the soldiers gave the name Mescaltitlan, believing that they had found themselves in the legendary place of origin of the Aztecs. In a word, Ruiz says, "Mescaltitlan was another name for Aztlán, the legendary place of origin of the Aztecs or Mexican people. The Aztecs described it as a terrestrial paradise." (p. 11)

What interests us is not determining where Aztlán is found, but documenting the rebirth of the myth in Chicano thought. It is necessary to point out the fact that before March, 1969, the date of the Denver Conference, no one talked about Aztlán. In fact, the first time that it was mentioned in a Chicano document was in "El Plan Espiritual de Aztlán," which was presented in Denver at that time. Apparently, it owes its creation to the poet Alurista who already, during the Autumn of 1968, had spoken about Aztlán in a class for Chicanos held at San Diego State University.

"El Plan Espiritual de Aztlán" is important because in it the Chicano recognizes his Aztec origins ("We, the Chicano inhabitants and civilizers of the northern land of Aztlán, from whence came our forefathers..."); because it established that Aztlán is the Mexican territory ceded to the United States in 1848; and because, following one of the basic ideas of the Mexican Revolution, it recognizes that the land belongs to those who work it ("Aztlán belongs to those that plant the seeds, water the fields, and gather the crops"); and finally, it identifies the Chicano with Aztlán ("We are a nation, we are a union of free pueblos, we are AZTLÁN").

Those words were published in March of 1969. Beginning with that date, Aztlán has become the symbol most used by Chicano authors who write about the history, the culture, or the destiny of their people; and the same thing occurs with those who write poetic novels or short stories. During the spring of the following year, 1970, the first number of the journal *Aztlán* was published, and in it the *Plan* was reproduced in both English and Spanish. The prologue consists of a poem by Alurista called "Poem in Lieu of Preface," which united the mythical Aztec past with the present:

> it is said
>> that MOTECUHZOMA ILHUICAMINA
> SENT
>> AN expedition
> looking for the NortherN

                          mYthical land
            wherefrom the AZTECS CAME
                          la TIERRA
                                dE
                            AztláN
                    mYthical land for those
                    who dream of roses and
swallow thorns
                        or for those who swallow thorns
                    in powdered milk
            feeling guilty about smelling flowers
                            about looking for AztláN (p. ix)

In the following year, Alurista published the anthology *El ombligo de
Aztlán*, and a year later his *Nationchild-Plumaroja* appeared, published in
San Diego by Toltecas de Aztlán. The title "Nationchild" refers, of course,
to the Chicanos of Aztlán. From here on books in whose title the word
Aztlán appears would multiply.

    In fiction also, especially in the novel, the symbol has been utilized with
advantage for artistic creation. The novels of Méndez, *Peregrinos de Aztlán*
(1974), and of Anaya, *Heart of Aztlán* (1976), are works representative of
that tendency. It is fitting to point out that both works have antecedents in
Mexican narrative. In 1944 Gregorio López y Fuentes published his novel
Los peregrinos inmóviles, and in 1949 María de Lourdes Hernández printed hers, *En el nuevo Aztlán*. There is no direct influence between these Mexican and Chicano novels. Nevertheless, the elements that they have in
common are significant and permit us to make a comparison. The theme of
Los peregrinos inmóviles is the search for the promised land; in that novel
López y Fuentes recreates the mythical pilgrimage of the Aztecs. In
Peregrinos de Aztlán the theme is identical, only that the pilgrimage is in
reverse. We read in Méndez' novel: "My imagination got the best of me and
I saw a pilgrimage of many Indian people who were being trod upon by the
torture of hunger and the humiliation of despoilment, running back through
ancient roads in search of their remote origin." López y Fuentes had already
written: "We walked all afternoon and part of the night....We were going to
the land of abundance: that was the message of the eagle, and we were on the

right track." Another important coincidence is that in both works the narrator is an old Indian who remembers the history of his village. For the old Yaqui Loreto Maldonado, in Tijuana, the memories of his fallen and abused people torment him; and for the old Marcos, the memory of the original pilgrimage gives him courage to guide his own people. The first part of *Los peregrinos inmóviles* is entitled "Heart of the World." And years later, Rudy Anaya would publish his novel with the title *Heart of Aztlán*, in which there is also a pilgrimage which the protagonist makes in search of Aztlán in a vision. Here he has the help of a magic stone instead of the eagle.

A greater similarity exists between *Heart of Aztlán* and *En el nuevo Aztlán*. In both novels the theme is the search for Aztlán, the lost paradise. In the work of Hernández a group of Aztecs, immediately after the fall of Cuauhtémoc, takes refuge in a secret valley to which they can travel only by means of a mysterious river which runs inside the grottos of Cacahuamilpa. In that valley they founded a kind of Shangri-La, a perfect society. In the novel of Anaya, which develops in the barrio in Albuquerque, the protagonist Clemente Chávez, not an old man but a man of some years, goes to the mountains, guided by the blind minstrel Crispín, in search of Aztlán on a truly imaginary pilgrimage:

> They moved north, and there Aztlán was a woman fringed with snow and ice; they moved west, and there she was a mermaid singing by the sea...They walked to the land where the sun rises, and...they found new signs, and the signs pointed them back to the center, back to Aztlán. (1976: pp. 129-30)

It is here where they find Aztlán, Aztlán is the center:

> Time stood still, and in that enduring moment he felt the rhythm of the heart of Aztlán beat to the measure of his own heart. Dreams and visions became reality, and reality was but the thin substance of myth and legends. A joyful power coursed from the dark womb-heart of the earth into his soul and he cried out I AM AZTLÁN! (p. 131)

The search, for Clemente, has ended. And that is the way it must be for all Chicanos: whosoever wants to find Aztlán, let him look for it, not on the maps, but in the most intimate part of his being.

The Archaic, Historical and Mythicized Dimensions of Aztlán

Michael Pina

According to Cecilio Robelo's *Diccionario de mitología náhuatl,* Aztlán is a synizesis or contraction of the Nahuatl word *Aztatlan: aztatl,* heron; *tlan,* together; close together: (place near/of the [white] herons) or place originally occupied by *los mexicanos,* from which came their name of *Aztecas.* Its location has been the object of innumerable investigations, and remains unknown even today. It is generally believed to have been north of the gulf of California.[1]

Aztlán constitutes the primordial homeland of the Aztec people whose location and nature have been investigated over the past five-hundred years. Throughout this span, individuals from radically different temporal, ideological, and existential contexts have explored various dimensions of this myth. Most frequently their questions have focused on discovering the geographical location of Aztlán. First sought by religious emissaries dispatched by Moctezuma Ilhuicamina from Tenochtitlan in the mid-fifteenth century, the Aztec quest for Aztlán can be interpreted as an attempt to reconnect with their remote origins and the ancestors left behind as they journeyed southward to establish their empire and fulfill their destiny. They were seeking the power and authority that resides in that time-space interval that Mircea Eliade designates as *in illo tempore* or "in the beginning," perhaps to sanctify their reign over Anáhuac "the land encircled by water." A much different quest for Aztlán has been pursued by scientific investigators working throughout the past three centuries. This search for the "historical" Aztlán has been conducted by academics from various disciplines who approach myth from a more skeptical, interpretive context. Their perspective can be collectively referred to as Historicism. This approach assumes the ability to *de-mythologize* the myths of others, that is, to reduce myth to allegorical tales, proper to a prescientific worldview, but inadequate as a contemporary mode of understanding. The most recent search for Aztlán occurred within the decades of the nineteen sixties and seventies as Chicano nationalists sought Aztlán as a spiritual homeland and the object of nation-building. They romanticized their cultural connections to the primordial inhabitants of Aztlán and relied upon them as a metaphysical justification for their political program. They lived within the horizon of a mythicized history that identified Aztlán as a Chicano nation. These individuals believed Aztlán to exist as a spiritual reality, and it was their duty to establish it as a political-territorial entity.

These three hermeneutic approaches to the myth of Aztlán illustrate the difficulty involved in myth interpretation. Each approach attaches a different significance to the myth and offers competing assertions concerning its truth. Rather than attempting to discern the relative merit of these approaches this study will utilize them as an analytical framework with which to explore archaic, historical, and living dimensions of this myth. These approaches to the myth of Aztlán provide useful distinctions with which to engage in a thorough descriptive analysis of the myth. This analysis aims to contribute to a more insightful understanding of the myth of Aztlán, in particular, and the phenomena of myth in general.

Part I of this study will engage in an exegesis of the available historical documents in order to reconstruct the Aztec narrative of the myth of Aztlán. This effort will be guided by a methodological attitude known as structured empathy.[2] This attitude attempts to get "inside" Aztec experience of this myth through relying on knowledge of their cultural, historical, and religious contexts, the use of neutral descriptive categories and language, and the avoidance of evaluative bias through the suspension of judgment. The effort is to arrive at a narrative that resonates with the truth of the archaic believers, while expressing it in a language that communicates with the non-believer.

Tezozómoc's *Crónica Mexicáyotl* will serve as the main reference source in reconstructing this narrative, as it is representative of the information provided by other colonial-era chronicles. However, information from other documents contemporary to Tezozómoc's, such as the *Códice Aubin, Códice Ramírez, Anales de Tlatelolco* and *Historia Chichimeca* will be included. In addition to the chronicles there are the historical monographs composed mainly by Spanish ecclesiastics. Although these texts were written with the intention of stamping out any traces of indigenous spirituality, if approached from a critical perspective they can provide a wealth of information concerning indigenous thought and culture. The value of these texts stems from the fact that they relied extensively on indigenous informants with access to pre-Hispanic picturebooks most of which have long since disappeared. The texts that this study will draw from are: Fray Diego Durán's *Historia de las Indias de Nueva España e Isla de Tierra Firme* and Fray Bernardino de Sahagún's *Historia de las cosas de la Nueva España*. In addition to these previously mentioned texts, this study will consider historical works that were penned in a more contemporary era, such as the Jesuit Clavijero's *Historia antigua de México*, and Manuel Orozco y Berra's *Historia antigua de la conquista de México*, that was published in the early 1880's. This collection of texts provides ample information from which a descriptively accurate account of the Aztec narrative concerning the myth of Aztlán can be established.

Part II of this study will analyze the manner in which the myth of Aztlán has been interpreted from the perspective of historicism or what might be referred to as the "myth of history." This approach stands in contrast to the archaic consciousness from which the *sacred history* of Aztlán issued. This modern tradition of myth interpretation is implicit to the historical monographs patterned after the investigative methods of the European Enlightenment and their intellectual precursors. It is a perspective that is largely concerned with questions of an empirical nature which explains the emphasis that these types of studies place on discovering the "historical" location of Aztlán. This question involves utilizing scientific reasoning to extract "historical" facts from the mass of myths inherent to a "primitive" consciousness. This approach operates from a worldview that remains phenomenologically "outside" of archaic mythologies such as Aztlán. The reconstruction of this type of historical analysis of the myth will work with the same documentary sources as in Part I, however, their contents will be interpreted in light of the critical attitude implicit to contemporary works such as volumes fourteen and fifteen of the *Handbook of Middle American Indians: A Guide to Ethnographic Sources*, and Benjamin Keen's *The Aztec Image In Western Thought*. These additional sources reveal the theoretical framework inherent to modern academic approaches to myth interpretation, as well as providing critiques of the main historiographies concerning the Aztecs and the myth of Aztlán.

Part III represents a radical departure from the empathetic reconstruction of the archaic myth of Aztlán and the antagonistic analytical study of its historical nature. The concern in this instance lies with exploring Aztlán as a *living myth* within the context of the Chicano nationalist movement. During the height of this movement Chicanos were existentially situated *inside* a mythic horizon that interpreted Aztlán as a vital element of their cultural heritage and political ideology. To understand the power that this myth held during this volatile period of Chicano history, this study will critique three distinct Chicano nationalist documents which illustrate the influence this myth exercised upon this movement: 1) the political program known as *El Plan Espiritual de Aztlán*; 2) poems from the Festival de Flor y Canto thematically concerned with the myth of Aztlán; 3) the novel by Rudolfo Anaya entitled *Heart of Aztlán*. These documentary sources reveal the depth of the Chicano commitment to the myth and symbol of Aztlán. It was embraced by a community in search of self-knowledge and self-determination and emerged as an undeniable inspiration that manifested itself in art, literature, and politics. The ubiquitous nature of Aztlán's hold upon Chicano nationalist thought and imagination reveals its vitality as a *living myth*.

Reconstructing the Archaic Myth of Aztlán

Describing the myth of Aztlán in a manner that reflects the archaic consciousness of the Aztec people requires an empathetic venture into a distant worldview characterized by unfamiliar myths, doctrines, rituals, and experiences. It requires an awareness that the Aztec cosmos was dominated by supernatural forces which modern people have long since dismissed as "superstitious" or "mythological." In order to understand the Aztec relationship to the myth of Aztlán the modern attitude that assumes the ability to render judgment on the veracity of archaic myths must be suspended. The truth claims of the Aztec people must be taken seriously, as the intention of this reconstruction is to present the Aztec narrative of Aztlán as accurately as possible.

The discipline known as the History of Religions offers an approach well suited to the analysis of the structure and function of myth within archaic cultural settings. One of its foremost spokespersons, Mircea Eliade, offers the following definition which will serve as a frame of reference in the discussion of the myth of Aztlán in its archaic context:

> In general it can be said that myth, as experienced by archaic societies, (1) constitutes the History of the acts of the Super-naturals; (2) that this History is considered to be absolutely *true* (because it is concerned with realities) and *sacred* (because it is the work of the Supernaturals); (3) that myth is always related to a "creation," it tells how something came into existence, or how a pattern of behavior, an institution, a manner of working were established; this is why myths constitute the paradigms for all significant human acts; (4) that by knowing the myth one knows the "origins" of things and hence can control and manipulate them at will; this is not "external," "abstract" knowledge but a knowledge that one "experiences" ritually, either by ceremonially recounting the myth or by performing the ritual for which it is the justification; (5) that in one way or another one "lives" the myth, in the sense that one is seized by the sacred, exalted power of the events recollected or re-enacted.[3]

Eliade's schema for defining myth provides descriptive categories well suited to reconstruction of the myth of Aztlán. This myth corresponds to the general morphology which he outlines as it is concerned with the acts of the Supernaturals. One of the main figures in the unfolding of this *sacred history* is the cultural hero Huitzilopochtli (Hummingbird of the south or left). This figure is cast alternatively as an earthbound leader and all powerful deity as he guides the Aztecs on their peregrination from Aztlán to Tenochtitlan. The narrative surrounding this journey recalls how the ancient Aztecs acquired knowledge, technology, and sacred authority on their southward trek. Although centuries had passed between the time the Aztecs exited their primordial homeland and established themselves in the central valley of México, they continued to have faith in the truth of this myth. The strength of this faith was demonstrated when Moctezuma Ilhuicamina dispatched priestly emissaries to retrace the route travelled by the ancients and locate Aztlán. This event marked the powerful role that myth played in the lives of archaic civilizations and the worldview that did not separate the natural and supernatural realms.

The narrative of Aztlán recounts the events of the peregrination of the Aztec people from a northern homeland of Aztlán to the founding of their empire of Tenochtitlan. Aztlán, which is also referred to as *Chicomóztoc*, place of the seven caves, is described as a place surrounded by water from which seven *calpulli* [clans/peoples] set out in a southerly direction in search of their destiny. During the course of their journey the Aztecs experienced important cultural transformations which prepared them to fulfill their divine calling. Upon their exit from Aztlán, roughly around the tenth century A.D., the Aztecs were considered lowly Chichimecas [literally "sons of dogs" or more figuratively "barbarians"], but by the time of their Mesoamerican conquests they had assimilated many of the cultural traditions of the much esteemed Toltecas. The arrival of the Aztecs on the fringes of the central valley of Mexico roughly coincides with the waning years of the Toltec empire at Tollan or Tula, which falls around 1168 A.D. Although they shared many cultural features with other nomadic tribes making their way into this territory, they differed from them in one significant respect, they spoke the Nahuatl language, which was common to both the Toltecs and many Teotihuacanos. By the time the Aztecs established their initial temple at Tenochtitlan in 1325 A.D., they had already acquired knowledge of calendrics, astronomy, architecture, agriculture and had assumed the ubiquitous deity/cultural hero, Quetzalcóatl, into their religious system.

Even with these great cultural adaptations the Aztecs remained unwelcomed immigrants into pre-Hispanic Mexico's central valley. The

area surrounding the Texcoco lake system was already densely populated
by peoples with long established communities. There were a numer of city-
states, such as Culhuacan, that traced a direct descendance from the
Toltecs. As the last group to enter this area the Aztecs were seen as intruders
and were driven from place to place within the lake region. They finally
established their complete independence after defeating the Tepenacas of
Azcapotzalco in 1428. From that date on their imperial power grew until the
arrival of the conquistadores and the fall of Tenochtitlan in 1521.

One of the most indispensable documents in the reconstruction of the
mythic narrative surrounding Aztlán is known as the *Códice Boturini*. This
document is considered to reflect in style, content, and format the traditional
pictorial manuscripts of preconquest times. Composed during the sixteenth
century outside the accepted bounds of Spanish patronage, it is fortunate
that it did not fall prey to the zealous flames of colonial proselytization. It
became part of a collection of Mexican Indian documents gathered by
Lorenzo Boturini Benaduci during the years 1736-1743. This codex portrays *la tira de la peregrinación de los Aztecs*, that is, their exit from Aztlán
until their arrival at the hill of Chapultepec and subjugation by the
Culhuacanos. A series of glyphs, ideographs, and phonetic symbols codices
such as this one assisted the indigenous storytellers' memories. Although
produced after the conquest, this text evidences the retention of a strong
sense of historical consciousness and identity among the indigenous
population.

Another excellent source in establishing the narrative of Aztlán is the
Crónica Mexicáyotl, penned in 1609 by Don Fernando or Hernando
Alvarado Tezozómoc. Tezozómoc was of indigenous ancestry and intended
his work to demonstrate his status as a noble and thus preserve the privileges
associated with this status. He was the son of Diego de Alvarado Huanitzin,
who served as *tlatoani* or ruler of Tenochtitlan under the Spaniards, and of
Francisca de Moctezuma, daughter of Moctezuma II. Much of his chronicle
is an elaborate genealogy of Mexica nobility wherein he locates himself and
his direct progenitors. Tezozómoc had access to a wide range of pictographi-
cal writings, oral informants, and prose narratives. From these diverse sources the author weaves an epic account of Mexica history, from their lowly
beginnings as wandering *Chichimecas* to their triumph over Azcapotzalco
and the establishment of their dominance over Anáhuac. He writes from a

particularly indigenous point of view, however, he is careful to avoid heaping too much praise upon the glories of the fallen empire:

> Writing at the turn of the sixteenth century, Tezozómoc took care not to appear lukewarm in his Christian faith or in his loyalty to Spanish rule. He denounced the great devil and deceiver Huitzilopochtli; he expressed a proper horror at the cruelty of human sacrifice.[4]

Although Tezozómoc's version of history presents an interesting opportunity to study the influence of the colonial era's spiritual transculturation upon the indigenous consciousness, of particular interest to this study is the information he provides concerning the peregrination of the Mexica from Aztlán. His narrative is representative of the chronicles produced during this era; while discrepancies concerning dates, names, and minor events exist, the overall message of these accounts follows a consistent line.

According to the *Crónica Mexicáyotl*, the Aztecs began their long southward journey in the year 1069:

> Cuando salieron los chichimecas, los aztecas, entonces de allá hacia acá salieron de Aztlán su morada en el Uno-Pedernal, 1069 años...permanecieron allá por mucho tiempo, cuando estaban allá, yacían allá los chichimecas, los aztecas en Aztlán: por mil y catorce años como viene apareciendo en la cuenta de años de los viejos; entonces hacia acá vinieron andando.[5]

This date is comparable to those found in other historical prose sources, such as the *Códice Chimalpopoca* and the *Anales de Cuauhtitlan* which fix the date at 1090 A.D.; the *Anales de Tlatelolco* which places it at one *acatl* or 1155 A.D. and the *Códice Ramírez* at 902 A.D. According to the tradition Tezozómoc follows, the Aztecs had been long established in their homeland of Aztlán. This view is shared by other chroniclers and later historians who would concern themselves with Aztec antiquity. They believed Aztec origins to be rooted in the most remote past.

The idea that the Aztec possessed ancient origins is aptly if somewhat curiously, illustrated by the Dominican Diego Durán in his *Historia de las*

Indias de Nueva España e islas de Tierra Firme. In this work, published in the period from 1579-81, the good priest contends the Aztecs are one of the ten lost tribes of Israel who God had punished for their sins. Durán saw their life under the control of the devil and the Spanish conquest of their once grand empire as evidence of this view.[6] In spite of Durán's Christian centric worldview, he does provide important details concerning Aztlán as his work reflects an abundance of indigenous sources both oral and written. He offers the following description which portrays the richness of the primordial Aztec homeland, as told to Moctezuma Ilhuicamina by the royal historian Cuauhcóatl:

> ...nuestros padres moraron en aquel felice y dichoso lugar que le
> llamaron Aztlán, que quiere decir blancura: en este lugar ay un
> grand cerro, en medio del agua, que llamaron *Culhuacan*, por-
> que tiene al punta algo retuerta hacia abaxo, y a esta causa se
> llama *Culhuacan*, que quiere decir "cerro tuerto." En este cerro
> auia unas bocas o cuevas y concauidades donde auitaron nues-
> tros padres y aguelos por muchos años: allí tuvieron mucho des-
> canso, debaxo desde nombre *Mexitin y Azteca*: alli goçaron de
> mucha cantidad de patos de todo genero, de garzas, de cuervos
> marinos y gallinas de agua y de gallaretas; goçaron del canto y
> melodía de los paxaritos de las caueças coloradas y amarillas,
> goçaron de muchas diferencias de hermosos y grandes pescados;
> goçaron de gran frescura de arboledas que auia por aquellas
> riberas, y de fuentes cercadas de sauces y de sauinas, y de alisos
> grandes y hermosos: audauan en canoas y hacian camellones en
> que sembrauan maiz, chile, tomates, uauhtli, frisoles y de todo
> género de semillas de las que comemos y acá truxeron;[7]

In addition to this description of Aztlán, Durán and his informants introduce several synonyms or *segundo nombres* associated with Aztlán: *Culhuacan* "curved mountain;" *Chicomóztoc* "place/rock of the seven caves;" and *Quinehuayan* "the place from which one rises or sets out from." While Tezozómoc's text concurs with Durán's use of the place-name *Chicomóztoc* for Aztlán; he includes further details which indicate the possible locality of this distant land:

> ...Chicomóztoc se llama la roca, pues por siete partes hay agu-
> jeros, cuevas pegadas al cerro empinado, de donde vinieron a
> salir los mexicanos...en la población de Aztlán Aztátlan, lugar
> de las garzas, por eso se llama Aztlán; estaba allá en lo que ahora
> quizá esté muy junto, muy cercano de la muy grande margen, la
> muy grande ribera la que ahora llaman "Nuevo México" ellos
> los españoles, Aztlán Chicomóztoc.[8]

This view concerning the location of Aztlán is supported by the anonymous
author of the *Códice Ramírez*, who citing the authority of ancient paintings
and tradition, agrees with Tozozómoc's assessment that Aztlán is located in
the territory then known as Nuevo México:

> En esta tierra (Nuevo México) están dos provincias, la una
> llamada Aztlán, que quiere decir lugar de garzas, y la otra le
> dicen Teuculhuacan, que quiere decir tierra de los que tienen
> abuelos divinos, en cuyo distrito están siete cuevas de donde
> salieron siete caudillos de los Nahuatlaca, (gente que se explica
> y habla claro), que poblaron esta Nueva España, según por
> antigua tradición y pinturas.[9]

Based on the textual sources cited, Aztlán existed as a northern land
encircled by water where the seven *Calpulli* lived in caves on a curved or
twisted mountain. It was a paradisiacal place where the ancestral Aztecs
lived in comfort and ease. Aztlán is referred to as the place of "whiteness" or
herons, which indicates a lush setting teaming with flora and fauna. This
land appears to have offered an environment capable of nurturing and sustaining a people without any difficulty. If this is the case, then what could
possibly motivate or cause the Aztecs to leave its security and pleasant sur-
roundings for the uncertainty of distant and unknown lands? This question
leads to two distinct answers that do not necessarily contradict one another,
but point to divergent streams within a wide ranging narrative.

Following the account of the *Crónica Mexicáyotl*, the Aztec exit from
Aztlán is precipitated by a conflict in leadership between two male heirs that
ensues upon the death of a primordial king Moctezuma. A son named
Chalchiuhtlatónac, or called *Mexi* leads the *Mexica* out of Aztlán because

their *Acxoyates* or *acxoyatl* [a ritual tree used to adorn temples and to place the thorns used in auto-sacrifice or penance] were scattered by the followers of an older brother whose name is not known:

> Y los mexicanos ya hacen penitencia allá en el lugar de su nom-
> bre Quinehuayan Tzotzompan; cuando acá depositaban sus
> 'acxoyates' o 'Acxoyatls' volvieron allá cuatro veces; vienen
> una vez cuando acá ve que están esparciéndose sus 'acxoyates'
> el acá los dispera; luego allí dijo el Mexi, el Chal, 'amigos nues-
> tros,' les dijo a los mexicanos, 'ya por eso reunimos, ya por eso
> salgamos hacia acá de nuestra morada Aztlán' y por eso luego le
> obedecieron los mexica.[10]

The event of desecrating or violating ritual objects within a cultural setting dominated by a religious consciousness is obviously a serious offense. In protest to this violation of ritual propriety the Aztecs decide to leave Aztlán. Yet, they were not leaving as a dejected or demoralized people, rather they left in pursuit of a destiny that was filled with promise and anticipated glory. The deity Huitzilopochtli instructed the Aztecs to leave Aztlán; under his guidance they would come to conquer new lands and rule over new peoples who would serve their needs and pay them tribute:

> ...fuertes mexicanos, ya que bien muy...numerosos, pues que
> muchos naturales, porque pues iremos, nos iremos a colocar,
> nos iremos a sentar, e iremos a conquistar a quienes están
> establecidos en el grande universo, a los naturales; y porque yo
> verídicamente os digo, allá os iré a hacer vosotros reyes, voso-
> tros seréis señores de todo cuanto hay por todas partes del
> mundo, y cuando seréis reyes, habrá allá, vosotros guardaréis
> nomás sin cuenta, sin término, sin fin serán los naturales que
> pagarán tributo.[11]

Huitzilopochtli inspires the Aztecs to embark upon their epic journey. This all-powerful deity promises them conquest and infuses them with the spirit to undertake this campaign without fear or doubt. They are a people who, according to the *Códice Ramírez* are in search of lands promised to them by their idol. The intervention of Huitzilopochtli into Aztec history sharply contrasts the conflict laden incident involving the destruction of the *acxoyates* as the impetus behind their exit from Aztlán. It reflects the Aztec view of themselves as a people favored with divine guidance. Within this context the Aztec journey from Aztlán does not correspond to an escape from disgrace, nor a nomadic wandering, but rather assumes the sacred aura of a pilgrimage directed by a supernatural being:

> ...la nación mexicana, la cual como los demás salió de las tierras de Aztlán y Teuculhuacan, gente belicosa y animosa, que emprendió sin temor de grandes hechos y hazañas, política y cortesana, que salieron buscando tierras prometidos por su ídolo Huitzilopochtli, por ese hicieron su peregrinación.[12]

The figure of Huitzilopochtli plays a prominant role in the series of events that lead the Aztecs from Aztlán to the founding of Tenochtitlan. While integral to the unfolding narrative of the Aztec's peregrination, he remains a rather enigmatic figure within its course. His status is never unam- biguously fixed; at times he is portrayed as the high god who communicates his will through his priests; in other instances, he acts as a divine being who displays human qualities. Regardless of the guise he assumes, Huit- zilopochtli functions as a cultural hero imparting vital knowledge as he inter- venes into the collective experience of his people. This god-man motif runs throughout most of the chronicles concerned with this history. Tezozómoc, perhaps inadvertently, seems to capture a sense of Huitzilopochtli's dual nature as his descriptions [of Huitzilopochtli] move back and forth across the line that separates the natural and supernatural worlds. This metaphysi- cal quality which is characteristic of archaic cultures is alien to modern cultures which stress the separation of these two realms. The following passage bears witness to Huitzilopochtli's supernatural identity, as the Aztecs carry a bundle with them that they adore and communicate with; it is identified as the god Tetzahuitl Huitzilopochtli:

> Y cuando salieron de allá del mencionado, que se donomina Quinehuayan, Chicomóztoc, los que se llamaban teochichi- mecas, aztecas, mexi, algo traían que era depósito de ellos, bulto

de ellos al que adoraban, oían que hablaba, y le contestaban los
aztecas, que les llamaba Tetzahuitl Huitzilopochtli.[13]

As a god Huitzilopochtli transforms and shapes the nature of Aztec
identity, thought, and culture. Early in the course of their journey he
instructs his people to change their name from *aztecas* to *mexicanos*. This
illustrates his ultimate power as he possesses the authority to name things, in
this instance an entire people, and thus can control their destiny. Huitzilopochtli also provides his people with technological innovations such as
the deadly *atlatl* [spear thrower], bows and arrows, as well as nets for hunting and fishing.[14] Although Huitzilopochtli clearly commands the power and
authority of a god, he is often anthropomorphically depicted in human terms.
For example, Tezozómoc records an event along the trek from Aztlán where
Huitzilopochtli, in the guise of a priest, must abandon his sister named
Malinálxoch due to the disruptive consequences of her malevolent ways.[15]
This event perhaps reveals the importance of preserving the community in
Aztec life. In spite of the familial bond, Huitzilopochtli was willing to banish
his sister in order to assure harmony within the community.

The abandonment of Malinálxoch, which on one level may indicate the
Aztec's willingness to put the needs of the community before individual
needs [an attitude essential for survival in a hostile environment], may also
indicate a sort of religious schism between the followers of Huitzilopochtli
and the members of a rival calpulli. While Huitzilopochtli is portrayed as
leading the Aztec pilgrimage from its beginnings, there are at least three
instances where his authority is challenged. The first is the abandonment of
his sister; the second is pictographically represented in the *Códice Boturini*
as a tree splitting and two groups going off in different directions;[16] the third is
conveyed in the story of Huitzilopochtli's birth. This third event undoubtedly confirms the dominance of Huitzilopochtli and his followers over the
other *calpulli*.[17]

The myth of Huitzilopochtli's birth introduces two elements vital to
Aztec religion and the development of their empire: 1) the identification of
Huitzilopochtli with the sun and the belief that the daily astral struggle of the
sun to push back the night is the "sun-god" battling his sister, *Coyol-
xauhqui* [the moon], and his brothers, the four hundred stars of the south;
and 2) the practice of taking of tribute, as the Aztecs follow the example of

their god who took possession of the insignias and attributes of his fallen brothers. These two events are integral to the development of the Aztec warrior psyche, which would prove an indespensable asset in the subjugation of Anáhuac.

With Huitzilopochtli firmly in control of the Aztec destiny they inauspiciously enter the central valley of Anáhuac which will soon become the heart of their empire. Following the *Crónica Mexicáyotl* in 1299 the Aztecs establish a settlement near Chapultepec [hill of grasshoppers]. However, they are soon driven from there by warriors from the city-states of Azcapotzalco, Xochimilco, and Culhuacan.[18] Unable to resist their combined forces the Aztecs put themselves at the mercy of the king Coxcoxtli of Culhuacan. They plead with him to grant them *"un poquito de tu tierrita allá en que iremos nosotros."*[19] Coxcoxtli relents and decides to send the Aztecs to a place called Tizaapan, a rocky inhospitable place filled with scorpions and snakes. However, instead of faltering in this harsh environment, the Aztecs flourish and grow stronger. For this accomplishment, as well as their fierce abilities in warfare [as they were often called on to serve as mercenaries], they gained the admiration and fear of the region's other city-states.

Through sheer determination and perseverance, the Aztecs assure themselves of physical survival as they gradually establish themselves on the fringes of the lake region's cultural milieu. They soon realize that their lowly Chichimeca origins relegates them to an inferior status in relation to their Toltec descended neighbors. Desiring to rise above the social niche assigned to them by the surrounding people, in 1323 the Aztecs ask king Achitómetl for his daughter, that she might become the wife of their god. The king grants their wish, but to his horror discovers that his daughter has been flayed, and that her skin now ritually adorns the priest of Huitzilopochtli. Although the Aztecs believed this mode of sacrifice a great honor to bestow upon the maiden, it was too much for her father to bear as he amassed the necessary forces to drive the Aztecs from their settlement.[20] To escape the wrath of the vengeful father the Aztecs take to hiding among the reeds along the shores of Lake Tezcoco. It was there among the reeds that the Aztecs discovered a small island upon which to take refuge. On this island they encountered the hierophany of an eagle perched upon the branches of a large cactus plant devouring a serpent. This sign informs them that they have indeed reached the "promised land." This is the place where they would establish their city of Tenochtitlan, "lugar de tunal en la piedra." Here they would re-create the center of time and space and ritually serve their deity: that his power might radiate to the four corners of the world and preserve the life of the cosmos.

The Search for "Historical" Aztlán

The search for an historical Aztlán is guided by a critical consciousness that stands in sharp contrast to the archaic belief in a cosmos dominated by supernatural forces. The historical approach to Aztlán is marked by a skeptical attitude that considers itself outside the realm of metaphysics. Within this empirically based setting, myth is somewhat pejoratively identified as:

> A purely fictitious narrative usually involving supernatural persons, actions, or events, and embodying some popular idea concerning natural or historical phenomena. Myth is properly distinguished from legend or allegory which implies a nucleus of fact.[21]

This modern conception of myth has been narrowly defined within the parameters of a tradition referred to as historicism. The attitudes implicit to this tradition have uncritically assumed a preeminence in our contemporary thinking and now lie at the foundational level of a modern consciousness. This consciousness believes that by virtue of reason, science, and above all history, it can rid itself of the "mythological" survivals of previous ages. It assumes the contemporary sources of knowledge and analysis as a standard against which the truth of a previous age can be discerned. The dominance of science, and by extention historicism, in contemporary Western consciousness has led to the emergence of a new myth. This is the myth of no myth; that "we" alone as rational beings have rid ourselves of the last vestiges of "mythological" thinking. This myth feeds a sense of superiority that has precipitated the emergence of a myopic sort of cultural imperialism that claims to be able to *de-mythologize* the myths of others. From this perspective the events of *in illo tempore* [in the beginning] appear as untenable fictions, non-realities, or as allegorical tales that no one is expected to believe.

This attitude reflects the widespread conception that only "primitive" peoples have myths. This view has its roots in the hermeneutics of "Classical" Greece which sought to *demythologize* the myths of an earlier epoch. This tradition can be traced to Xenophanes' criticisms and rejection of Homer's and Hesiod's "mythological" expressions of divinity. The Greeks steadily continued to empty *mythos* of all religious and metaphysical value. Contrasted both with *logos* and, later, *historia*, *mythos* came in the end to denote "what cannot really exist."[22] As Mircea Eliade states, "If in every European language the word "myth" denotes a 'fiction,' it is because the Greeks proclaimed it to be such twenty-five centuries ago."[23] This is the intellectual legacy that the West has inherited for analyzing myth. It is a particularly one-dimensional approach that has severely handicapped our attempts to come to grips with non-Western worldviews that retain a sense of their mythic past.

Armed with this perspective, investigators ranging from the colonial-era ecclesiastics to twentieth century historians have attempted to separate "fact" from "myth" concerning the myth of Aztlán. This archaic myth has proved a source of tremendous intrigue and interest as investigations seek to unveil the mystery that shrouds it in uncertainty. Their primary concern has focused on discovering the historical location of this primordial Aztec homeland, if in fact, it ever existed. The cautious stance which characterizes their efforts is perhaps conveyed in the following statement Frances Berdan makes concerning the nature of the Aztecs mythic journey: "Although numerous pictographic manuscripts and texts recorded the migration, it is now difficult to separate fact from myth, and to establish clearly many details."[24] While Berdan's statement concerning the Aztec pilgrimage reflects a normative academic stance toward myth, it takes on an added significance if viewed in light of what Sahagún's informants report concerning the nature of the Aztec historical record. It seems that in 1433, shortly after the Aztecs had consolidated their victory over the Tepanecas of Azcapotzalco and began their rise to power, they burned their picturebooks and rewrote their history:

Se guardaba su historia.
Pero, entonces fue quemada...
Los señores mexicas dijeron:
no conviene que toda la gente

conozca las pinturas.
Los que están sujetos (el pueblo),
se'echan a perder
y andará torcida la tierra,
porque allí se guarda mucha mentira,
y muchos en ellas han sido tenidos por dioses.[25]

Under the direction of Tlacaélel, counselor to rulers of Tenochtitlan, both the Aztec and the Tepaneca books were destroyed.[26] A new history more fitting to the new imperial power of Anáhuac was composed.

This revelation implies that many documentary sources that have survived into the present-day contain embellished versions of the Aztec past. Modern investigators struggling to make sense of a distant cultural world must take this knowledge into consideration in their research. Their work with the documentary sources of the pre-Hispanic record must be guided by an attitude that explores them without rendering judgment. They must be open to what each particular source may have to offer. David Carrasco, in his study *Quetzalcóatl and the Irony of Empire*, classifies the sources available to investigators into seven major categories: 1) pre-Hispanic storybooks–pictorial manuscripts, largely sacred historical, genealogical, and ritual-calendrical manuscripts, dependent on oral tradition as final interpretive authority; 2) post-Hispanic storybooks–done in native style they primarily deal with pre-Hispanic historical and cosmological traditions, many were commissioned by Spaniards while others were produced independently; 3) transitional prose documents–early postconquest documents, written in Nahuatl, Spanish or French consist of ancient songs, storybook images and oral traditions woven into a single narrative; 4) mestizo sources–authored by the descendants of the preconquest royalty they tend to incorporate both the native and the European view; 5) Spanish letters and descriptions–valuable sources in that they represent eyewitness accounts of Aztec society and culture, however, between the seeing and telling various personal, political, and literary agendas are interjected; 6) priestly writings–these texts reveal a strong influence of a foreign worldview with its ideological requirements, although constantly riddled with Christian polemics that are an indispensable source of information; 7) archeological evidence–through the symbolism of the stela associated with Aztec ceremonial centers much of their mythology, history, and genealogy can be reconstructed.

These textual and plastic sources inform modern investigators in their attempts to reconstruct, and at times unravel, the Aztec past. Their primary task when interpreting the various materials is to clarify the relationship of text to its context. The essential point is that the investigators suspend their interpretation until they have examined the historical and hermeneutical factors that have influenced the configurations that the surviving records of pre-Hispanic life have assumed. According to Carrasco in this situation the investigator needs to practice a special form of the "hermeneutics of suspicion:"

> Hermeneutics of suspicion means that before we show a willingness to listen and try to make something meaningful out of the material available, we must first ask penetrating questions about the nature, reliability, and intentions of the material itself.[27]

This methodological attitude attempts to balance a healthy skepticism with the need to work with the existent documentary sources, however dubious they may appear. It reflects a maturity–that has not always been characteristic of Western thought–in the way it approaches the problem of understanding archaic traditions. This approach runs counter to the past tendency to scrutinize myth from a predisposed stance that refuses to take its contents seriously. Operating from this limited stance the very questions investigators pose are circumscribed by the unexamined assumptions that inform their theoretical approaches. These questions tend to be framed in terms that the investigator believes to be empirically determinable. The relationship between the questions raised and the existent verifiable evidence to a large degree accounts for the fact that the search for "historical" Aztlán has been the focus of numerous studies throughout the past two hundred years. Investigators have displayed an unflagging confidence that they could separate "historical facts" from the "fictitious contents of myth" when attempting to determine the precise geographical location of Aztlán.

The first critical studies concerning Aztec antiquity appeared in the eighteenth century. These works tended toward literal interpretations of the historical sources with which they were dealing. A prime example of this first effort at historical analysis, as opposed to the methods of the earlier chroniclers, is Franciso Clavijero's *Historia antigua de México*, published in 1789. Clavijero was a Jesuit priest who intended to write a "natural history," wherein supernatural powers did not intervene; however, given his Catholic worldview certain Christian interjections were unavoidable:

> Clavijero's historical method represented a fusion of the providential interpretation of history with a cautious rationalism. His opening lines sounded like the characteristic Enlightenment note of skepticism. The history of the first peoples of Anáhuac was so obscure, distorted by so many fables, that it was impossible to ascertain the truth.[28]

Concerning Aztlán Clavijero writes that the Aztecs:

> ...vivieron hasta más de la mitad del siglo XII en Aztlán, provincia situada en mucha distancia del Nuevo México hacia el noroeste, según se puede colegir del rumbo que siguieron en su peregrinación y de algunas noticias que adquirieron los españoles en las entradas que hicieron desde Nuevo México hacia aquellas partes.[29]

Although Clavijero supports the idea that the Aztec habitation of Aztlán dates to the most remote past, his interpretation of why they left their homeland sharply contrasts with the views expressed by earlier chroniclers. He sees the Aztec abandonment of Aztlán as an indication that their northern territory experienced a period of barrenness. He also takes issue at the claims that the Aztecs were led out of this land under the direction of the "devil"–Huitzilopochtli. Rather, the Aztecs were led by a person of great authority named Huiziton. Clavijero's view concerning the location of Aztlán is derived from the testimony of Torquemada, who bases his knowledge on native pictographs that were later destroyed. Working from the fact that the Aztecs first stop after leaving Aztlán was in Hueicolhuacan [present day Culiacan], he deduces that Aztlán's location must lie to the north of the Colorado river. However, he disputes the claims of Boturini that the large body of water found in the ancient pictographs represents the Gulf of California, it is none other than the image of the "Great Flood" that occurred in Old Testament times.[30] [So much for "natural history."]

In contrast to Clavijero, the historian Manuel Orozco y Berra, found the question concerning the location of Aztlán as "inextricable." In his *Historia antigua y de la conquista de México*, published in 1880, he cites the difficulties in untangling the mass of conflicting evidence supporting various locations. He cites the conflicting testimony of the experts in the field as support for his non-position. Orozco y Berra contrasts José Fernando Ramírez's view that Aztlán is to be found in the region of lake Chalco in the valley of Mexico, to that of Alexander von Humbolt who concludes that Aztlán had to be located no further south than forty-two degrees of latitude somewhere in the present-day states of Oregon, Idaho, and Wyoming. The former interprets the enormous distances travelled by the Aztecs, as recorded in the pre-Hispanic storybooks and colonial documents in an allegorical sense, whereas the latter bases his conclusion concerning the great distances on an etymological analysis of the name-place glyphs in these same documents to arrive at a much different view.[31]

Depending on the methods and approaches employed to interpret the existent documents, investigators often discover shockingly dissimilar answers. Working in the late 1800's, Edward Seler, the noted German anthropologist, was of the opinion that Aztlán existed only as an Aztec fantasy.[32] Seler's "mission" was to remove all hint of fantasy from the historical record concerning the civilizations of Mesoamerica. Based on his rigorous comparative study of Spanish and indigenous sources [mestizo prose manuscripts and pictographic writings], sculptures, and ceramics, his conclusion was that Aztlán existed as a "mythical" place where the dead went. According to Aztec beliefs, this place was situated somewhere to the northwest of Tenochtitlan. Seler's attitude toward the myth of Aztlán reveals the intransigence on the part of many scholars to approach the contents of archaic cultures with the credit they deserve.

Perhaps the most widely accepted conclusion concerning the location of "historical" Aztlán is offered by historian Alfredo Chavero in his 1887 monograph entitled *Historia antigua y de la conquista de México*. He proposes that by retracing the route of Nuño de Guzmán's 1530 expedition into the area of New Spain, then known as Nueva Galicia, the location of ancient

Aztlán would be discovered. The route that the conquistador followed inversed the order of the peregrination of the Aztec people as it was set down in the *Lienzo de Tlaxcala*.[33] Chavero traced this route north from the valley of Mexico identifying the various places the Aztecs had passed. This investigation led him to conclude that Aztlán was to be found on the Pacific coast of the present-day state of Nayarit. There an island named *Mexcaltitlan* or *Mexticacan* lies in the center of an extensive lagoon that connects to the ocean; he considers this place to be the primordial homeland of the Aztecs.

Although Chavero's view would later become adopted and supported by others in the field, the combination of philological and hieroglyphical evidence utilized to support his claim was somewhat erroneously constructed. For example, he points to the etymological coincidence that root *Mexi*, the name of a major Aztec deity, shared with *Mexticacan* and *Mexica*–the former being the island location pictured in such indigenous colonial documents as in the *Códice Aubin*, and the latter being the name given to them by their god Huitzilopochtli. This commonality serves as a key element in Chavero's assertion that a geographical coincidence exists between the island of *Mexcaltitlan* and the *Mexica*'s primordial homeland, Aztlán. This claim, while possessing a plausible connection, is refuted in Remi Simeon's *Diccionario de la lengua náhuatl*, as well as in Cecilio R. Robelo's *Diccionario de mitología náhuatl*. Robelo, citing inconsistencies in Chavero's philological argument, states that *Mexticacan* cannot signify, *"en donde se oye Mexi*," but rather, is an adulturation of the word *Metztitecacan*, that roughly might be translated to mean place of the people of the moon.[34] Simeon adds to this refutation by pointing out the diversity of meanings that can be attached to the roots *metztli* and *icacan* that Chavero uses to support his position. Chavero derives further evidence that would subsequently be refuted more by contemporary scholars from the *Lienzo de Tlaxcala*. After conducting an examination of the place names set down in this indigenous style document, he accepts it as factual proof that the journey of Nuño de Guzmán did pass through Aztlán. Through tracing the progression of names from the central valley of Mexico northward, Chavero identifies *Mexticacan* on the Pacific coast in between the towns of *Xalizco* and *Chimetla* as Aztlán. However, as Cecilio Robelo points out, that Aztlán, meaning "place of the herons," is a common place-name for the marshy regions along the Pacific coast and could not exclusively be associated with the Aztec homeland.[35]

Although some of the details in Chavero's investigation may be doubtful, his conclusion concerning the location of Aztlán has become a normative view accepted by most researchers involved in the study of pre-Hispanic culture. Much of the mystery surrounding the location and even existence has been cleared-up for many as a result of a series of "ethnohistoric" investigations conducted in the mid 1970s by Wigberto Jiménez Romero and Jorge Olvera. Relying on oral tradition recorded in Padre Antonio Tellos' *Libro segundo de la crónica*, they fix the span of the Aztec pilgrimage between the years 1111 and 1345 A.D. They follow Chavero's earlier view that Nuño de Guzmán did pass through Aztlán in 1530, but gave it little notice as it was devoid of the riches the conquistador had anticipated finding in the Aztec homeland. Given this information along with its corroboration by diverse sources, Jiménez Romero concludes that the *Mezcaltitlan* on the coast of Nayarit is the historic Aztlán:

> La isla de Mezcaltitlan que Jiménez Morena ha identificado con
> la antigua Aztlán o Aztatlan, se localiza en una laguna del
> mismo nombre, en la costa norte del Estado de Nayarit, al
> noroeste de la actual población de Santiago Ixcuintla.[36]

Although the prestigious nature of these studies has done much to resolve many of the questions surrounding the myth of Aztlán, given its elusive character, some would claim the location of "historical" Aztlán remains at issue.

The Search for the Mythicized Aztlán

Within a situation of political underrepresentation, economic disenfranchisement and cultural antagonism, Chicanos initiated their drive toward national recognition. While possessing many ideological and tactical weapons in its arsenal, myth, somewhat surprisingly, proved to be one of the most vital elements contributing to this movement's appeal and forcefulness. The mythic narrative of Chicano nationalism weaves two distinct strands of human understanding into a single fabric. It fuses the pre-Hispanic myth of Aztlán to the modern myth of history. On one level Chicano nationalism calls for the re-creation of an Aztec spiritual homeland, Aztlán; on another, it expresses the desire to politically reconquer the northern territories wrested from Mexico in an imperialist war inspired by American "Manifest Destiny." These two mythic narratives merged to form the living myth of Chicano nationalism. This myth spanned the diachronical chasm that separates the archaic contents of cultural memory from the contemporary struggle for cultural survival. Chicanos interpreted their nationalist cause as more than a political movement; they were involved in the regeneration of sacred time and space, as the ultimate concern of Chicano nationalism sought to transcend the existent temporal and spacial barriers and establish a homeland patterned after the primordial homeland from which the Aztecs originated. This would be a spiritual nation rooted in a sacred landscape charged with the power of an indigenous spirituality and justified by the validity of their national liberation struggle.

During the brief period in which this movement flourishes, from the late 1960's until the mid-1970's, the myth of Aztlán constitutes a key element within the political consciousness that guides its course. Chicanos are inspired by a romantically charged nationalist vision that claims the territory designated as the southwest United States to be Aztlán. This region, north of the central valley of Mexico, is said to coincide with the primordial landscape of Aztlán. Chicanos, as the *mestizo* inhabitants of this area and by virtue of their Aztec ancestry–however distant and removed–claim this territory as a spiritual homeland. They aspire to politically establish, and spiritually reestablish the nation of Aztlán. Although this movement is short-lived and falls short of its most radical goal, its demands echo the powerful calling of a distant mythology.

The Chicano nationalist movement's relation to the myth of Aztlán represents a radical departure from the previously analyzed historical approach, and while it echoes aspects of an archaic mythic consciousness, it remains ideologically distinct. Many Chicanos embrace this myth as a living dimension of their existential belief system. The following observation offered by Raimundo Panikkar in his *Myth, Faith and Hermeneutics* clarifies Chicano nationalism's relationship to Aztlán as a "living myth:"

> *The myth you live* is comprised of the ensemble of contexts you
> take for granted. Myth gives us a reference point that orients us
> into reality. The myth you live is never lived or seen as one lives

or sees somebody else's myth; it is always the accepted horizon within which we place our experience of truth. I am immersed in my myth like others are in their own. I am not critically aware of my own myth, just as others are not aware of their own. It is always the other who, to my ear, speaks with an accent. It is always the other whom I surprise speaking from unexamined presuppositions.[37]

Myth, therefore, constitutes a transparent horizon against which these individuals view reality. Every cultural group, nation, or people exist within a particular mythic horizon that corresponds to their particular vision of truth. This is the myth they live. It contains those aspects of their worldview that go without saying, that are given without hesitation and assumed to be true. From within the myth, there is no doubt or question concerning the validity of its claims; from without, these claims appear utterly absurd and patently false. Chicanos living within the myth of Aztlán experience their claims to nationhood as an implicit part of their daily consciousness. In this respect the myth of Aztlán functions to provide identity, location, and meaning for a people who were previously directionless in their collective existential pilgrimage through earth. This myth became an essential dimension of their everyday experience in terms of how their experience is organized, interpreted, and "lived out:"

A myth seen and lived from within is an ensemble of facts that forms the basic fabric where what is given stands out as if against a horizon. Myth thus serves as the ultimate reference point, the touchstone of truth by which facts are recognized as truths. Myth, when it is believed and lived from the inside, does not ask to be plumbed more deeply, i.e., to be transcended in the search for some ulterior ground; it asks only to be made more and more explicit, for it expresses the very foundation of our conviction of truth. Seen from the outside, however, the mythical appears a mass of legends, of 'myths' in which others believe, but which have nothing to do with 'factual' truth. Myth then recounts in its own way the ultimate ground of a particular belief: either of others' belief (myth seen from the outside), or of our own belief (myth lived from the inside). In the latter case we believe the myth without believing *in* the myth, since it is transparent for us, self-evident, integrated into that ensemble of facts in which we believe and constitute the real.[38]

The myth of Aztlán is self-evident to Chicano nationalists. It relates the sacred history of the Aztecs' peregrination from a northern homeland, Aztlán, to the founding of the empire of Tenochtitlan. This is a primordial time in the sense of *in illo tempore*, where the ancestors left all that was secure and certain in pursuit of their destiny. They were led by their fierce deity Huitzilopochtli, and the priests through whom he communicates his will. Although this myth is preserved for contemporary peoples in a number of primary sources that were composed early in Mexico's colonial period, among these *Crónica Mexicáyotl, Anales de Cuauhtitlan* and *Códice Ramírez*, most Chicanos are unaware of the narrative contents of these texts. However, an essential truth is gleaned from these texts: all that could be decisively stated concerning the geographical location of Aztlán was that it lay somewhere to the north of the central valley of Mexico[39] The indeterminate situation of Aztlán ignites a mythic consciousness that seeks to regenerate an indigenous past through establishing a Chicano homeland on the same sacred landscape from which the Aztecs drew life. Chicano nationalists drew inspiration from the prehispanic myth of Aztlán:

> Nationalism may be described as the myth of historical renovation. Rediscovering in the depths of the communal past a pristine state of true collective individuality, the nationalist strives to realize in strange and oppressive conditions the spirits and values of a Golden Age. The roots of the individual are buried in the history and ethos of his group, in its culture and institutions; and from these, and these alone, he can draw purpose and strength for the heroic deeds of the future.[40]

Aztlán became synonymous with the territory of the southwest United States. This is a spiritual homeland whose realization lay within the grasp of a determined nationalist program. The Chicano destiny is intrinsically linked to the realization of this "mestizo nation," where the cultural ways would flourish and brotherhood would be the guiding principle. This mythic narrative provides a spiritual grounding for one of the core elements of the national liberation struggle, that is, territorial acquisition as nationalism is an ideology and movement is very much concerned with the practical and symbolic uses of land; a nation without its 'homeland' is almost unthinkable.[41] Chicanos were unaware of any historical contradictions within their interpretation of the myth of Aztlán and their subsequent struggle to politically control it. This myth is inseparable from the consciousness that confirmed nationhood upon the Chicano people. It was an integral aspect of the Chicano nationalist worldview whose destiny was founded on the realization of Aztlán as a nation.

One of the most striking documents supporting the cause of Chicano nationalism is *El Plan Espiritual de Aztlán*. This document, produced at the 1969 Denver "National Chicano Youth Liberation Conference," reflects a wide range of Chicano social, political, and cultural concerns for improved housing, education, employment, self-determination, and self-defense. However, more striking than the particular demands this plan issues is the ideological base from which they are launched. Chicanos claim these rights as the ancestors of the "Aztec civilizers of the northern territories of Aztlán." Although this claim, with the benefit of a dispassioned hindsight, appears as utterly naive and fantastic at the time of its assertion it quivers with the power of a self-evident truth. *El Plan* weaves both strands of the Chicano nationalism's mythic horizon into a comprehensive program that calls for the geographical and spiritual resurrection of Aztlán. The following passage excerpted from *El Plan* illustrates the depth of conviction that is involved in the articulation of this mythic narrative.

> In the spirit of a new people that is conscious not only of its proud historical heritage, but also of the brutal "gringo" invasion of our territories, we, the Chicano inhabitants and civilizers of the northern land of Aztlán, whence came our forefathers reclaiming the land of their birth and consecrating the determination of our people of the sun, declare that the call of our blood is our power, our responsibility, and our inevitable destiny.[42]

El Plan articulates many of the nationalists' most heartfelt goals. It attempts to systematically address the most radical ambition of this social movement; the establishment of a Chicano nation: Aztlán. Even to Chicanos, largely unversed in the chronicles and histories concerned with this myth, Aztlán symbolizes a spiritual homeland that was rightfully theirs. Chicanos emphasize the indigenous side of their mestizo heritage while denying their European roots. This romanticism fuels their political aspirations which are not removed from their cultural, social, and economic concerns:

> El Plan Espiritual de Aztlán, sets the theme that the Chicanos (La Raza de Bronze) must use their nationalism as the key or common denominator for mass mobilization and organization. Once we are committed to the idea and philosophy of the Plan de Aztlán, we can only conclude that social, economic, cultural, and political independence is the only road to total liberation from oppression, exploitation and racism.[43]

A "cultural renaissance"[44] inspired by the powerful ideological thrust of cultural nationalism swept through the barrios of the Southwest. One of the central motifs of this "renaissance" is the Chicano identification with ancient cultures of Mesoamerica. Chicanos turned to pre-Hispanic myths and symbols as a source of spiritual inspiration in their struggle for national self-determination. These myths and symbols still pulsate with a living energy. They were revived by a people who sought to draw from them as a reservoir of strength within the course of their political struggles. The most outstanding example of this practice is illustrated by the vital role that the Aztec myth of Aztlán played in the development of Chicano nationalism. The following poem, which appears in the first edition of the Chicano journal *Aztlán*, illustrates the essential function of the arts in conveying a sense of a nationalist spirituality:

> it is said
>   that Moctecuhzoma Ilhuicamina
>   sent...
>   an expedition
>   looking for the northern
>   mythical land

> where from the Aztecs came
>   la tierra
>   de
>   Aztlán
>   mythical land for those
>   who dream of roses
> swallow thorns
>   or for those who swallow thorns
>
>   in powdered milk
>   feeling guilty about smelling flowers
>   about looking for Aztlán.[45]

This poem links the pre-Hispanic mythology of Aztlán to the Chicano mythology of nation-building. The poet draws from a knowledge of Diego Durán's *Historia de las Indias de Nueva España e islas de tierra firme* to relate the event of Moctecuhzoma sending an expedition in search of a distant homeland, and the Chicano search for that same homeland. The romanticism of this image is sharply contrasted to the powdered milk that symbolizes the government programs that hand out surplus commodities to the poor. The extended metaphorical meaning of this poem serves to drive home the point that in their own spiritual homeland Chicanos suffer pain inflicted by the thorns of deprivation.

The above poem, just as many other artistic creations produced during the height of the Movement, is intended to raise Chicano consciousness while inspiring them to political action. Chicano nationalism demanded that Chicano artists create works that reflected the cultural heritage and political situation that they found themselves immersed in. Chicano art had to have a social theme; it was not just art for art's sake. In 1976 Rudolfo Anaya published a novel entitled *Heart of Aztlán*. Although this novel appears in the waning days of the nationalist movement, it brings together themes concerning the Chicano political struggle for equality and their reliance on pre-Hispanic myths and symbols for inspiration.

The protagonist in this novel is a man of the New Mexican *llano*, Clemente Chávez, who is forced through economic necessity to move his family from the land into the *barrio* of Barelas in Albuquerque. He fears this move as it will erode the cultural ways that nurtured and supported his family on the sacred landscape of the llano. He suffers the indignities of menial labor at the Santa Fe railroad yard under the control of corrupt union officials who contribute to the workers' exploitation. However, Clemente refuses to be pushed and is fired from his job. This is a tremendous blow to Clemente's pride as he no longer is able to fulfill his role as a head of household and support his family. Cut-off from the land that could sustain him, Clemente falls into the depths of drink. He alienates himself from his family, the men of the barrio and even becomes a stranger to himself. One night at a meeting of striking union members this all changes suddenly. Clemente hears the legend of Aztlán as it is told by a mystical figure, Crispín, a blind poet:

> '...We are the fruit of the people who wandered from the mythical land of Aztlán, the first people of this land who wandered south in search of a sign.'...'It is a simple story,' Crispín continued, 'a burning god fell from the sky and told the people to travel southward. The sign for which they were to watch was a giant bird in whose claws would be ensnared the poisonous snakes which threatened the people. In that place, under the protection of that plumed bird, the wanderers from Aztlán were to build their new civilization. There they would meet the second part of their destiny–But the important thing,' Crispín leaned forward so that all could listen, 'is to know how to interpret the signs. The legend renews itself with each generation, and we must know how to unravel the meaning of the sign–'[46]

Clemente is captivated by this legend of Aztlán as it awakens within him memories of stories about men who could fly that he had heard during his youth. He wants to know what this story has to do with the strike. Crispín draws analogies between the winding trains and the serpents that threatened the people. But the question arises, 'Where will a man find the power to melt the steel?' Crispín responds, "In his heart, in the heart of Aztlán." Clemente is disturbed by this event and can no longer find an escape in his drinking. He wants to know if he is the man to lead the workers in the strike. He is compelled to search for the heart of Aztlán.

In his efforts to discover the significance of the legend of Aztlán for himself and the workers of Barelas, Clemente embarks upon a mystical journey that nearly takes his life. Assisted by Crispín and an old woman versed in "witchcraft," he journeys to Aztlán and experiences the bond of a comaraderie with the suffering masses that he encounters in its waters. Clemente emerges from this experience knowing that the power that can defeat the railroad lies in a unity based in love. Rejecting violence, Clemente imparts the following message to the strikers at the novel's end:

> There is a heat more intense than the fire of a torch! And it can be rekindled at a moment's notice! Wherever discrimination and injustice rear their ugly heads the fire can be called upon to burn them away! Wherever there is an honest man, a poor man, an oppressed man, the fire smolders within his heart ready to ignite and light his path! It is the fire of love that burns in each man and woman and child: it is the fire of the soul of the people which must serve us now![47]

This novel, although criticized in Marxist circles for its mystical vein, does illustrate the effort to link the still vibrant myths of an archaic consciousness to contemporary political events. It also embodies one of the cardinal requirements of the Chicano nationalist movement; that art should have a political content. But more than this, it demonstrates the extent to which the mythic consciousness of Aztlán has survived into the present-day and pervaded the depths of Chicanos' twentieth-century thinking.

Summarizing Three Approaches to Aztlán

Through analyzing the myth of Aztlán from three distinct vantage points: the archaic; the historic; and the living, a more complete view of the myth's various dimensions comes to light. The first approach corresponds to an empathic reconstruction of the narrative that seeks to recapture a sense of the primordial flavor of this myth as the touchstone of a people's identity. Aztlán, as sacred history, provided the Aztecs with a meaning for their existence and a knowledge of their origins in the age of the fifth sun. It constituted an indispensable dimension of a worldview which remains separated by time, place, and being from the current age. The second perspective consists of a rationally verified interpretation of the myth which relies on the investigative methods of modern history as the arbiter of truth and meaning. This historical view of the myth represents a contemporary venture into a distant world which was predicated on a set of radically different assumptions concerning the nature of being and reality. The untranscended void between the categories and language of history and the unity and silence of myth testify to the existence of a narrative outside the limits of an academically derived comprehension. The third view reflects a modern attempt to flesh-out the meaning of the myth within the context of a search for spiritual identity and political self-determination. The myth of Aztlán was rediscovered by people of Mexican descent living within the United States in their struggle to understand themselves as Chicanos. This new identity reflected the cultural metamorphoses and nationalist aspirations which Aztlán came to symbolize. As a living myth Aztlán's truth stood as a horizon against which to interpret all thought and action. It was the source of a powerful, romantic vision that appealed more to the Chicano heart than mind as Aztlán became the focus of Chicano nationalism's plan to achieve self-determination.

These distinct interpretations of the myth of Aztlán emerge from very different existential relationships to the myth. The first corresponds to a theoretical attitude termed structured empathy, that is, a descriptive analysis that suspends evaluative judgments concerning the myth and its content while it attempts to reveal the "inner facts" of a given myth. Although this approach relies heavily on traditional academic sources it avoids their inherent bias and predisposition to impose Western categories of experience and thought over distinctly non-Western patterns of being. Structured empathy strives to respect the integrity of the myth by always couching its analysis in the historical context which gave it life. If this approach does have a bias it falls sharply on the side of non-bias. The second approach which has been identified as historicism exercises a tremendous influence over the way modern people understand and relate to myth. Historicism utilizes its "superior" knowledge and experience to explain away the myths of others while denying the existence of its own. What has happened is that history has become the supreme myth of the modern age. From this vantage point what was once sacred is emptied of its power and rendered mere superstition. The third view belongs to the province of myth as a living phenomenon. It involves a process described as the passage from *mythos* to *logos*, that is, the mystery of myth is made more explicit through its articulation and revelation. The myth becomes part of daily life and in some sense loses the fascination and awe which fed the narrative in its original form. The myth, now transformed into the basis of an ideological system, is no longer the Aztec myth of Aztlán, nor the historical view of Aztlán, it emerges as a distinctly modern narrative. It reveals the beliefs, aspirations, and fears of a people who draw from a distant past in the creation of a new mythic consciousness. This *transmythification* represents the myth's most dynamic dimension as it retains a powerful core that continues to resonate with meaning for people struggling to come to grips with their destiny in the modern world.

NOTES

1. Robelo, Cecilio, A., *Diccionario de mitología náhuatl* (México, D.F.: Ediciones Fuentes Cultural, 1951), p.28.
2. See Ninian Smart's *Worldviews* (New York: Charles Scribner's Sons, 1983) and *Beyond Ideology* (New York: Harper & Row Publishers, 1981) for a full discussion of the term.
3. Eliade, Mircea, *Myth and Reality* (New York: Harper & Row Publishers, 1963), p. 18.
4. Keen, Benjamin, *The Aztec Image in Western Thought* (New Brunswick, New Jersey: Rutgers University Press, 1971), p. 133.
5. Tezozómoc, Fernando, *Crónica Mexicáyotl*, (México: Imprenta Universitaria, 1949), p. 14.
6. Durán Diego, *Historia de las Indias de Nueva España e islas de tierra firme* ed. José Ramírez, 2 Vols, (México: Imprenta de J.M. Andrade y F. Escalante, 1867), Vol. II, p. 71.
7. *Ibid.*, Vol I., p. 220.
8. Tezozómoc, Fernando *op. cit.*, pp. 21-22.
9. *Códice Ramírez*, ed. Manuel Orozco y Berra (México: Editorial Leyenda, 1944), p. 17.
10. Tezozómoc, Fernando, *op. cit.*, p. 17.
11. *Ibid.*, pp. 23-24.
12. *Códice Ramírez*, ed. Manuel Orozco y Berra (México: Editorial Leyenda, 1944), p. 24.
13. Tezozómoc, Fernando, *op. cit.*, p. 17.
14. *Ibid.*, p. 23.
15. *Ibid.*, p. 31.
16. *Colección de documentos conmemorativos del DCL aniversario de la fundación de Tenochtitlan* (México, D.F.: Secretaría De Educación Pública, 1975).
17. See Miguel León-Portilla's *Las literaturas precolombinas de México*, p. 41, for a full explanation.
18. Tezozómoc, *op. cit.*, pp. 46-47.
19. *Ibid.*, p. 49.

20. *Ibid.*, p. 58.

21. *Oxford English Dictionary* (Oxford University Press, 1971), p. 1889.

22. Eliade, Mircea, *Myth and Reality* (New York: Harper & Row, 1963), p. 3.

23. Eliade, Mircea, *The Quest* (Chicago: University of Chicago Press, 1969, p. 73.

24. Berdan, Frances, *The Aztecs of México* (New York: Holt, Reinhart, and Winston, 1982), p. 3.

25. *Textos de los informantes de Sahagún*, Vol. III, fol. 192, in Miguel León-Portilla, *La filosofía náhuatl* (México: Universidad Nacional Autónoma De México, 1979), pp. 251-252.

26. *Ibid.*; See chapter 5; "Cosmovisión místico-guerrera de Tlacaelel," for a treatment of this issue.

27. Carrasco, David, *Quetzalcóatl and the Irony of Empire* (University of Chicago Press, 1982), p. 12.

28. Keen, Benjamin, *op. cit.*, p. 294.

29. Calvijero, Francisco, Javier, *Historia antigua de México, (México: Editorial Porrúa S.A., 1968), p. 65.*

30. *Ibid.*, p. 67.

31. Orozco y Berra, Manuel, *Historia antigua y de la conquista de México*, (México: Editorial Porrúa, S.A., 1960), Chapter 7.

32. "Aztlán." *Enciclopedia de México* (1978 ed.). I. p. 1077.

33. See Article 23, p. 214-216 of the *Handbook of Middle American Indians: Guide to Ethnographic Sources,"* Part 3.

34. Robelo, Cecilio, *Diccionario de mitología náhuatl* (México, D.F.: Ediciones Fuentes Cultural, 1951), p. 28.

35. Robelo, *op. cit.*, p. 29.

36. "Aztlán." *Enciclopedia de México*, (1978 ed.), I, p. 1077.

37. *Ibid.*, p. 20.

38. Panikkar, Raimundo, *Myth, Faith and Hermeneutics*, (New York: Paulist Press, 1979), pp. 98-99.

39. Although there are a number of conflicting perspectives concerning the "historical" location of Aztlán, which range from Lake Chapala in the state of Jalisco, México to Puget Sound near Seattle, Washington, the most consensus evoking determination is on the island of Mezcaltitlan in the state of Nayarit, México. See *Enciclopedia de México*, Director

Alvarez, José Rogelio Alvarez (México, D.F.: Impresor y Editora Mexicana, 1978), pp. 1078-1082.

40. Smith, Anthony, *Theories of Nationalism* (London: Gerald Duckworth & Company Limited, 1971), p. 22.

41. Smith, Anthony, *op. cit.*, p. 63.

42. *Aztlán*, I, No. 1, Spring 1970, p. iv.

43. "A Program of the Chicano Movement," *The Militant*, February 27, 1970.

44. Ortego, Philip, "The Chicano Renaissance," *Introduction to Chicano Studies*, edited by I. Durán, & Bernard (New York: Macmillan Publishing Co., Inc., 1982).

45. Alurista, F.A. Cervantes, J. Gómez-Quiñones, M.A. Pacheco, G. Segade (eds.) *Festival de Flor y Canto* (Los Angeles: University of Southern California Press, 1976), p. 3.

46. Anaya, Rudolfo, *Heart of Aztlán* (Berkeley: Editorial Justa Publications, Inc., 1976), pp. 83-84.

47. *Ibid.*, pp. 207-208.

Aztlán, Cíbola, and Frontier New Spain

John R. Chávez

The distant ancestors of Chicanos and other indigenous American peoples arrived in the Western Hemisphere in small groups beginning from forty to seventy thousand years ago. Since by that time human beings had existed in the Old World for millions of years already, the discovery of the Americas was clearly the finding of a "New World," and the discoverers would certainly have been justified in viewing it as a "Virgin Land." Over the millennia the descendants of the first arrivals spread south from the point of entry, at what we now call the Bering Strait, to the tip of South America, where they arrived about 11,000 B.C.[1] During this migration, of course, countless groups broke off from the general movement south to establish themselves in local areas, which in time became their homelands. Despite the occurrence of these events in prehistoric times, this migration through and occupation of the Americas would later form an important part of the Chicanos' image of themselves as a native people of the Southwest, their ancient, as well as modern homeland. Because Chicanos would know their Native American ancestry by the color of their own skin, they could be sure that their forefathers had in the distant past crossed over from Siberia and moved south. And on their way south generations of these ancestors would necessarily have entered the Southwest, inhabited it permanently, or occupied it temporarily before moving on to Mexico proper.

These early ancestors probably had no conception of the Southwest on the scale visualized by their descendants. Southwestern cultures from earliest times until after the coming of the Europeans undoubtedly regarded their particular territories as sacred lands that provided sustenance as well as space,[2] but these homelands were always local areas corresponding to specific tribes. Since the Indian tribes of the Southwest were never united,[3] they most likely perceived the region as a whole about as much as modern man would perceive the world as a whole. The conception of the region as such began from a distant perspective, from central Mexico after the arrival of Cortés in 1519. Even though the history of Chicanos already lay deep in the Southwest itself, their modern image of the region would develop from the perspective of Mexico City.

After taking Tenochtitlan (Mexico City) in 1521, the Spanish looked to the north for new lands to conquer and projected their own myths onto the unknown region that was to become the Southwest. They imagined that to the north there was a rich land of warrior women, that in that direction there were silver cities, or that at the very least the unexplored region touched on a waterway that would link Europe to the wealth of the Orient. All these myths manifested Edenic aspects which when viewed together formed the first general myth of the Soutwest as a whole—the myth of the region as a land of golden promise. While this image was the invention of the foreign Spaniards, it soon influenced and was influenced by Indians both in the North and in central Mexico. The Indians on the northern frontier, probably to encourage the Spanish to move on to other areas, sometimes agreed with the invaders' conceptions of the region and elaborated on them. In this way the European legend of the Seven Cities of Silver, which led to Spain's exploration of the Southwest, became the native legends of the Seven Cities of Cíbola and the riches of Quivira.

In central Mexico the Spanish myth of the golden northern land aroused interest in the legend of Aztlán, the Edenic place of origin of the Mexica (the Aztecs). Aztlán, meaning either "land of the herons" or "land of whiteness," was an old name by Cortés' arrival. According to their own histories, the Aztecs had left that homeland, located somewhere in the north, in 1168 and journeyed to the lakes where in 1325 they founded Tenochtitlán.[4] After the Spanish conquest Indian, mestizo, and Spanish chroniclers, relying on native informants, recorded the legend of Aztlán along with the rest of the history of the Aztecs. However, in their histories the chroniclers, influenced by the myth of the golden north, placed Aztlán in the Southwest; in fact it was probably in Nayarit, only four hundred miles northwest of Mexico City. This error would later lead Chicanos to refer to the Southwest as Aztlán, an application of the name that would, nevertheless, be paradoxically appropriate.

By the middle of the seventeenth century the Edenic picture of the north had disappeared at least from the minds of the authorities in Mexico City. By then the region was seen as a series of frontier outposts established to defend central New Spain from northern intruders. On the other hand, Spanish missionaries still viewed the borderlands as golden areas of opportunity for spiritual conquest and agricultural development. But most significant for the future Chicano image of the Southwest was the increasingly popular belief among the settlers that the region was their homeland. To be more exact, the *descendants* of the first settlers apparently came to perceive the land in that way—especially by the late eighteenth century. Since most of the settlers from the very beginning had been Indians and mestizos from central New Spain and had intermarried with the northern natives, it was not surprising that they eventually pictured the borlderlands as home, much as their indigenous ancestors had perceived their own northern tribal lands.

The oldest evidence of these ancestors in the Southwest has been found in Texas and dates back to about 35,000 B.C. Some of the earliest evidence of a clearly distinguishable culture has been found in southern Arizona and dates back to about 8,000 B.C.[5] Significantly, according to anthropological studies of Indian languages, social organization, material culture, and origin myths, the Cochise culture of southern Arizona was the parent culture of peoples as far apart as the Ute of Colorado and the Aztec of the Valley of Mexico.[6] The ancestral Cochise people apparently spoke the language from which the Uto-Aztecan lingustic family derives. In addition to the Ute, the Gabrielino of California, the Pima of Arizona, some of the Pueblo peoples of New Mexico, the Comanche of Texas, and many other southwestern tribes have spoken Uto-Aztecan languages and probably descend from the

Cochise people. In Mexico, besides the Aztec, Uto-Aztecan tribes include the Opata of Sonora, the Tarahumara of Sinaloa and Durango, the Huichol of Jalisco, and many others, forming an almost unbroken line from the Southwest to Mexico City. This together with other cultural evidence indicates that at about 1,000 B.C. descendants of the original Cochise people migrated south and became the direct ancestors of many of the Mexican people.[7] Thus, while Aztlán, the Aztecs' homeland of 1168, was relatively close to Mexico City, their more distant homeland in both time and space was in the Southwest.

Contact between the Southwest and the Valley of Mexico increased after 1,000 B.C. because just as Uto-Aztecan speakers were moving south, the technology of maize cultivation was moving north. The introduction of maize to the Southwest from Mexico led to the replacement of the hunting-and-gathering Cochise culture by the sedentary cultures of the Mogollon, Hohokam, Anasazi, and Pueblos. These cultures, which overlapped a great deal in time and space from about 300 B.C., existed largely in Arizona and New Mexico but also across the present border in Sonora and Chihuahua. As time passed, communication in the form of indirect trade became common throughout the Southwest and Mexico, and the cultural influence of the civilizations of central Mexico became dominant. After introducing squash, beans, and irrigation methods to the Southwest, the peoples of central Mexico—especially the Teotihuacanos, Toltecs, and Aztecs, from A.D. 200 to 1520—had an important impact on cloth making, pottery, architecture, and government in the region to the north.[8] Interestingly, the Indians of both the Southwest and Mexico reached their cultural high points at roughly the same time, between A.D. 900 and 1520. Clearly even in ancient times the Southwest was an extension of Mexico.

This interconnection became more pronounced with the capture of Tenochtitlan by the Spanish under Hernán Cortés in 1521. Though the Southwest had felt the effects of the rise and fall of Mexican cultures for two thousand years, the founding of New Spain would lead to closer ties than ever before between that northern region and the Valley of Mexico. While many of these new ties would be provided by a foreign European power, many others would be renewals of ties that had already existed for thousands of years. The most important of the renewed bonds would be racial, for as the

Spanish expanded toward the north, they would be accompanied by central Mexican Indians more numerous than the conquerers themselves.

The importance of Spain's Indian allies for the expansion and unification of New Spain can hardly be exaggerated since it was as much they as the Spaniards who toppled the Aztecs. Anthropologist Eric Wolf has convincingly argued the importance of these allies to the capture of Tenochtitlan:

> [Cortés] enlisted on his side rulers and peoples who had suffered grievously at the hands of their Mexica enemies...Spanish firepower and cavalry would have been impotent against the Mexica armies without the Tlaxcaltec, Texcocans and others who joined the Spanish cause. They furnished the bulk of the infantry and manned the canoes that covered the advance of the brigantines across the lagoon of Tenochtitlan. They provided, transported, and prepared the food supplies needed to sustain an army in the field. They maintained lines of communication between coast and highland, and they policed occupied and pacified areas. They supplied the raw materials and muscular energy for the construction of the ships that decided the siege of the Mexica capital. Spanish military equipment and tactics carried the day, but Indian assistance determined the outcome of the war.[9]

Just as the demolition of the Aztec state had been accomplished by an alliance of Spaniards and Indians, the creation of New Spain, racially and culturally, would be the accomplishment of these two groups and their descendants, the mestizos. This would be as true in the northern borderlands as in the center of the viceroyalty. Later this fact would lead to much uncertainty in the Chicanos' image of themselves in both Mexico and the Southwest, for being descendants of both conquered Indians and conquering Spaniards and Indians, Chicanos would vacillate between a self-identity as foreigners and a self-identity as natives.

The fall of Tenochtitlan was only the beginning of a series of explorations and conquests that was to expand New Spain. From the ruins of the Aztec capital, expeditions moved out in all directions, and interest in the distant north was soon aroused. Although the coast of present Texas had been sighted by Spaniards as early as 1519,[10] some of the more exciting news concerning territory that was probably within today's Southwest was heard in 1524. In *De Orbe Novo*, one of the earliest European histories of the New World, Peter Martyr wrote that when a group of Spanish explorers was

> wandering through the region that separates the great Panuco River from the Rio de las Palmas [along the Gulf Coast, two hundred miles south of Texas], they enquired of the natives what existed beyond the lofty mountains [the Sierra Madre Oriental] which bounded the horizon....They answered that beyond those mountains existed vast plains and great cities ruled by warlike caciques [chiefs].[11]

To look beyond the mountains, the Spaniards had to look west or northwest; in both directions there were plains and deserts, and the only "cities" unknown to Spaniards in those directions were the Pueblo villages of New Mexico, a thousand miles to the northwest. While the coastal Indians may actually have heard of the Pueblos, it is possible they were giving the Spaniards a golden picture of distant lands just to get them to leave.

During the sixteenth century, especially after the conquest of the fabulously wealthy empire of the Aztecs, Spaniards were quite willing to believe any tale of golden lands, whether they heard these tales from Indians or read them in books. Consequently, in their minds the unknown north was filled with mythical peoples and cities surrounded by riches. A few years after his capture of Tenochtitlan, Cortés wrote, regarding the Mexican coast across from present Baja California,

> I am told that down the coast [meaning "to the north," since his expeditions went in that direction]...are many provinces ...where, it is believed, are great riches and that in these parts of it there is one which is inhabited by women, without a single man, who have children in the way which the ancient histories ascribe to the Amazons.[12]

In a letter to Charles V, Cortés remarked that he was given this report by the Indian "lords of the province of Ciguatán [country of women]."[13] Since no such place existed, clearly the Spanish were projecting images derived from Greek mythology onto a real landscape, and most likely these images were simply being reflected by the Indians.

Interestingly, a novel involving Amazons, entitled *Las sergas de Esplandián* by Garci Ordóñez de Montalvo, had been popular in Spain since 1510. This romance spoke of an island of gold called California ruled by an Amazon queen named Calafia, and located "on the right hand of the Indies...very near the Earthly Paradise...." That the Spaniards took their reading literally is evident since one expedition after another went into the northwest seeking the realization of this fantasy. At first the explorers went by land up the western coast of the Mexican mainland, and then they went by sea. By 1535, Cortés himself had landed on the shore of present Baja California, and the peninsula received the name of Montalvo's imaginary island. Juan Rodríguez Cabrillo carried the name north when he led the first Spanish expedition to the coast of present California in 1542. Although Cabrillo encountered no Amazons in the northwest, the impact of those mythical women on the Spanish mind was such that in South America during the same decade, one Spaniard actually claimed to have seen a tribe of female warriors along what he named the Amazon River.[14]

Ever seeking golden lands, the Spaniards chased more than one dream into the distant north. They had barely entered Tenochtitlan in 1519 when they first heard mention of the Aztecs' wondrous land of origin, Aztlán. The description and legend of this place were preserved in the oral tradition and pictorial manuscripts of the Mexica during their rule; after the conquest Spanish chroniclers relied on these sources when they wrote histories of the Indians for the information of the king and church. In one such history, entitled *Historia de las Indias de Nueva España* (1579-81), Fray Diego Durán provided a vivid picture, derived from native informants, of this place called Aztlán:

> Our forebears dwelt in that blissful, happy place called Aztlán,
> which means "Whiteness." In that place there is a great hill in
> the midst of the waters, and it is called Colhuacan because its

summit is twisted; this is the Twisted Hill. On its slopes were caves or grottos where our fathers and grandfathers lived for many years. There they lived in leisure, when they were called Mexitin and Azteca. There they had at their disposal great flocks of ducks of different kinds, herons, water fowl, and cranes.... They also possessed many kinds of large beautiful fish. They had the freshness of groves of trees along the edge of the waters. They had springs surrounded by willows, evergreens and alders, all of them tall and comely. Our ancestors went about in canoes and made floating gardens upon which they sowed maize, chilli, tomatoes, amaranth, beans and all kinds of seeds which we now eat and which were brought here from there.[15]

Such an Edenic description must certainly have excited the imaginations of the Spaniards, and after seeing the gold of Tenochtitlan, they must certainly have assumed the wealth of Aztlán to be in precious metals as well as in flora and fauna. The water imagery of this description indicates that Aztlán was in a semitropical location, and early sixteenth-century pictorial manuscripts place the Aztec homeland on an island.[16] Equipped with such descriptive details and having been told that Aztlán lay to the northwest, the Spanish sought that place where they sought the Amazons—along the Pacific coast of the Mexican mainland. In 1530, about four hundred miles northwest of Mexico City, the conquistador Nuño de Guzmán encountered a place called Aztatlán, whose name and environment resembled those of the legendary Aztlán. Though the evidence indicated (and still indicates) that Aztatlán and Aztlán were one and the same place, it must have seemed too mundane a location for a land that had been idealized to the point of a paradise on earth. Furthermore, storytellers had recounted that in Aztlán there were caves, specifically the Seven Caves, the totemic shrines of the Aztec clans. Since these caves had not been found in Aztatlán, the Spanish decided Aztlán must be farther to the north.[17]

As a consequence, in 1538 Juan de la Ascunción and Pedro Nadal, two Franciscan friars, set out in search of Chicomoztoc, another name for Aztlán meaning "place of the seven caves." Together with their Indian porters, these explorers marched west from Mexico City to the coast, then to the distant north, possibly as far as the Colorado River, which today forms the boundary between Arizona and California. If they actually went that far, they may have been the first formal expedition to reach the Southwest by land. In any case they were the first to seek Aztlán in that vicinity, and their search would lead to the centuries-old myth that Aztlán was in the Southwest. More than anything else, their expedition caused the image of the Aztec homeland to become the first known Native American image to be applied to the region as a whole. While the friars found no signs of the Seven Caves, on their return they reported hearing word from the Indians of great cities farther north—thus keeping alive the myth of the Southwest as a land of golden promise.[18]

Ascunción and Nadal had not been the first to hear of cities in the distant north. As we have seen, such news had been heard by Spaniards as early as 1524 on the coast south of Texas. Moreover, in 1536 Alvar Núñez Cabeza de Vaca had made similar reports from the same area the friars visited in 1538 (in fact his reports were partially responsible for their journey). In an almost unbelievable adventure, Cabeza de Vaca had set sail in 1528, had been marooned on the Florida shore, had sailed by raft along the Gulf of Mexico, and had landed on the Texas coast. From there he and a few companions had wandered across the width of what is now Texas, traveled along the present border between Mexico and New Mexico, and then turned south for six hundred miles before reaching a Spanish outpost on the Gulf of California. There they finally came back into contact with other Europeans. As a result of this journey, Cabeza de Vaca became the first European to explore extensively the territory of the Southwest, and his observations were eagerly noted in Mexico City.

Somewhere near modern El Paso, Indians had presented Cabeza de Vaca with arrowheads and other gifts, some made of turquoise, a stone common in the present Santa Fe area of New Mexico. "These [arrowheads] looked quite valuable," Cabeza de Vaca later reported. "I asked where they came from. They said from lofty mountains to the north, where there were towns of great population and great houses." He had received the first definite information to reach the Spanish concerning the Pueblo Indians. Interestingly, Cabeza de Vaca's report was simple; he gave a straightforward account of what the Indians had said. Having seen a great deal of the

Southwest and having encountered little that resembled civilization, Cabeza de Vaca was less likely than other Spaniards to cherish a fantasy of golden cities in the region. And having lived among the Indians for years, he was also less likely to misunderstand or be misled by the stories they told. Cabeza de Vaca did indeed understand that the new land had potential for wealth, but that wealth would be in mines, rather than treasure rooms:

> The people who made it [a copper material] lived in fixed dwellings. We conceived the country they spoke of to be on the South Sea [the Pacific ws thought to be quite close], which we had always understood was richer in mineral resources than that of the North [Atlantic].[19]

Naturally, Cabeza de Vaca's return from the wilderness caused excitement in Mexico City, and the less he said about the north, the more exaggerated became its image. People linked all sorts of fables with the north, the most common of which was the legend of the Seven Cities. According to the legend, sometime in the Middle Ages seven Portuguese bishops had fled the advancing Moors and founded the Seven Cities of Antilia or Silver in a land across the Atlantic. When the Spaniards arrived in the New World, they brought the legend, as can be seen in the name they gave the West Indian islands—the Antilles. As the West Indies failed to produce any cities, the locale of the tale was naturally assumed to be elsewhere, though still in the Americas. This locale was situated in northwest New Spain when the Spaniards began to associate the Seven Cities with the Seven Caves of the Aztecs. In fact when Nuño de Guzmán entered Aztatlán in 1530 he had probably been seeking both the caves and the cities. Since neither was found there, the location was shifted farther north. When Ascunción and Nadal sought the caves in the distant northwest and returned with news of cities matching Cabeza de Vaca's report, the myths of the Seven Caves and the Seven Cities merged.[20]

These superimposed images formed the guiding myth of the Spanish exploration of the Southwest. As fairness would have it, that myth was a combination of legends pertaining to the two peoples that would participate in the exploration and conquest—the Spanish and their central Mexican auxiliaries. The Indians of the north, not to be left out, would make their own distinct contribution to the myth during the 1539 expedition of Fray Marcos de Niza. Having taken Cabeza de Vaca's account seriously, the Spanish viceroy selected a friar to verify the report because friars, such as Ascunción and Nadal, had shown themselves to be good explorers and diplomats. Fray Marcos, moreover, had already served in Peru with Pizarro. Esteban, an African slave who had accompanied Cabeza de Vaca on his journey, was to guide the friar.[21]

Esteban moved ahead of the main expedition and sent reports and directions back to Fray Marcos. At one point Esteban reported that he had news from the Indians of "the greatest thing in the world." He reported that ahead of him was a city called "Cíbola" (bison)—the first of seven cities. Thus, a southwestern Indian conception of a local homeland was joined to the Spanish and Aztec image of the Seven Cities to form the broader regional myth of the Seven Cities of Cíbola. The nomadic and seminomadic Indians south of the Pueblo villages were probably being truthful when they described such towns to Esteban, but these nomads did not conceive of cities as did the Europeanized mind. In the process of translation, exaggeration was almost inevitable. The description of the Pueblo villages was fairly accurate; their houses were of stone and mortar and of multiple stories. Yet it was a general description that gave rise to fantastic pictures in the minds of the explorers.[22]

All along the march north Fray Marcos continued to receive news from Esteban that further excited his imagination. Then, while in southern Arizona, Fray Marcos learned to his dismay that Esteban had been killed on reaching the first of the Seven Cities. Although his own life was now in danger, Fray Marcos claimed that he went ahead anyway until he came within sight of the first city itself, a city

> which is seated on a plain at the bottom of a round hill. It has the appearance of a beautiful town, the best that I've seen in these parts; the houses are just as the Indians described them to me, all of stone with storeys and flat roofs, so it appeared to me from the height where I had placed myself to see. The population is greater than that of Mexico City;...in my opinion [Cíbola] is the largest and the best of all [the lands] discovered.

For one who had seen both Mexico and Peru to claim that a Pueblo village was larger and better than Mexico City is surprising. Probably Fray Marcos, frightened by the news of Esteban's death, turned around and fled toward home without seeing Cíbola at all. Too ashamed to admit his failure, he most likely wrote a description of the town based on Esteban's reports and his own memories of Mexico and Peru. In any case the authorities in Mexico City soon pictured the northwest as a "new" Mexico, and before long the famous Coronado expedition of 1540-42 was on its way.[23]

This expedition, which explored much of present-day Arizona, New Mexico, Texas, Oklahoma, and Kansas, did a good deal to make the Spanish conception of the distant north more realistic, at least for a time. With one of the largest expeditions in the history of Spanish exploration, Francisco Vázquez de Coronado marched north only to be disappointed. When the "Seven Cities" were seen to be small villages, Fray Marcos was severely criticized by everyone concerned. In a letter to the viceroy, Coronado put the matter bluntly: "To make a long story short, I can assure you he [Fray Marcos] has not told the truth in a single thing he has said,...except the name of the cities and the large stone houses."[24] Later, in a letter to the king, Coronado added,

> there wasn't a thing of those which Fray Marcos had men-
> tioned,...the best that I have found is this river of Tiguex where I
> am and its settlements, which cannot be colonized because
> besides being four hundred leagues from the Sea of the North,
> and two hundred from the South Sea...the land is so cold,...that it
> seems impossible to be able to pass a winter in it.[25]

To his further embarrassment, after Coronado discovered the mundane reality of Cíbola, the local Indians convinced him that a far richer land called Quivira existed beyond the Pueblo villages in the plains to the northeast. Led on another futile search, Coronado trekked through vast sections of what we now know as Texas, Oklahoma, and Kansas, only to realize the Pueblo Indians had lied to him. A fabulously rich Quivira had probably never been part of the local Indian conception of the plains areas, but had been invented purely for the imaginations of the Spaniards. Since the Spanish had conquered and brutally occupied the Pueblo villages, the Indians most likely fabricated the urban wealth of Quivira in order to lure Coronado into a wilderness from which they hoped he would never return. They must have realized he would believe the tale because they doubtlessly understood only too well that the Spanish image of the region was of a land of great cities and valuable metals, a land the Spaniards expected to conquer and exploit. Following Coronado's disappointing experiences, Spain heeded his reports and left the region unsettled for another fifty years. The golden image of the north had tarnished.[26]

Even though the myth of the Seven Cities disappeared before the reality of the Pueblo villages, the accompanying myth of the Seven Caves of Aztlán lived on, at least in the collective mind of the Aztecs and their descendants in central Mexico. In fact, for some Aztecs and mestizos the Spanish discovery of the Pueblos confirmed the existence and location of Aztlán because, unlike the Spaniards, the Indians had seen Aztlán more as an Edenic land of the past than a golden land of the present. The Pueblo villages were, therefore, present evidence of past Aztec civilization in the distant north, evidence which was incorporated into the sixteenth- and early seventeenth-century chronicles of the Aztecs. The anonymous *Códice Ramírez* (1583-87), for example, recounted that the Aztecs had come "from another land toward the north, where recently has been discovered a kingdom which is called New Mexico." Furthermore, the ancestral Aztecs had been "a very civil people as can be readily seen from the ways of those [the Pueblos] of New Mexico from where they [the Aztecs] came." We can infer from this that if the contemporary Pueblos were civilized, the ancestral Aztecs must have been even more so. According to the *Códice Ramírez,* the Aztecs in their ancient homeland had had houses and farmland, an orderly government, a complex religion, and an elaborate social organization.[27] Such descriptions caused the myth of Aztlán to take on utopian qualities, in addition to its traditional Edenic features. It was such qualities that Chicanos would later see then they chose Aztlán to symbolize their own ideal society in the Southwest.

While the Pueblos came to be seen—with some justification according to modern anthropology—as distant relatives of the Aztecs, the utopian features that had been included in the myth of Aztlán made it difficult for the chroniclers and their informants to view the Pueblo villages and Aztlán as the same place. The villages indicated that Aztlán had been in the region, but they could not be *the* ancestral homeland. Just as Nuño de Guzmán's Aztatlán had earlier seemed too mundane to be the mythical homeland, the Pueblo villages now also seemed too ordinary. Since the north, even after the Coronado expedition, was largely unknown terrain, there were still many other possible locations in that region for the mysterious Aztec homeland.

Because accurate information about California, New Mexico, and Florida was poorly disseminated, the chroniclers and their informants frequently confused those places with one another; with the result that Aztlán, even after being linked to the Pueblo villages, could be placed anywhere as long as it was to the north. In his *Historia de las Indias* (1579-81) Durán's informants actually located Aztlán "toward the north and near the region of La Florida."[28] More often in the chronicles, Aztlán would appear in New Mexico, but the site would only be indirectly associated with the Pueblo villages. In the *Crónica Mexicáyotl* (1610), for instance, the mestizo chronicler Alvarado Tezozómoc said the homeland of his ancestors "was out there, where, today it perhaps lies very close to the extensive coasts, the extensive shores, which today the Spaniards call New Mexico."[29]

In 1652, after the Pueblo areas of New Mexico had been colonized by Spain, another chronicler took up the issue of Aztlán. In his *Crónica miscelánea* Fray Antonio Tello placed the original Aztec homeland "between the north and the west," but he meant territory beyond what we now call the Southwest, for the frontiers of the unknown had moved farther north by the mid-seventeenth century. Tello stated that the Aztecs on their journey to central Mexico had "passed the strait of Anián, and that the province of Aztatlán [Aztlán] lies on the other side of the strait." The Spaniards had long believed in the existence of a strait cutting across North America, a strait that could, if found, link Europe directly to the riches of the Orient. Given the constant interchange between Spanish and Indian myths, it is no surprise that Tello placed Aztlán beyond the mythical waterway, the last important image of the golden north to interest the Spanish. Ultimately, however, Tello admitted that he was merely speculating concerning the Aztec homeland; "even *now*," he wrote, "no one knows exactly where the province of Aztatlán is, nor have any of our Spaniards seen it; we only know we have heard of it and that it lies *toward* the north."[30]

While the Indians of central Mexico during and after the late sixteenth century conceived of the north as an old land to which they were somehow indigenous, by the 1580s the Spaniards once more viewed the region as a new land of riches, a "new" Mexico. By then the disappointment of the Coronado expedition had abated. The Spanish still remembered that New Mexico had been found "poor in provisions and minerals; but beyond, it was said, was a great salt river, and lakes where the people used gold and silver." Once again a major expedition moved north. The expedition of Juan de Oñate, which began in 1596, was especially significant because it established the first permanent colony in what is now the Southwest.[31] Moreover, the first literary work concerning this frontier region of New Spain resulted from the colonization; in 1610 Gaspar Pérez de Villagrá, a Spanish officer under Oñate, published an epic poem entitled *Historia de la Nueva México* in Spain.

This work dealt with the first stages of the conquest and colonization and discussed the preparations for the expedition at length. Emphasizing that the purpose of the expedition was settlement and not the acquisition of quick riches, the poet chastized those in the Coronado venture (1540-42) who he believed had earlier forced the abandonment of New Mexico "because they did not stumble over bars of gold and silver immediately upon commencing their march into these regions, and because the streams and lakes and springs they met flowed crystalline waters instead of liquid golden victuals."[32] Nevertheless, Oñate did search for riches beyond the Pueblo villages, but again to no avail. When the colonists realized that the chance of their leading the life of landed gentry was small, many fled, almost causing the colony to fail. Finally, the settlement was solidly established, and a new, much less glamorous image of the northern borderlands began to form in the Spanish mind.

Although explorers such as Juan Rodríguez Cabrillo had followed fables into other parts of the north, New Mexico was first conquered and settled because there was some truth to the myth of the Seven Cities. In California there were no Amazons and there was no strait of Anián, but in New Mexico there were sedentary Indians who, while not rich in precious metals, could provide an agricultural base for a colony. Above all they could provide the disciplined labor unobtainable from nomadic peoples in other areas. Once the Spanish colony became established in New Mexico, it settled into a frontier life based on subsistence farming, and the north gradually lost its glossy image. Life in the borderlands was by no means luxurious, for difficulties between the Indians and colonists were continual, and starvation and disease were always a threat. Nevertheless, except for a brief period in the late seventeenth century, the colony survived and finally prospered. Reflecting these changed conditions, later descriptions of the northern frontier spoke of the land and its produce, rather than of silver cities.

In 1773 a number of settlements on both sides of today's international boundary formed the environs of El Paso, which at that time was much more closely linked to New Mexico than Texas. In that year a resident of the area described the vicinity in words that embodied the later Spanish picture of the borderlands:

> This settlement includes five Indian missions....The Mansos were its first inhabitants, but they are totally extinguished, and on their lands our citizens are living with their farms and homesteads, some by purchase, and some by gift from their chiefs. In these places Indians and Spaniards live commingled.

By the late eighteenth century the authorities in Mexico City perceived the borderlands as a series of outposts designed to keep intruders far from the core of New Spain. Missions were part of this defensive system because they helped pacify uncivilized Indians on the frontier. In this respect El Paso fit Mexico City's picture of the north, even as it fit the missionaries' conception of the borderlands as a territory ripe for spiritual conquest. Of course, the Spanish authorities also saw the north as a colonial acquisition, and the sad facts concerning El Paso's Mansos justified that view. The lands of those Indians had been turned over to the settlers for agriculture which, as the Spaniards now realized, would produce much of the real wealth of the distant north. But the most interesting aspect of the description of El Paso was the intermingling of Indians and Spaniards.[33]

"The number of its [El Paso's] inhabitants," continued the anonymous author of the town's description, "reached 9,363 [*sic*] adult persons and a little over 500 children, including all classes of people, Indians and whites. In the last group are included the few Spaniards that are there and about eight or nine Europeans." This comment revealed that while the Mansos may have been extinguished as an identifiable tribal group, many of them most likely intermarried with the Indians and mestizos who always accompanied the Spaniards north on their marches from central Mexico. Furthermore, the existence of five missions meant that a significant number of local Indians were still part of El Paso's population in 1773. Since few of the people were identified as Spaniards, hispanicized Indians and mestizos made up the majority of the population.[34] Thus, despite the "extinction" of the Mansos, the population could still claim to be indigenous to El Paso, in much the way Chicanos would later claim to be native to the Southwest. Since so many of the town's people were Indians and related to local Indians, it could not have been much of a conceptual transformation for them to see the area as home. Indeed by the late eighteenth century the "Spanish settlers" of El Paso and other localities throughout the borderlands undoubtedly saw the region as their homeland and were more at home than most people have since realized.

Although New Mexico and El Paso were colonized in the late sixteenth and early seventeenth centuries, efforts in other areas were delayed. Once the Spanish authorities realized that the riches of the north would take great effort to develop, their enthusiasm for the region waned. While missionaries had been anxious to push the frontier northward, only in the late seventeenth century did the secular authorities permit missions in eastern Texas and Arizona, and not until the late eighteenth century in California. The Spanish missionaries had a sincere interest in the conversion of the Indians and were willing to undertake the tremendous effort necessary to gather nomads into civilized, Christian communities. Since farming was a necessary base for such communities, the missionaries saw the north as a potential agricultural as well as spiritual conquest. If their plans were to succeed, the missionaries realized that they would need to grow crops and were therefore always grateful for any good soil they found in the borderlands.

Father Eusebio Kino, who founded the first missions in what is now Arizona, raved about the bountiful land his converts worked:

The greater the means the greater our obligation to seek the
salvation of so many souls in the very fertile and pleasant lands
and valleys of these new conquests and conversions. There are
already very rich and abundant fields, plantings and crops of
wheat, maize, frijoles, chick-peas, beans, lentiles....

Father Kino went on to list the fruit, stock, and climate that made the region a
golden land for economic as well as spiritual conquest.[35] Father Junípero
Serra, the first missionary to Upper California, also saw the intrinsic
economic and social value of the borderlands. The Spanish secular
authorities, however, were reluctant to invest much of their treasury in the
region, an attitude that contributed to the later loss of the borderlands to the
United States.

Ironically, California and Texas were ultimately colonized as defensive
measures to ward off foreign threats against Spain's empire from the north:
Texas was established as a buffer against the French in Louisiana, California as a barrier against the English and Russians on the northwest coast.
California and Texas, therefore, were perceived by the secular authorities as
outposts, as frontiers rather than as colonies having intrinsic value. During
the late eighteenth century, for instance, Spain abandoned all its outposts
northeast of San Antonio because they were seen as unnecessary after
Louisiana had come under Spanish control. Despite this official view, the
people of the northeastern settlements themselves were incensed at being
forced to move south, and eventually many returned north—the residents
had come to perceive this region as home.[36] Nevertheless, the indifferent
attitude of Spanish officials had important consequences for the future of
Chicanos. Seen as less valuable than areas farther south, the borderlands
received less money, fewer colonists, and in general less attention from
Mexico City. Consequently, their development as integral parts of New
Spain and Mexico was retarded, a situation which eventually worked to the
advantage of the United States.

Yet Spain's advance into the region left an indelible mark on the
Southwest, a mark that, paradoxically, was as much Mexican Indian as
Spanish. While Anglo-Americans would later imagine the period of Spanish
rule in terms of conquistadores and Franciscans, Chicanos would revive the

facts of Indian and mestizo participation in the settlement of the region. They would note that for every conquistador and missionary who went north, ten or twenty Indians and mestizos, carrying their own customs and languages, went along as porters, soldiers, servants, and small farmers. The important expedition of Marcos de Niza, for example, was led by that friar but was composed almost entirely of central Mexican Indians. And Juan de Oñate, conquerer and colonizer of New Mexico, was himself married to a mestiza, the great-granddaughter of Moctezuma (she was also the granddaughter of Cortés).[37]

Chicanos would also point out the bonds that were felt between the Indians from central Mexico and those of the borderlands. For instance, when Vázquez de Coronado left New Mexico, he left behind several Mexican Indians who apparently felt sufficient affinity for the Pueblos to choose voluntarily to live among them. In 1680 when the Pueblos carried out a temporarily successful revolt, they were joined by many central Mexican Indians who were also disenchanted with Spanish rule. And, of course, throughout the colonial period there was a constant intermarrying between the Indians of north and south, as well as between Indians and Spaniards. All these facts would link modern Chicanos to southwestern Native Americans and would lend credibility to the Chicanos' image of themselves as indigenous to the Southwest, their homeland, both ancient and modern.[38]

NOTES

1. Victor Barnouw, *An Introduction to Anthropology*, vol. 1: *Physical Anthropology and Archaeology*, The Dorsey Series in Anthropology, 3rd ed. (Homewood, Ill.: Dorsey Press, 1978), pp. 128, 139, 186.
2. Edward H. Spicer, *Cycles of Conquest: The Impact of Spain, Mexico, and the United States on the Indians of the Southwest, 1533-1960* (Tucson: University of Arizona Press, 1962), pp. 576-77.
3. Robert F. Berkhofer, Jr., *The White Man's Indian: Images of the American Indian from Columbus to the Present* (New York: Alfred A. Knopf, 1978), p.3.
4. Lowell Dunham, trans., Introduction to *The Aztecs: People of the Sun*, by Alfonso Caso, The Civilization of the American Indian Series (Norman: University of Oklahoma Press, 1958), p. xiv.
5. Barnouw, p. 186; and Lynn I. Perrigo, *Our Spanish Southwest* (Dallas: Banks Upshaw & Co., 1960), p. 1.
6. Florence Hawley Ellis, "What Utaztecan Ethnology Suggests of Utaztecan Prehistory," in *Utaztekan Prehistory*, ed. Earl H. Swanson, Jr., Occasional Papers of the Idaho State University Museum, no. 22 (Pocatello: Idaho State University, 1968), p. 96.
7. James A. Goss, "Culture-Historical Inference from Utaztekan Linguistic Evidence," in Swanson, pp. 3, 5 14; see also Eric R. Wolf, *Sons of the Shaking Earth* (Chicago: University of Chicago Press, Phoenix Books, 1959), pp. 34-41.
8. C.W. Ceram [Kurt W. Marek], *The First American: A Story of North American Archaeology*, trans. Richard Winston and Clara Winston (New York: Harcourt Brace Jovanovich, 1971), p. 165; Carroll L. Riley, "Early Spanish-Indian Communication in the Greater Southwest," *New Mexico Historical Review* 46(October 1971) :286-87; and Matt S. Meier and Feliciano Rivera, *The Chicanos: A History of Mexican Americans*, American Century Series (New York: Farrar, Straus & Giroux, Hill & Wang, 1972), pp. 4-5.
9. Wolf, pp. 154-55.
10. Perrigo, p. 15.

11. Peter Martyr D'Anghera, *De Orbe Novo: The Eight Decades of Peter Martyr D'Anghera*, trans. Francis Augustus Macnutt, Burt Franklin: Research & Source Works Series 642, Philosophy Monograph Series 44, 2 vols. (1912; reprint ed., New York: Lenox Hill, Burt Franklin, 1970), 2:350.

12. Hernando Cortés, "Instrucciones dadas...a Francisco Cortés...," in *Colección de documentos inéditos...de Indias*, ed. Joaquín F. Pacheco, Francisco de Cárdenas, and Luis Torres de Mendoza, 42 vols. (1864-84; reprint ed., Vaduz, Liechenstein: Kraus Reprint, 1964-66), 26:153, my translation.

13. Hernán Cortés, *"Hernan Cortes: Letters from Mexico*, trans. and ed. [Anthony] R. Pagden, with an Introduction by J.H. Elliott (New York: Grossman Publishers, Orion Press, 1971), p. 298.

14. Garcí [Rodríguez] Ordóñez de Montalvo, "Las sergas de...Esplandián," in *Libros de caballerías*, ed. with a Foreword by Pascual de Gayangos, Biblioteca de autores españoles desde la formación del lenguaje hasta nuestros días, vol. 40 (Madrid: Ediciones Atlas, 1963), p. 539, my translation; and Neil Morgan, *The Pacific States: California, Oregon, Washington,* Time-Life Library of America (New York: Time, 1967), p. 33.

15. Fray Diego Durán, *The Aztecs: The History of the Indies of New Spain*, trans. with Notes by Doris Heyden and Fernando Horcasitas, with an Introduction by Ignacio Bernal (New York: Orion Press, 1964), p. 134.

16. See *Códice Boturini* and *Mapa Sigüenza*, best located through Robert Wauchope, gen. ed., *Handbook of Middle American Indians*, 16 vols. (Austin: University of Texas Press, 1964-76), vol. 14: *Guide to Ethnohistorical Sources: Part III*, ed. Howard F. Cline, pp. 100-101, 197-98.

17. Heyden and Horcasitas, Notes to Durán, p. 330, n. 5; and Durán, p. 134.

18. Perrigo, p. 18.

19. Alvar Núñez Cabeza de Vaca, *Adventures in the Unknown Interior of America*, trans. Cyclone Covey (New York: Crowell-Collier Publishing Co., Collier Books, 1961), pp. 119, 110.

20. Herbert E. Bolton, *Coronado: Knight of Pueblos and Plains* (New York: McGraw-Hill Book Co., Whittlesey House, 1949; Albuquerque: University of New Mexico Press, 1949), p. 6; and T.H. Watkins, *California: An Illustrated History*, The Great West Series (New York: Imprint Society, Weathervane Books, 1973), p. 20.

21. Bolton, *Coronado*, pp. 18-19.

22. Fray Marcos de Niza, "Relación," in Pacheco, Cárdenas, and Torres de Mendoza, 3:333, my translation.

23. Ibid., pp. 347-48; and Bolton, *Coronado*, pp. 34-35.

24. Quoted in Bolton, *Coronado*, p. 128.

25. Francisco Vázquez de Coronado, "Carta...al Emperador...," in Pacheco, Cárdenas, and Torres de Mendoza, 3:368, my translation.

26. Ibid., pp. 363-69.

27. *Códice Ramírez, manuscrito del siglo XVI intitulado: Relación del origen de los Indios que habitaban esta Nueva España, según sus historias,* ed. Manuel Orozco y Berra (Mexico City: Editorial leyenda, 1944), pp. 17-18, my translation.

28. Heyden and Horcasitas, p. 330, n. 5; and Durán, p. 6.

29. Fernando Alvarado *Tezozómoc, Crónica Mexicáyotl*, trans. from Nahuatl to Spanish by Adrián León, Publicaciones del Instituto de Historia, 1st ser., no. 10 (Mexico City: Imprenta Universitaria for the Universidad Nacional Autónoma de México with the Instituto Nacional de Antropología e Historia, 1949), p. 22, my translation from Spanish to English.

30. Fray Antonio Tello, *Crónica miscelánea de la sancta provincia de Xalisco: Libro segundo* Instituto Jalisciense de antropología e historia, Serie de historia, no. 9, vol. 1 (Guadalajara: Gobierno del Estado de Jalisco for the Universidad de Guadalajara, [1968]), pp. 31, 22, my translation.

31. Herbert E. Bolton, ed., *Spanish Exploration in the Southwest: 1542-1706*, Original Narratives in Early American History ([New York]: Charles Scribner's Sons, 1908; reprint ed., New York: Barnes & Noble, 1969), pp. 199-200, 202.

32. Gaspar Pérez de Villagrá, *A History of New Mexico*, trans. Gilberto Espinosa, Rio Grande Classics ([Los Angeles: Quivira Society], 1933; reprint ed., Chicago: Rio Grande Press, 1962), pp. 58-59.

33. "Description of...El Paso...," in *Historical Documents Relating to New Mexico...,*" ed. with an Introduction by Charles Wilson Hackett, 3 vols., Papers of the Division of Historical Research (Washington, D.C.: Carnegie Institution of Washington, 1923-37), 3:506-8.

34. Ibid.

35. Eusebio Francisco Kino, "Report and Relation of the New Conversions...," in *Spanish Exploration*, Bolton, p.457.

36. Charles Edward Chapman, *The Founding of Spanish California: The Northwestward Expansion of New Spain, 1687-1783* (New York: MacMillan Co., 1916; reprint ed., New York: Farrar, Straus & Giroux, Octagon Books, 1973), pp. 173-86; and Herbert E. Bolton, *Texas in the Middle Eighteenth Century: Studies in Spanish Colonial History and Administration*, University of California Publications in History, vol. 3 (Berkeley: University of California Press, 1915), pp. 1-2, 375-446.

37. Jack D. Forbes, *Aztecas del Norte: The Chicanos of Aztlán* (Greenwich, Conn.: Fawcett Publications, Premier Books, 1973), pp. 23-29; and Bolton, *Spanish Exploration*, p. 201.

38. Forbes, pp. 70-76.

Aztlán: Mito y Conciencia Histórica del Pueblo Chicano

Cosme Zaragoza

La primera acepción de Aztlán, en un contexto semántico amplio, parece encuadrar dentro de la etnohistoria, disciplina reciente que, a través de descubrimientos arqueológicos, interpreta su posible significación cultural. En este caso se intentaría desentrañar y describir el legendario lugar de origen del pueblo azteca con futuros descubrimientos arqueológicos.

No obstante lo anterior, se sabe que los aztecas se llamaban así:

> Porque eran originarios de Aztlán: uno de los modos de formar los nombres de los habitantes de un pueblo era suprimir la última sílaba del nombre de éste, y agregar técatl, que quiere decir persona. Así de Tlaxcallan se forma tlaxcaltécatl, de Chololan chololtécatl, y de Aztlán aztécatl y en plural azteca (Chavero 1955: 8).

Los aztecas o mexicanos pertenecían a la familia nahuatlaca y decían haber vivido en un mítico Chicomóztoc con otras seis tribus de la misma rama lingüística: chalcas, xochimilcas, tecpanecas, tlahuicas, acolhuas y tlaxcaltecas. Así lo consigna la *Crónica Mexicáyotl* de Alvarado

Tezozómoc que, al referirse al territorio de los aztecas, dice:

...y allá la morada de ellos, el lugar de nombre Aztlán, y allá la morada de ellos, por segundo nombre Chicomóztoc, y son sus nombres Aztecas y Mexicanos (Tezozómoc 1949: 14).[1]

Los que han rastreado el vocablo Aztlán, lo describen también como una etimología: síncopa de *azta-tlán*; de *aztl*, garza y *tlán* desinencia abundancial (Cabrera 1974: 39). El significado sería: tierra de las garzas:

...las designadoras del nombre de una raza que no se sabe a punto fijo de donde vino, sino vagamente de Aztlán, de la tierra de las garzas, que la precedieron y la siguieron en sus peregrinaciones periódicas a las tierras intertropicales de un valle llamado en el tiempo a cumplir grandes destinos. Al errar con la raza emigradora, trasladaban con ella el nombre de su procedencia, adondequiera que fuesen; y en el bello idioma aglutinante sería Aztlán, la tierra de las garzas, la residencia definitiva de los aztecas...(Campos 1935: 29).

Hay quien afirme también, que por epéntesis, *Atlán*, pronunciado erróneamente por los españoles Aztlán, en un contexto situacional, evocaba una dimensión espacial al "Norte," que en el pensamiento de los indígenas significaba universo: *Atl*, agua y *an*, tierra. Por lo tanto, Aztlán, o mejor dicho Atlán, equivaldría a tierra rodeada por agua, y por extensión abarcaría el universo formado por los elementos vitales de tierra, agua, aire y fuego:

Aquí les contaré, hermanos
en donde comenzó
la tierra de Aztlán
vino de las aguas del cielo
vino de la tierra del fuego
del aire (Macías 1974: 146-147).

Las cartografías a que hemos tenido acceso registran estos dos nombres: Aztatlan, en el primer Atlas Teatrum Orbis Terrarum (Ortelius 1570) y

Aztablan, en el mapa Orbis Terrarum Nova et Accurantissima Tabula (Visscher). El primero de los nombres indicados es compatible con la etimología descrita por Cabrera; sin embargo, el segundo de ellos aparece como una tercera variante, lo cual complica más el rastro de su posible descripción, y nos obliga a desistir, por ahora, de dicho rastreo. Además, esta incidental cuestión etimológica sólo nos interesa de forma complementaria. Así que, sin más, pasamos a otra no menos intrincada faceta: la localización de Aztlán.

Uno de los historiadores que mejor resume esta inextricable cuestión, que hoy sigue despertando interés y confusión en los científicos sociales de la materia, es Alfredo Chavero, quien documenta el problema en los siguientes términos:

> Comencemos por decir que en el códice mexica de M. Aubin se le representa como una isla rodeada de agua, sobre la isla se levanta un cerro, tépetl, y en él el carácter figurativo hombre, de pie. El carácter calli, casa, está dos veces a cada uno de los costados del cerro: El intérprete ha puesto sobre cada uno los cuatro calli, la palabra azteca y debajo de téptetl y en una orla, Aztlán. Veamos las diferentes opiniones. Humboldt presume que debió estar hacia el 42° de latitud norte. Luphan lo coloca en Wisconsin, en la parte norte de los Estados Unidos. Vetancourt, Clavigero y Bourbourg creen que estaba al norte de California. En la península de California lo ponen Boturini, Aubin y Bancroft. Más al norte de Sonora, Veytia, Acosta y el Códice de Ramírez. Al noroeste de México, el códice de Zumárraga y Tezozómoc. En el norte de Xalisco, Mendieta y el mismo Tezozómoc...Presumimos en el señor Orozco que, según lo indican los lugares de la peregrinación, Aztlán debía estar en Xalisco, y escogimos la isla de Mexcalla que se encuentra en medio del lago de Chapala...(Chavero 1955: 9).

Lo último, y novedoso por cierto, es la investigación de los antropólogos que, echando mano de la lingüística, y comparando los idiomas indígenas de México y del Suroeste de los Estados Unidos, han logrado fijar ciertos nexos lingüísticos que corroboran la teoría de que los orígenes de los aztecas se encuentran en el norte, específicamente en Arizona. Según esta investigación, los orígenes de los idiomas indígenas de estas áreas explicitan un idioma antecedente, el cual fue hablado por los antiguos antecesores del pueblo azteca que, de acuerdo con los antropólogos, vinieron de la región de Arizona. Aunque al respecto existe infinidad de teorías, los científicos sociales insisten en que Aztlán está en el norte y en que los aztecas emigraron desde allí (Morales 1975: 4).

De todos los argumentos esbozados, lo único que podemos deducir es que estas manifestaciones referenciales sólo describen parcialmente algunos de los aspectos relacionados con la etimología, localización y posible origen de los habitantes de Aztlán. Ante tan variadas conjeturas, y relacionando esos inciertos y desglosados indicios que existen del rastro de la peregrinación azteca, hoy por hoy, lo único que se acepta y se repite, y de manera controversial, es que los aztecas vinieron de Asia por el estrecho de Bering: que se les puede localizar en el lago de Chapala; o en última instancia, que su origen está en los núcleos de los hombres rojos del Suroeste de los Estados Unidos de Norteamérica.

Ahora bien, por lo que hasta este momento hemos descrito, y como lo indicamos inicialmente, Aztlán parece ser mero anteproyecto de una posible descripción etnohistórica del legendario lugar de origen del pueblo azteca. Sin embargo, y casi cual un desafío, a esta actitud mayoritaria que sospecha de Aztlán, y cuya legalidad histórica se regatea a fin de cuentas, se enfrenta la actitud minoritaria de los "chicanos y civilizadores de la tierra norteña de Aztlán," quienes además de redescubrirlo, lo legitiman como un símbolo necesario dentro de la problemática social en que les ha tocado vivir. Aztlán, como signo, recibe condicionamiento simbólico y real a la vez, ya que es motivo de identificación dentro de una contienda social que reclama concientización del origen cultural, tal cual se puede apreciar en este discurso programático, catalizador de los valores de la raza, de la cultura, de la lengua y del lugar geográfico propio:

> En el espíritu de una raza que ha reconocido no sólo su orgullosa herencia histórica, sino también la brutal invasión gringa de nuestros territorios, nosotros los chicanos, habitantes civilizadores de la tierra norteña de Aztlán, de donde pro-

vinieron nuestros abuelos sólo para regresar a sus raíces y con-
sagrar la determinación de nuestro pueblo del Sol, declaramos
que el Grito de la Sangre es nuestra fuerza, nuestra respon-
sabilidad y nuestro inevitable destino. Somos libres y soberanos
para señalar aquellas tareas por las cuales gritan justamente
nuestra casa, nuestra tierra, el sudor de nuestra frente y nuestro
corazón. Aztlán pertenece a los que siembran la semilla, riegan
los campos y levantan la cosecha, y no al extranjero europeo. No
reconocemos fronteras caprichosas en el Continente de Bronce.
El carnalismo nos une y el amor hacia nuestros hermanos nos
hace un pueblo ascendente que lucha contra el extranjero
gabacho que explota nuestras riquezas y destroza nuestra
cultura. Con el corazón en la mano y con las manos en la tierra,
declaramos el espíritu independiente de nuestra nación mestiza.
Somos la Raza de Bronce con una cultura de Bronce, somos una
nación, somos una unión de pueblos libres, somos Aztlán
(*Bibliografía de Aztlán* 1971: V).

Aztlán como entidad geográfica es litigio de aquellos derechos que
teóricamente le fueron adjudicados al pueblo chicano por los tratados de
Guadalupe Hidalgo al terminar la guerra anexionista de los Estados Unidos
contra México en 1848. El Suroeste de los Estados Unidos de Norteamérica significa para los chicanos, Aztlán, la tierra del chicano.

En relación con este tratado leonino, una revista que se especializa en
diseñar posibles capítulos de la historia del futuro (analizando el
crecimiento de la población de extracción mexicana en los Estados Unidos,
sin ser necesariamente un pronóstico de lo que pueda ocurrir), al referirse a
esta situación, específicamente a la región del Suroeste, expresa:

Grupos de tendencias radicales demandan la devolución de
Aztlán a México (territorios tomados a México al término de la
guerra de 1848). Un escuadrón suicida de militantes extremistas
mexicano americano asalta el Capitolio; un senador y dos
diputados mueren; 31 personas son lesionadas... Conforme
crece la agitación en pro de la devolución de territorios mexi-

canos, un nuevo presidente mexicano propone la 'revisión' del tratado del siglo XIX. Los hispanoamericanos de Estados Unidos presionan a la Administración para que entable negociaciones (Ettore Pierre 1979: 191-194).

La región geográfica que para unos es el Suroeste de los Estados Unidos, para otros, para los chicanos, es simplemente Aztlán, no importa que se diga que un incierto rastro de una legendaria peregrinación azteca, en alguna medida, haya sido su generador, ya que las asequibles, constantes e imborrables huellas históricas que han estampado manos y pies de trabajadores documentados e indocumentados en esta región de que hablamos, pareciera desvirtuarlo, pues este peregrinaje daría cumplimiento, a lo que Rendón llama "ciclo cósmico" y lo expresa en estas palabras:

> My people have come in fulfillment of a cosmic cycle from ancient Aztlán, the seed ground of the great civilizations of Anáhuac, to modern Aztlán, characterized by the progeny of our Indian, Mexican, and Spanish ancestors. We rediscovered Aztlán in ourselves. This knowledge provides the dynamic principle upon which to build a deep unity and brotherhood among Chicanos (Armando B. Rendón 1971: 10).

Aztlán explicita, además de geografía, fuerza de unión espiritual, y, al igual que sus ancestros aztecas, los chicanos llevan con ellos el nombre de su procedencia: Aztlán. La presencia de Aztlán como lo hemos constatado se manifiesta a través de la historia de distintos modos: en el pasado es vislumbre de la residencia del pueblo azteca; desde los años 1960s hasta nuestros días es reencuentro concientizador de autodeterminación del pueblo chicano; en el futuro parece ser predicción de un pueblo nuevo.

Aztlán como mito o como historia es un concepto influyente en el porvenir del chicano. La recuperación de Aztlán como fenómeno cultural está ligada a la problemática social del chicano, ya que la reaparición y aceptación de este vocablo, al igual que chicano o raza, como fenómenos lingüísticos responden, a la vez que son eco, a una profunda exigencia, o necesidad cultural de identidad individual y colectiva que está enraizada en una tradición legendaria y convencional, tal vez, tradición que es anterior a la existencia misma de otro término, con menos tradición e igualmente convencional, como es la palabra Southwest, nombre con que Charles F. Lummis rebautiza esta misma región de que hablamos, en el año 1884.[2]

Que los términos Aztlán o Southwest expliciten convenciones situacionales "Norte-Sur" en general, importa bien poco; sin embargo, es de todos conocido que los puntos cardinales casi siempre son orientadores, tanto en el espacio como en la historia. La hipotética dualidad Aztlán-Southwest, Norte-Sur que parece explicitar este mismo escenario geográfico, conforma también casualmente entre sus habitantes tangibles oposiciones en lo económico, en lo social, en lo cultural y en lo político. Si al escenario geográfico se le da uno u otro nombre, esto en el fondo aclara la situación pero no la modifica, como tampoco la modifican el uso de los nombres que se les asignan a las personas que actúan en este mismo escenario:

> Chicanos y anglos son también etiquetas convencionales que en el presente corresponden a papeles que han sido siempre desempeñados por los mismos actores. Los que ahora son anglos también han sido gringos, gabachos, bolillos, patones, gadamers; los que ahora son chicanos también han sido latinos, hispanos, mexicano americanos, mexicanos, etc. Para estos últimos ha habido términos específicamente peyorativos tales como greaser o mescans usados por los anglos; sin embargo, cualquiera de los anteriores pueden adquirir connotaciones peyorativas capaces de provocar violencia según las circunstancias del encuentro entre dos miembros de ambos grupos. Lo objetivamente verificable en términos generales, es que un grupo ha sido siempre de piel blanca, religión protestante, de ascendencia anglosajona, de mayores ingresos, de más alto nivel de escolaridad y de ocupaciones más prestigiosas; en tanto que el otro grupo ha sido siempre de piel morena, religión católica, ascendencia mexicana, de más bajos ingresos, de menor nivel de escolaridad y de ocupaciones de menos prestigio social. En términos estructurales, el primero ha estado por lo general en posiciones de dominación en tanto que el segundo ha estado en

posiciones de subordinación. (Jorge A. Bustamante 1979: 9).

Es necesario recalcar que estas terminologías no dejan de reflejar ciertas actitudes mentales que, en su oportunidad, son utilizadas provechosamente por ambos grupos. Antes de dar algunas de las pinceladas históricas que determinan estas contraposiciones sociales, es necesario abrir un paréntesis y exponer brevemente lo que se entiende por el gentilicio chicano, designación que, como ya se explicó, no excluye automáticamente otras usadas en el pasado, ya que el término no es nuevo y ha explicitado a través del tiempo diversos sentidos que van desde igualdad, hermandad hasta estratificación y desprecio. Actualmente, sin embargo, el término chicano está cobrando un número de usuarios cada día más alto, lo cual se explica por la premisa de autodeterminación que lo conforma; es decir, dicho vocablo expresa conjuntamente lo autóctono y lo sincrético, meollo de la experiencia histórica chicana.

Chicano, al igual que Aztlán, es considerado por algunos como una voz ideológica, "aglutinante" del orgullo étnico cultural que idealmente, a partir de los años sesenta, solidarizó a todo "habitante norteño" de extracción mexicana. Tino Villanueva, en el prólogo que precede a su antología, después de documentar y comentar ampliamente estos aspectos a que estamos haciendo referencia y las principales meditaciones que intentan describir la posible etimología de la palabra chicano, concluye que se hace insoslayable un estudio integral que se aproxime al tema de manera más sistemática, tomando en consideración que el aspecto filológico, las perspectivas antropológicas, las socioculturales, así como el enfoque histórico-lingüístico que se describen en dicho prólogo, no han agotado del todo la historia de dicho vocablo. Aunque al respecto existe infinidad de teorías que tratan de explicar la etimología de Aztlán, seguimos la interpretación filológica sustentada en el prólogo de Tino Villanueva: se llega a chicano por aféresis del gentilicio mexicano, considerando que la consonante velar (x) es un fonema palatal (s) con ortografía (sh) que de acuerdo con el sistema fonomático indígena de los mexicas (pronunciado meshicas), se obtendría 'meshicano' 'mechicano' (Tino Villanueva 1980: 7-34).

Con la descripción anterior cerramos nuestro paréntesis, ya que también el rastreo de esta etimología genera infinidad de controversias que escapan a nuestro propósito. Aunque la etimología engendra controversia entre los mismos chicanos, sin embargo, no existe discrepancia entre los mismos en lo que respecta a la existencia de una conciencia comunitaria. Las necesidades más urgentes siempre han sido conocidas; es decir, la situación de este grupo denominado chicano, latino, mexicano americano, hispano, etc., en relación con este otro denominado anglo, gringo, etc., ha sido una relación de subordinación, dominación, resultado de la guerra entre México y los Estados Unidos.

Ahora enumeramos los momentos más significativos de la historia de Aztlán o del pueblo chicano. Para ello partimos de los planteamientos teóricos de Juan Gómez-Quiñones, quien presenta críticamente las posibilidades interpretativas de dicho proceso histórico a través de dos postulados básicos: la identificación de aquellos factores que desligaron a la comunidad chicana de la sociedad en su conjunto, y una útil definición del tema histórico.

El postulado inicial lo reduce a ocho factores que reproducimos textualmente:

El primero de estos factores es que tanto el territorio como la comunidad chicana fueron resultado de una guerra y de sus consecuencias sociales e institucionales.

El segundo factor, que es muy importante, es que la comunidad chicana se diferencia racialmente de los demás sectores de la sociedad.

El tercer factor es la práctica del racismo y su impacto particular sobre la gente de sangre mexicana.

El cuarto factor de diferenciación es que existe una región considerada como tierra natal que ha tenido una población numerosa en forma ininterrumpida en el tiempo.

El quinto es la aparición de una cultura sincrética.

El sexto es que se presenta un intenso conflicto en un gran número de planos.

El séptimo factor es que, desde el punto de vista económico, la enorme mayoría de los chicanos han sido jornaleros y han tenido ingresos comparativamente bajos.

El octavo aspecto que diferencia a este grupo es la condición de subordinación en que durante tanto tiempo ha estado (Gómez-Quiñones 1975: 23).

En el postulado final define y explica el tema histórico en estas palabras:

La historia chicana es la suma de las experiencias de las comunidades de origen mexicano (indígenas, mestizos y mulatos) en los Estados Unidos. Esta situación es el resultado de la guerra entre México y los Estados Unidos. La comunidad ha aumentado mediante el crecimiento natural, la asimilación y la inmigración. No obstante hay un pasado anterior a la guerra mexicano-norteamericana que debe ser tomado en cuenta para explicar la actual diversidad de la comunidad, su localización geográfica y sus referencias culturales tanto con respecto a la sociedad estadounidense como a la mexicana. Sin embargo, para explotar el pasado anterior a 1848 hay que reconocer y comprender un proceso dinámico bifurcado, cuyos elementos son la formación de la moderna nación mexicana y la diferenciación de su parte segregada, es decir, la comunidad hispanohablante de indígenas, mestizos y mulatos que residen en el suroeste de los Estados Unidos (Gómez-Quiñones 1975: 25).

La sugerencia de estos factores deslindantes permite apreciar y enfocar la historia del pueblo chicano desde un punto de vista más objetivo, ya que al reconocer al pueblo chicano como una entidad distinta, tanto del pueblo de México como de los Estados Unidos, se legitima la expresión cultural del mismo como una manifestación con unicidad propia, no obstante el dualismo cultural y lingüístico que la conforma.

Así, iniciados en estos postulados básicos y considerando la citada periodización, la historia del pueblo chicano se divide en dos períodos principales, el primero de 1598 a 1848 y el segundo de 1848 al presente. Lo anterior a 1598 cae dentro de lo que el historiador ha denominado etnohistoria. Sin embargo, dicho período es ineludible, ya que aparece formando parte integral de la conciencia histórica del pueblo chicano. Los años que van de 1965 a la fecha es propiamente el llamado Movimiento Chicano.

Los acontecimientos que preceden al año 1848 pueden ser descritos resumidamente en tres períodos: el primero de 1600 a 1810 que comprendería la colonización de los territorios situados al norte de la Nueva España y el proceso de la formación de los territorios de lo que sería la nación mexicana.

El segundo período se centraría en los años 1810-1830 que incluiría los preparativos de la Guerra de Independencia y el Grito de Dolores. Aquí se hace necesario destacar que, al nivel internacional, la adquisición de la Florida facilitó el programa de expansión territorial de los Estados Unidos, iniciado con anterioridad en Louisiana. Si a estos acontecimientos internacionales, sumamos la desolación y la enorme distancia que separaba a la región norteña de su centro, la Nueva España, es fácil explicarse la entrada de los primeros angloamericanos a lo que posteriormente sería la república mexicana, país que a los pocos años de su independencia política sería nueva víctima, ahora del expansionismo norteamericano, legitimado por el "Destino Manifiesto."

Era de esperarse que el período de 1830 a 1848 fuese de conflicto abierto y de gran agitación. La dictadura de Santa Anna impulsaría inmediatamente a los anglotexanos a proclamar un gobierno provisional a favor del liberalismo mexicano, lo cual motivaría en forma indirecta la guerra texana contra México y que traería como consecuencia la independencia de Texas, seguida de su anexión a la Unión Americana. Dicha anexión desencadenaría la guerra entre los Estados Unidos y México, perdiendo este último una parte importante de su población y del territorio que comprende actualmente los estados de Nuevo México, Arizona, California, Nevada, Utah, parte de Colorado, Wyoming, Kansas y Oklahoma.

Aunque han transcurrido muchos años, este incidente le duele al mexicano que, como conciencia y memoria histórica, nos da la voz de alerta. México, nos recuerda:

> Perdió cerca del 45 por ciento del territorio original del país: 1.528,241 kilómetros cuadrados, dentro de los cuales se encontraban las inmensas riquezas petrolíferas de Texas, el oro de

California, descubierto dos días después de firmando el tratado,
¡y más de cien mil personas que habitaban en los territorios
"vendidos" en la miserable suma de quince millones de dólares,
que ni siquiera se pagó al contado! ¡Pocas veces un pueblo fue
despojado de tanto en una guerra! (Gilberto López 1971: 28).

El período que va de 1848 al presente también se subdivide en varios
momentos que el historiador citado ordena más o menos así:

La resistencia mexicana a la dominación norteamericana,
1848-1875.
Marginación política, social y económica, 1875-1900.
Regeneración, revolución y urbanización, 1900-1920.
Segunda Guerra Mundial, agresión cultural, 1920-1941.
Guerra fría y acomodamiento, 1945-1965.
Reconquista, resistencia y Movimiento Chicano, 1965-.

Resumiendo las ideas de este período, se puede afirmar que desde 1848,
con el tratado de Guadalupe Hidalgo, documento simbólico que
teóricamente garantizó los derechos y bienes de la población arrancada por
los Estados Unidos y también abandonada por México, hasta fines del siglo
XIX, la gente de extracción mexicana fue víctima de una cadena ininterrumpida de explicaciones supuestamente científicas, de índole biológica
algunas veces, y culturales otras tantas. Todas tendían al rebajamiento y
regateo humano de los conquistados y a la absolución, si no moral, por lo
menos legal, con que los dominadores han intentado siempre documentar el
despojo y la explotación de sus semejantes.

El desarrollo del capitalismo norteamericano en el territorio anexado se
fructificó gracias al despojo que se hizo a los mexicanos de los medios de
producción. Esto los transformó en una minoría étnico-nacional de mano de
obra superexplotable, marginándoles, consecuentemente, social y econó-
micamente en la sociedad dominante.

En México, las facilidades otorgadas por el Porfiriato a las inversiones
norteamericanas iniciaron la industrialización del país por las vías férreas
que se tendieron, permitiendo así una más rápida comunicación entre el cen-

tro y las regiones norteñas. Posteriormente, estas mismas vías agilizaron la salida de mexicanos que, como consecuencia de la industrialización del país, de la Revolución Mexicana o de la Primera Guerra Mundial, tuvieron que servir como mano de obra barata en los Estados Unidos, especialmente en el Suroeste. Esta masiva aportación y avalancha de refugiados políticos fortificó culturalmente a la población de ascendencia mexicana y restableció los lazos con México.

La activa participación de un contingente de ascendencia mexicana en la Primera y Segunda Guerra Mundial poco a poco conscientizó socialmente a su comunidad en los Estados Unidos. Los soldados participantes, sobre todo en la Segunda Guerra, se dieron cuenta de que mientras ellos se inmolaban por lo que consideraban su patria, allí mismo, en Los Angeles, California, sus hermanos menores eran atacados brutalmente por marineros pomposos, solapados por las instituciones oficiales y el medio publicitario (McWilliams 1979: 283-305). Los chicanos sobrevivientes de la Segunda Guerra Mundial regresaron a los Estados Unidos, intentando utilizar sus experiencias en busca de un mejor acomodo dentro de la sociedad dominante. No obstante, muy pocos lo lograron satisfactoriamente. En este período de la postguerra, aparte de la pobreza y la discriminación, se desplegó una campaña de redadas en donde el grupo minoritario se vio acosado por distintas agencias oficiales que, prontas a sofocar cualquier inquietud social, lo tachaban de radical o de comunista.

Dicho período, también fue conocido como la era de McCarthy, la cual se diluye con la administración de John F. Kennedy, quien a través de su campaña política presidencial inició un período, si no liberal, por lo menos más abierto en trato y relación con el grupo minoritario. Kennedy logró despertar simpatía y esperanza en la minoría de ascendencia mexicana, tanto en la masa como en sus representantes. Pero, la poca ayuda en el renglón económico no originó cambios substanciales en la infraestructura socioeconómica de la comunidad chicana. Desilusionada ésta optó por medidas más efectivas que canalizó indistintamente a través de un movimiento de lucha y protesta social.

Así, llegamos a lo que se ha llamado el Movimiento Chicano, que parece ser el punto más alto de los mexicanos asentados en los Estados Unidos, tanto por sus logros materiales como por la concientización social de la problemática de los chicanos dentro y fuera de los Estados Unidos. El Movimiento fue y ha sido considerado por propios y extraños como un movimiento heterogéneo, es decir, es epítome de los diferentes sectores que conforman su conglomerado social:

> Rural y urbano, norteamericanos nativos e inmigrantes mexicanos, inmigrantes recientes y más antiguos, trabajadores temporales y en tránsito, inmigrantes legales e indocumentados, etc., con problemas específicos en cada sector...(Miguel Abruch 1979: 14).

No obstante esta complejidad, el Movimiento ha poseído un núcleo motivacional que gira en relación de dos metas muy claras: liberación de la opresión e igualdad social. El Movimiento difiere mucho de otras etapas anteriores de lucha y desarrollo político-social. De este Movimiento han nacido organizaciones militantes con participación activa y con énfasis, sobre todo, en la confrontación y utilización de tácticas directas para dar a conocer su lucha y sus objetivos. El Movimiento ha explicitado un nacionalismo cultural y político, palpable en un orgullo étnico y en una reafirmación de arraigo de lo autóctono.

De los muchos eventos sociales que probablemente influyeron y determinaron la gestación del movimiento chicano, se han señalado y rastreado el bandolerismo social del siglo XIX; los efectos socio-políticos de la Revolución Mexicana de 1910; la actitud rebelde de los llamados "pachucos" de la década de los años cuarenta; la huelga de la uva en Delano, California, en 1965; la serie de conferencias sustentadas en la Universidad de Loyola, en el verano de 1966; la conferencia del Partido "La Raza Unida," en El Paso, Texas, en 1967, etc. Dichos sucesos, ya históricos, generaron concientización cultural a través de textos programáticos como el Plan de Delano en 1966; El Plan de la Raza Unida en 1967 y el Plan Espiritual de Aztlán en 1969. Las ideas de un César Chávez, un Reies López Tijerina o un 'Corky' Gonzales, expuestas concretamente en estas publicaciones, sirvieron de efecto estímulo para la acción común y la ideología del Movimiento Chicano. Así desafió y desafía las creencias tradicionales de la estereotipia de muchos angloamericanos que, como justificación para la dominación, invocan la existencia pobre y humillante de la gente conquistada, carente de cultura y, lo que es peor, sin posibilidad de expresión cultural alguna.

El movimiento, a fin de repudiar y contrarrestar estas distorsiones históricas, viene utilizando a sus propios científicos sociales para ir reconstruyendo poco a poco la imagen propia que convalide oficialmente su ideología cultural y política dentro y fuera de los Estados Unidos.

Se ha calado tan hondo que los chicanos se han reencontrado culturalmente en lo que ellos llaman Aztlán, un concepto que explicita, por un lado, una geografía étnica conocida "oficialmente" como Suroeste de los Estados Unidos, y por el otro, simboliza la unión espiritual de hermandad de los chicanos.

Aztlán se remonta a un pasado que los chicanos reconocen como su antecedente común, su conciencia histórica y su posible liberación, es decir, la recuperación del derecho a ejercer y conducir su propio destino. Aztlán, en la tradición oral, siempre ha sido memoria de los asentamientos anteriores y motivo recurrente en la búsqueda de un Edén perdido. Esto implica que, al conservar memoria de una edad precolonial, como parte de la historia propia que los une y que llega hasta el presente, se relativiza la colonización, cualquiera que ésta sea. Es decir, se asume la colonización como un movimiento de esa historia que tiene principio y que tendrá fin. Aztlán como símbolo aparece irremediablemente ligado al destino y saber histórico y cultural del pueblo de extracción mexicana asentado en los Estados Unidos.

Esta conciencia de que Aztlán existe como un soporte histórico cultural se ha reforzado a través de la expresión artística. El escritor mexicano y el chicano la han utilizado como motivo literario que denota mítica, búsqueda y localización geográfica. Sin embargo, Aztlán, para el escritor chicano, aparte de esta búsqueda y localización geográfica, señala límites espaciales concretos a un tipo de vida humano en el cual los chicanos se han encontrado actuando ininterrumpidamente desde hace muchos años.

Luis Leal, entre otros, ordenando los primeros indicios literarios sobre Aztlán, comenta:

> What interests us is not determining where Aztlán is found,
> but documenting the rebirth of the myth in Chicano thought. It is
> necessary to point out the fact that before March, 1969, the date

of the Denver Conference, no one talked about Aztlán. In fact, the first time that it was mentioned in a Chicano document was in "El Plan Espiritual de Aztlán," which was presented in Denver at that time. Apparently, it owes its creation to the poet Alurista who already, during Autumn of 1968, had spoken about *Aztlán* in a class for Chicanos held at San Diego State University ("In Search of Aztlán" 1981: 20).

Luego cita y comenta la importancia de dicho plan:

> 'El Plan Espiritual de Aztlán' is important because in it the Chicano recognizes his Aztec origins ('We, the Chicano inhabitants and civilizers of the northern land of Aztlán, from whence came our forefathers...'); because it establishes that Aztlán is the Mexican territory ceded to the United States in 1848; and because, following one of the basic ideas of the Mexican Revolution, it recognizes that the land belongs to those who work it ('Aztlán belongs to those that plant the seeds, water the fields, and gather the crops'); and finally, it identifies the Chicano with Aztlán ('We are the nation, we are a union of free pueblos, we are AZTLÁN'). ("In Search of Aztlán:" 20)

Los correlatos señalados por Luis Leal nos parecen aclarar la tradición histórica del chicano, pero, deja sin comentar un aspecto relacionado directamente con el fenómeno literario, mencionado en otro de los apartados de dicho plan, y que contiene esto:

> Debemos procurar que los escritores, poetas, músicos y artistas produzcan literatura y arte para el pueblo chicano y que se relacionen con la cultura revolucionaria (*Bibliografía de Aztlán* 1971: v).

De estas imprescindibles líneas se desprende claramente la conciencia literaria del locutor de este discurso que manifiesta la necesidad de una literatura que exprese el mundo cultural del chicano de Aztlán a través del vate chicano.

Sin lugar a dudas, algunos de estos puntos programáticos y otros acontecimientos sociales, ya comentados, acuñaron literariamente términos y conceptos como Aztlán, Raza, chicano, etc., manifestados en la expresión literaria de los años siguientes:

Those words were published in March of 1969. Beginning with that date, Aztlán has become the symbol most used by Chicano authors who write about the history, the culture, or destiny of their people; and the same thing occurs with those who write poetic novels or short stories. During the spring of the following year, 1970, the first number of the journal *Aztlán* was published, and in it the Plan was reproduced both in English and Spanish. The prologue consists of a poem by Alurista called 'Poem in lieu of Preface,'' which united the mythical Aztec with the present:

> it is said
>   that MOTECUHZOMA ILHUICAMINA
> SENT
>
>   AN expedition
>   looking for the NortherN
>   mYthical land
>   wherefrom the AZTECS CAME
>   la TIERRA
>   dE
>   AztláN
>   mYthical land for those
>   who dream of roses and
> swallow thorns
>   or for those who swallow thorns
>   in powdered milk
>   feeling guilty about smelling flowers
>   about looking for AztláN (Leal: 21-22)

También se menciona que:

In the following year, Alurista published the anthology *El ombligo de Aztlán*, and the year later his *Nationchild Plumaroja* appeared, published in San Diego by Toltecas de Aztlán. The title "Nationchild" refers, of course, to the Chicanos of Aztlán. From here on books in whose title the word Aztlán appears would multiply (Leal: 21-22).

Otros indicios literarios de Aztlán pueden ser rastreados en la narrativa:

> In fiction also, especially in the novel, the symbol has been utilized with advantage for artistic creation. The novel of Méndez, *Peregrinos de Aztlán* (1974), and of Anaya, *Heart of Aztlán* (1976), are works representative of that tendency (Leal 1981: 21).

Aunque dichas obras aparecen inscritas dentro de las coordenadas de la tradición literaria mexicana, Leal duda que exista una influencia directa entre estas novelas y dos de las tres obras mexicanas[3] que las anteceden:

> It is fitting to point out that both works have antecedents in Mexican narrative. In 1944 Gregorio López y Fuentes published his novel *Los peregrinos inmóviles*, and in 1949 María de Lourdes Hernández printed hers, *En el nuevo Aztlán*, (Leal 1981: 21).

La opinión de Leal es que, tanto el discurso narrativo de los escritores mexicanos, como el de los chicanos, expone como tema central la recreación del mítico peregrinaje de los aztecas en busca de la tierra prometida; claro está, con sus respectivas variantes.

Los comentarios de Leal nos parecen acertados en ralación con el estrato temático que plantean las mencionadas obras, sin embargo, y en esto seguimos los lineamientos bosquejados por Gustavo Segade, quien enmarcando o demarcando el símbolo de Aztlán dentro de la expresión literaria de los escritores chicanos, comenta:

> The Aztlán of the Chicano artist is, like the Troy of Homer,

the Macondo of García Márquez, La Mancha of Cervantes, or the Omeyocan and Yóllotl of Netzahualcóyotl, a mythic time-space, a symbolic elaboration of a basic human relationship which exists as an ever-potential experience in literature. As literature, Aztlán in all its facets initiates a process each time that symbolic word is experienced within the context of an image or expressed in thought-rhythm, making reference to the dialec-tical human relationships in which Chicanos find themselves thinking and acting (*Floricanto* 1976: 3).

Aztlán, para el escritor chicano representa indiscutiblemente una realidad evocadora del mito, ya que políticamente su noción no es clara. Sin embargo, la presencia de un conglomerado social, vinculado a un espacio relativamente concreto, con manifestaciones culturales propias a través del tiempo, responde a una realidad concreta, es decir:

Aztlán is as real as the United States of North America and México (Segade 1976: 5).

NOTES

1. El segundo nombre Chicomóztoc es también un lugar legendario, más mítico que histórico, cuya ubicación no se ha precisado, que se suponía ser la cuna o punto de partida de las tribus nahuatlacas en su peregrinación hacia el sur. Hay quienes relacionan este lugar con las siete cuidades que se buscaban en Nuevo México. La etimología: en las siete cuevas; de chicome, siete, y oztotl, cueva y la desinencia c, de lugar (Cabrera 1974: 65).
2. El mencionado autor declara que: "For nearly forty years I have been writing in and of the million square miles which include New Mexico, Arizona, Southern California, and adjoining parts of Colorado, Utah, Texas, and Northern Mexico–an area to which I was first to apply, over a third of a century ago, the generic christening by which it is now commonly known–THE SOUTHWEST" (Lummis 1925: VII).
3. La otra novela que no menciona Luis Leal es la de Rubén M. Campos, *Aztlán, tierra de las garzas.* Santiago: Ediciones Ercilla, 1935.

BIBLIOGRAFIA SELECTA

Abruch Lender, Miguel. *Movimiento chicano; demandas materiales, nacionalismo y tácticas.* México: Acallan, 1979.

Alvarado Tezozómoc, Fernando. *Crónica Mexicáyotl.* México: Imprenta Universitaria, 1949.

Barrios, Ernie. *Bibliografía de Aztlán: An Annotated Chicano Bibliography.* San Diego: Centro de Estudios Chicanos Publications, San Diego State University, 1971.

Bustamante, Jorge A. *Mi lucha por la tierra: Reies Tijerina.* México: Fondo de Cultura Económica, 1979.

Cabrera, Luis. *Diccionario de aztequismos*. México: Ediciones Oasis, 1974.

Campos, Rubén. *Aztlán, tierra de las garzas*. Santiago Ediciones Ercilla, 1935.

Chavero, Alfredo. *Los aztecas o mexicas: fundación de la ciudad de México*. México: Imprenta Universitaria, 1955.

Gómez-Quiñones, Juan. "Hacia una perspectiva de la historia chicana." En *Aztlán: historia del pueblo chicano (1848/1910)*. México: Sepsentas, 1975. 21-47.

Leal, Luis. "In Search of Aztlán." *Denver Quarterly*, 16, 3 (Fall, 1981) 16-22.

López y Rivas, Alberto. *Los chicanos: una minoría nacional explotada*. México: Editorial Nuestro tiempo, 1971.

Lummis, Charles L. *Mesa, Cañon and Pueblo*. New York: The Century, 1925.

Macías, Isidro R. "Nuestros antepasados y el Movimiento." *Aztlán*, 5, 2 (Spring and Fall, 1974) 143-155.

Morales, Alejandro D. "Visión panorámica de la literatura méxico americana (sic) hasta el boom de 1966." Ph.D. Dissertation: Rutgers University, 1975.

Pierre, Etorre. *Chicanos: el poder mestizo*. México: Editores mexicanos Unidos, 1979.

Rendón, Armando B. *Chicano Manifiesto*. New York: Colliers Books, New York, 1971.

Segade, Gustavo. "An introduction to Floricanto." *En Floricanto: An Anthology of Chicano Literature*. Los Angeles: University of Southern California, 1976.

Villanueva, Tino. *Chicanos: antología histórica y literaria*. México: Fondo de Cultura Económica, 1980.

Return to Aztlán:
The Chicano Rediscovers His Indian Past

Guillermo Lux and Maurilio E. Vigil

The Chicano Movement with its revitalization of the Mexican cultural origins of *La Raza* has indirectly resulted in the regeneration of interest in our Indian origins which in the past have been denied or played down. This essay will show, by outlining the historical experience of the Mexican American in the United States, how the melting pot concept has affected our people. Frequently displaced in the milieu of mainstream society, many Chicanos typically now behave as though they were Anglo-Americans, sharing with many of the latter a disdain for the Indian. Some Chicanos, obviously mestizo, struggle to divorce themselves from that heritage, while others proudly embrace it. Inasmuch as myth clouds this facet of the total cultural heritage of the Chicano people, the purpose of this essay is to explain to what extent the Indian was and is an influence on the Chicano. We will show that the traditional rejection by Mexican Americans of their Indian origins is part of a larger rejection of their entire antecedent cultural identification which is both Mexican and mestizo. We will show that the reasons for this rejection are partly the result of the Mexican American's struggle to accommodate himself to a very hostile environment in the United States. That environment first of all has stressed assimilation into the Anglo society with its use of the English language and Anglo values and normative systems. For Mexican Americans in this environment, becoming American has clearly meant rejecting one's own cultural background.

In addition to this has been the Mexican American's struggle to overcome pernicious, cruel and misleading stereotypes which have been created by Anglo society through motion pictures and other mass media. The Mexican has been portrayed as the dirty Mexican, the greaser, the pot-bellied "bandido," or the complacent, placid, fun loving quaint personality. The Indian, on the other hand, has been cast as savage, mean, and treacherous. As such, not only was the Mexican American impelled to shed his Mexicanness because of the stereotyped picture he was exposed to, but he has not been able even to begin to consider his Indian origins. In Mexico of the 1930s, during the presidency of Lázaro Cárdenas, the Indian origin of the Mexican people was accepted with pride. Yet the Mexican American, because his picture of the Indian was the same highly distorted one held by the Anglo, could not accept his Indianness. The socializing institutions in American society—the schools and the mass media—and even some organizations like the accommodationist-oriented League of United Latin American Citizens (LULAC), all stressed to the Mexican American that the way to succeed in America was to enter the mainstream of American life by emulating Anglos. In American life the "melting pot," actually an amalgam, a blending of different racial and cultural groups and creation of a new one, was a majority ideology substituted for the more conspicuous term "assimilation," even though the social processes dictated an assimilationist mold to which non-Anglo-Saxon groups were expected to conform.

The Chicano Movement with its emphasis on pride in being *La Raza* is, at least partially, a reaction to the pressure toward assimilation that stems from dissatisfaction with the social order of mainstream American society and results in a refusal to be absorbed. The concept of *La Raza* can be traced to the ideas and writings of José Vasconcelos, the Mexican theorist who developed the theory of *la raza cósmica* (the cosmic or super race) at least partially as a minority reaction to the Nordic notions of racial superiority. Vasconcelos developed a systematic theory which argued that climatic and geographic conditions and mixture of Spanish and Indian races created a superior race. The concept of *La Raza* connotes that the mestizo is a distinct race and not Caucasian, as is technically the case. *La Raza* is the term most universally accepted by Mexican Americans when referring to themselves.

Another quite opposite Chicano reaction to the pressure toward assimilation was to affiliate, or at least to accommodate, as stated before, to the extent necessary to maintain their status, or to establish rapport, in some cases, with the conqueror. This was accomplished more easily in some instances than others. For example, there existed commonalities in attitudes between the conquered and the conqueror such as those toward the *indios bárbaros* (savage Indians), the nomadic Utes, Navajos, Apaches, and Comanches, the enemies of *La Raza* for the past three hundred years. Both the Mexican and Anglo settlers shared that hatred, and the frontier policy of violence of both Spain and the United States coincided. Spain adopted this policy once it was determined that the previous Christianizing program of the mission was ineffectual with the *indios bárbaros*, the nomads. The newly arrived American settlers held that the "only good Indian was a dead Indian," as the frontier slogan demonstrated. That same feeling had been held in the outermost reaches of the colonial frontier by Mexican colonists who had suffered for over a century from the savage raids of Navajos, Apaches, and Utes and who had carried out considerable, though largely ineffectual, campaigns against *los indios bárbaros* before the Americans came. In fact, part of the reason for the bloodless conquest of New Mexico was that many Mexicans welcomed the military might and technology which the Americans could contribute against the rampaging Indians. The Anglo conquerors were quickly emulated by *La Raza* who gained status by association. It became a matter of good form for mestizos to become as Spanish as possible, thus disassociating themselves from their Mexican origins which necessarily implied Indian origins. Unfortunately, the universal designation given erroneously by Columbus to all Native Americans— Indians—did not allow for distinctions to be made between the sedentary Indians such as the Aztecs (from whom some Mexicans derived) and the Pueblos (with whom they later intermarried), and the nomads such as Apaches, and Utes, the arch-enemies of Mexican colonists. To the Americans an Indian was an Indian and the popular stereotype soon became one in which the Indian was viewed as an uncivilized savage, as popularly depicted in dime novels and later motion pictures. Another factor in the Mexican American's rejection of his Indianness pertained to attitudes relative to feelings of racial and social inequality among Anglos, Mexican American mestizos, and Indians.

Though it is not widely acknowledged by contemporary American social thought, the 1776 American Revolution was not for the establishment of democracy in the New World—that came later on. One could not imagine the Virginia aristocratic, patrician families of the Tidewater accepting the small farmer of the Piedmont as their equal. Neither did the *patrón* class of New Mexico nor the wealthy landed families of California accept the Indian or the mestizo as an equal (Valdés 1971, pp. 1, 30.) Under the patina of mythological colonial grandeur, there subsisted, in a state of vile servitude, the masses. The wealthy families designated themselves with pride as *castizos*, of pure blood lines, meaning no mescegenation, often claiming a genealogy dating back to the conquistadores. The colonial tradition of being pro-White (Spanish or other European) and anti-Indian was deeply ingrained. Once the Anglos arrived, the *patrón* class which dominated the lower classes quickly formed an alliance and collaborated in many instances with the recently arrived oppressor. This was manifested in land frauds such as the various intrigues of the Santa Fe Ring in New Mexico, the origins of the Maxwell Land Grant and so on. The miscegenated, colonial masses were again the object of racial discrimination.

Anglo-Americans shared this disdain for the half-breed—for miscegenation. Faced by such hostile attitudes the Mexican Americans embraced Anglo-American values. Like their counterparts, the black Americans, Hispanos considered güeros (fair-skinned mestizos) especially lucky since they would generally be more readily accepted by the dominant society.

The growth of democracy in the nineteenth and twentieth centuries and its social leveling tendency has had its impact on *La Raza* too. As Anglo America learned about equality, so did brown America. The Chicano Movement is the most recent stage of this democratizing evolution. It embraces all *Raza*. It frequently assumes a common enemy—the gringo. In its extremes it is a counter-racist surge. Those who do not comply are harshly labeled as *vendidos* or *agringados*, an anglicized term for a Mexican American who has assumed the characteristics of the "gringo," sell-outs, or politically naive or unaware. The colonial hierarchy based on color, pedigree, and wealth is summarily dismissed.

The descendants of the prestigious colonial families still frequently have difficulty in accepting democratic ideas and so they find it difficult to embrace concepts of ethnic community which would embrace the Indian as a brother. This would be a hard step to take inasmuch as the Indian was an enemy long before the Anglo arrived in the Southwest. Liaison with the controlling Anglo class has been more attractive.

There is substantial evidence of acculturation among our people today due to pressure from the dominant society. The Mexican American can become a different person by immersing himself "in the mirror image reflected by others," by acting as a person accepted by the mainstream society. This self-rejection focuses on color and nationality and hence community. For the person who may not physiologically appear distinctive or different it is relatively easy to pass for white. For the distinctive person, the mestizo, the recourse must be "my family descended from the conquistadores; we are Hispanos, Spanish" (Weiss 1962, p. 471). The mestizo demonstrates his obvious shame of his Indian heritage by introducing himself as Spanish. How often have Spanish-surnamed people been told "but you don't look Spanish!" The reference is, of course, to the mestizo and Indian characteristics and to the brown skin pigmentation. Little does the Anglo realize the heterogeneity of *La Raza* whose physical characteristics are a mosaic.

More significant is the image these persons strive to project. It is through community relationships with others that one has being, context, and self-realization in the social milieu. Individuals and groups constantly react and adjust to society. To quote the social psychologist George H. Mead:

> We cannot realize ourselves except insofar as we can recognize the other in his relationship to us. It is as he takes the attitude of the other that the individual is able to realize himself as a self. (Mead 1934, p. 194.)

An example of this would be expression of nationalism and patriotism voiced with a sense of superiority or domination over others who may therefore be deemed inferior. This may be an unconscious adjustment, but basically it is a reaction. Individuals perform as they are seen by others, as they are expected to perform, and as they see themselves. This is the "looking-glass self," a "self-image."

Consequently, until the 1960s, when the great awakening of *La Raza* occurred, the people of various shades of brown who spoke Spanish and lived primarily in the Southwest were called, by outsiders, Mexicans, Mexican Americans, and even Latin Americans (Twitchell 1911-12, p. 259). Yet many of them introduced themselves as Spanish and Hispanos. One could detect very definite attitudes concerning the implied and misunderstood Indianness of these people of Mexican ancestry. They introduced themselves as Spanish because that was synonymous with white (Casavantes 1969, p. 1). Anglos called them Spanish because it was considered polite to do so. Mexican was a name used in a pejorative sense.

In the 1960s the term "Chicano" took on a new meaning and gained acceptance. It connotes people who believe in self-determination. Chicano is still a controversial term worn by some as a badge of honor and rejected by others because of the activism and militancy with which it is associated. Even among the Chicano activists some make an unconscious adjustment vis-à-vis their Indian heritage and cling tenaciously to their Spanish past; yet the term Chicano itself has Indian origins. Chicano derives from a tribe of the Aztecs known as *Mexicas*. In time references to the tribe in the Nahua language as *Mexicanos* led through contraction and prounciation to the present spelling and pronunciation—*Mexicas, Mexicano, Xicano, Chicano* (Meier and Rivera 1972, pp. xiv, 8).

La Raza's journey towards recognition of *Chicanismo* has been one of struggle. In the year 1846 the Mexican army, much more numerous and powerful than that of the Americans, should have easily vanquished its enemy which arrived to revel in the Halls of Moctezuma, but the ancient Aztec cycle of history had completed its revolution again. As before, Huitzilopochtli, the Aztec god of war, and the other Aztec gods had abandoned the Mexican people. According to the ancient legend of the white god Quetzalcóatl, it was futile to resist the white gods who were more powerful than the brown gods of Aztlán.

In New Mexico, General Stephen Watts Kearny greeted the Mexican people saying that the army had come as their friend to better the conditions of the people. It was reminiscent of the words of Hernán Cortés three and a quarter centuries earlier, in 1519, on the occasion of his first meeting with the Aztec monarch Moctezuma: "Tell Moctezuma that we are his friends. There is nothing to fear....We have come to your house in Mexico as friends." Before the conquest of Tenochtitlan was over, more than 240,000 Aztecs would be sacrificed to propitiate the white gods from Spain (Valdez and Steiner 1972, pp. 28-29, 30).

The Corteses and Kearnys were carriers of new technologies, the representatives of different civilizations which profoundly changed the worlds of Mexico and Aztlán—modifying but not annihilating them. The Indian and mestizo world of Aztlán, now the Southwest of the United States, has metamorphosed into a different civilization. Arthur Campa has described very well the influence of Mexican culture, already tinged by Indian influence, on the Southwest and on the Anglo-American immigrant to Aztlán:

> ...These newcomers [Anglo-Americans], learned from the inhabitants to use water for irrigation, to break the wild *mesteño* into a serviceable mount, to work the longhorn cattle of the *ranchos*, to eat *frijoles, chile,* and *charqui* and to build with *adobe* in a land where timber was non-existent. In California, they learned to shout *chispa* not gold....they learned to pan the streams with a *batea*, to process quartz with an *arrastra* after bringing it up from the mine over *escaleras* [ladders]....Many Anglo-Americans whether trappers, prospectors, or traders, built upon a Mexican base, much of the culture what we call today southwestern. Take the *ranchos* and the cattle industry of a century ago from the Texan, remove his *chaparreras* [chaps] and *tapaderas* (leather stirrup cover), relieve him of his *lazo* (lasso), his *reata* (lariat), his *remuda* (relay of horses), his *sombrero*, his *mostranco* (mustang)...and his *rodeo*, and he is reduced to the midwestern farmer he was before he came into contact with the civilization that made him different from the rest of the *Americanos*...and incidentally, the American folk hero, the cowboy, vanishes (Campa 1973, p. 20).

In the Southwest the Spanish language remains as the spoken, if not official, language of the people of Aztlán. Chicanos speak Spanish, the language of the conquering European, and consider it part of the Chicano cultural heritage even though Spanish had earlier replaced Nahuatl, the language of the sixteenth century Mexican Indian. Much of the earlier Indianness of pre-Spanish culture also remains as a part of our heritage. Indian Mexico is an integral part of the Chicano culture on the north side of the arbitrary cactus curtain that separates Chicanos from their Mexican mestizo and Indian brothers. Buffer worlds such as Indian Aztlán are destined by history to surface once again.

Most Chicanos are likely more Indian than European, because relatively few Spaniards came to the New World. Initially, the Spaniards married Indian women creating the mestizo, who in turn married Indians or other mestizos. The Spanish villa of Santa Cruz de la Cañada, surrounded by three pueblos—San Juan, Santa Clara, and San Ildefonso—in what is today New Mexico, offers an interesting study of this intermarriage. The 1790 census of the town reveals that nearly the entire population listed itself as either *castizo* or mestizo; and almost none declared themselves to be *indios*. It is likely that many who called themselves mestizos were *indios*, but because they spoke Spanish and lived apart from the nearby pueblos they no longer referred to themselves as *indios*. This is a logical conclusion, given the Spanish social scale, which encouraged Hispanicization. If they were indeed mestizos, they offer evidence of considerable miscegenation. In any case, the high percentage of mestizos demonstrates the strong Indian influence on this Spanish colonial town. At the time of independence from Spain, in 1821, the population of New Mexico was approximately half mestizo. Yet one hundred and fifty years later, most of the Mexican Americans of northern New Mexico prefer to be called Hispano or Spanish American.

Evidence of the Indian culture of Aztlán is abundant. The Indian name "Aztlán" has a universal meaning that connotes a spiritual union, the beginning of Chicano cultural nationalism. Aztlán was the mythological homeland of the Aztecs, the Nahua-speaking people before their migration southward to Yucatan. The gods of Aztlán then must be Indian. Today, the *huelgas* (labor strikes), the processions, and other solemn occasions of the Chicanos are conducted under the sacred banner of the brown Virgen de Guadalupe, the patron saint of the Mexican campesino, who is the Christian counterpart of the gentle Indian goddess Tonantzín. Tonantzín was worshipped at the place where the Basilica of the Virgen de Guadalupe now stands in the Valley of Mexico. The brown Virgen protected the Indian and mestizo masses in 1810 when they struggled to throw off the cruel yoke of the Spanish gachupín oppressors who worshipped the white Virgen de los Remedios.

In Mexico, during the Conquest, the Spanish gained domination over the country and maintained their control for 300 years. Control meant maintaining a world of privilege for the gachupín and Creole overlords of colonial society. In 1810 the masses spoke and the outcry was deafening. Mexico saw blood run as it had during the reign of terror in the French Revolution. The old order was threatened even more with the rise to political power of the Indian and mestizo in the 1850s with the emergence of the *Reforma* of Benito Juárez and other Indians who ended, temporarily, the unequal position of the masses in Mexico. Later, in 1910 this struggle for real freedom was continued. Again the Virgen de Guadalupe symbolized this second struggle for independence. She is an Indian symbol.

When the Revolutionary movement was institutionalized in the Partido Revolucionario Institucional (PRI), presidents such as Lázaro Cárdenas officially declared the mestizo as the main component of the Mexican population. The Indian origins were discovered and reemphasized. This rediscovery undoubtedly touched the Mexicans who lived "north from Mexico."

Today many Indian symbols in Mexican and Mexican American culture are interpreted as Chicano. Some are the Aztec figures on Chicano magazine covers; the Aztec eagle on the *Huelga* banners of César Chávez and the United Farm Workers; Emiliano Zapata, an Indian, is one of the historical figures most commemorated by Chicanos in the movement. These and other unconscious symbols affirm a new trend among Mexican Americans to accept the Indianness in their heritage.

To illustrate the prevalence of the Indian influence on Mexican and Mexican American culture it is appropriate to single out highlights in the language, traditions, beliefs, and customs traceable primarily to Aztec origins and to a lesser degree to the Maya, Toltec, Olmec, Zapotec, and

Tarasco Indians who also lived in pre-Columbian Mexico.

More subtle, but pervasive, are the many foods, words, place names, beliefs, and legends that are still replete in Mexican American culture. It is important to note that current pronunciations of the Hispanicized Aztec words usually drop the "l" or "i" endings from the original Aztec spelling due to the phonetic differentiation in pronunciation between the two languages. Aztec words ending in "tl" usually end in Spanish "te" (*cax-itl=cajete*) and Aztec words ending in "li" end in Spanish "le" (*tamalli=tamale*).

The most familiar to most Americans are the Mexican foods and drinks which are largely Aztec. Primary among these are the maize derivative foods such as corn tortillas, pinole, *gordas* (thick corn tortillas), tamales, *nixtamal* (cooked corn), *chicos*, and *pozole*. *Atole*, a porridge made from corn meal; *pozole*, usually prepared with pigs' feet or shanks; *menudo*, prepared out of hominy and beef tripe; and *chicos*, made of dried corn, constitute the Chicano equivalent of Black soul food. Chili, probably the best known Mexican dish, is traceable to the Aztecs as are dishes such as enchiladas, tamales, and tacos. Other common foods, fruits, drinks, vegetables, or dishes are : *cacahuates* (peanuts), chicle (gum), chocolate, *ejotes* (green beans), *camotes* (sweet potatoes), guacamole (avocado salad), *mezcal* (corn liquor), tequila (a strong liquor derived from the agave plant), *tomates* (tomatoes), and *quelites* (spinach) (Thomas 1974, pp. 49-54).

The Aztec influence is manifest in many words thought to be Spanish, but which are actually of Aztec origin. Examples are *nopal* (cactus), *elote* (ear of corn), *chapulín* (grasshopper), *aguacate* (tropical fruit tree), *gua-jolote* (salamander), mesquite, *mitote* (gossip), *papalote* (kite), *zoquete* (mud), *metate* (grinding stone), *cajete* (water drum), *mecate* (rope or string), *milpa* (sown field), and *chiche* (breast).

Interestingly, the slang used by the young zoot-suit Mexican separatist subgroup *pachuco* in the 1940s and 1950s in the barrios included Aztec origin words such as *calco* (shoe), *cuate* (friend), *chante* (home), and *ruco* (old man) (Thomas 1974, pp. 49-54).

Also common are Aztec or other Indian origin words which appear as place names. In New Mexico (the name of the state itself is of Aztec origin) alone there are towns named Montezuma, Tecolote, Capulín, Aztec,

Analco, Chilili, Coyote, Cuates, Mesquite, Petaca, and Toltec (Thomas 1974, p. 55).

That the Indian influence goes beyond language and words is manifested in the many and varied beliefs and legends still current in New Mexico which are traceable to Aztec origins. They were transmitted like much of Mexican culture, in stories handed down through generations. Two examples are the legend of *La Llorona* and the legend of *Malinche*.

The legend of *La Llorona* exists in several variations but all tell of a woman who roams the streets and fields at night wailing and pursuing wayward children. The story, frequently told and implanted in the minds of young children, is used to scare them and keep them at home after dark. One popular version of the story concerns Luisa, a beautiful but poor young maiden, who falls in love with Nuño de Móntez, a handsome and wealthy bachelor. Luisa bears him children out of wedlock but is kept from marrying Nuño because of class barriers. When Nuño marries another woman, Luisa goes mad, and in a rage kills her children. As a result she is tried, convicted, and scourged. By strange coincidence her lover dies the same day she is scourged. As the story goes Luisa's soul is *La Llorona* searching for children to replace those whom she killed. As the cry of the *lobo* or wind is similar to the cry of a wailing woman, the story is clearly fixed in the mind of the young Chicanito who would dare wander out at night.

The story of *La Malinche* bears some resemblance and has on occasion been confused with that of *La Llorona*. *La Malinche* was the Indian mistress of Hernán Cortés and bore him sons. When Cortés abandoned her, she killed the two sons in her misery. Tradition has it that she spent the remaining years roaming the streets of Tenochtitlan in the dark of night, dressed in white, wailing over the loss of her sons (Thomas 1974, pp. 58-61).

Other aspects of Mexican Indian folklore and beliefs manifest themselves in contemporary Mexican American behavior. Manuel Gamio, in describing some folklore from Michoacán and Jalisco from whence many Mexican immigrants came, describes the Indian belief systems. The strong tradition of veneration of elders by the young Mexican American could be linked to certain Indian customs. For example, in the village of Cheran the natives bury in their fields, idols called *tares* which are the symbolic remains of old men. They believe that the idols will help ensure a good harvest.

The virtue of chastity is still comparatively strong among Mexican American women in spite of the more liberal sexual mores of the contemporary period. Undoubtedly, this was influenced by Mexican customs, many of which in turn can be traced to our Indian origins. For example, one custom in Angagua and other pueblos in Mexico traceable to Aztec origins was the placing of a clean white sheet on the marriage bed by an old woman of the village on the day of the wedding. The following morning the woman discreetly enters the bedroom and removes the bed sheet. If the sheet contains the virginal blood, the happy announcement is proclaimed to the village whereupon the wedding feast continues. If the sheet is spotless, however, this indicates that the bride was not a virgin. The celebration would cease immediately. The guests in reproach of the bride would break the pottery (the perennial wedding gift) thus making it unserviceable (Gamio 1930, pp. 217-19).

Many beliefs relative to pregnancy and newborn children have roots in Indian culture and are also strong among Mexican Americans. One belief is that if a pregnant woman looks at an eclipse of the moon, she will give birth to a lame child. Another belief, perhaps less current, is that a pregnant woman does not carry salt, chili, or lime for fear that her child will be born deaf or blind. New mothers do not like strangers to fondle their children for fear that they will give the child "el ojo" (the evil eye), which could lead to violent illness in the child. To avoid the evil eye, a mother may tie a ribbon on the child's blouse, put a coral necklace around its neck, or otherwise distract the "eye of la bruja." Mothers still practice the custom known in Jilotlan of pulling the noses of children during the first two months of life to prevent the child from being pug-nosed (Gamio 1930, pp. 217-223).

Another practice common in some homes of Mexican Americans is that of having a religious area, usually a small niche or altar, for a special patron saint such as Saint Jude. Votive candles burn constantly and incense may burn to commemorate the saint on special religious holidays (Gamio 1930, p. 220).

Indian influence is also present in mystical beliefs surprisingly strong among some Mexican Americans today. In addition to the preceding examples, belief in *brujería* (witchcraft) and *curanderas* (folk healers) is common among Mexican Americans in the Southwest. Rudolfo Anaya's work *Bless*

Me, Ultima, one of the most popular recent Mexican American novels, reflects these aspects of our culture. Indian influence is pervasive in folk medicine, particularly in the use of herbs and other remedies. Our people use herbs to cure ailments ranging from ulcers and headache, to stomach irregularities and colic in newborn babies. Medicinal herbs are often stocked along with modern drugs in drugstores serving Mexican American clientele.

The significance of such beliefs, legends, and language to Mexican American values, attitudes, and socialization patterns is well described by Jorge Thomas who observes that "superstitions and legends, whether based on fact or fiction continue to be a very important element in the life of the Mexican American...A belief does not have to be fact to influence the thinking of the young....These legends and language indicate the survival of Indian and Mexican culture among Mexican Americans in New Mexico today" (Thomas 1974, p. 62).

Other influences of our Indian past on Mexican and Mexican American culture may have been more covert or gone unnoticed because they were generally consistent with Hispanic cultural traits. Among these are the patriarchal tradition in which the father is the unchallenged head of the family. In Indian cultures the woman walks behind the man and generally performs most of the chores including such tasks as plastering the adobe hut. In the Spanish tradition the male is also dominant as manifested by the patronymical origin of some Spanish names such as Martínez [los hijos de (sons of) *Martín*].

In their political culture the Indian societies were characterized by a hierarchical structure where the leadership was inherited and usually the province of an elite group (such as the supremacy of Moctezuma over the Aztecs); this, likewise, reinforced the Hispanic monarchical tradition. Spain in the sixteenth century was one of the most absolutist of the European monarchies. These traditions continued and manifested themselves in the patrón-peón system of nineteenth century New Mexico territorial politics and are even visible in the strong-man rule of jefes políticos in the twentieth century. In social interaction, the Indians of New Mexico, like the Spaniards, had a definite caste or class structure. Together these contributed to the near feudal social structure which was instituted in the Southwest by the Spaniards.

In religion, the Christian piety of the Spanish Catholic is still evident in the strong adherence of the Mexican American to the Roman Catholic Church. There is, however, evidence of Indian influence. Although the religious rites of the Mexican American Penitentes have been traced to Spanish and Franciscan Third Order origins, there is evidence that flagellation was a common religious rite among some tribes of Indians (Weigle 1976, pp. 26-29). Although Ross Calvin lacks an understanding of the Penitentes, he, too, substantiates an Indian influence in their rites. "...Popular ignorance left without the guidance of the Church relapsed naturally into fanaticism, and the Mexican zealot, inheriting from the Spaniard a tragic interpretation of Christianity, and from his Indian forebears a recent and thinly covered savagery, evolved presently a cruel and schematic cult of scourge" (Calvin 1965, p. 217).

In familial ties, the Spanish *compadrazgo* system of the extended family was likewise consonant with the Indian tribal structure. Both contributed to close familial and tribal relationships but militated against formation of larger group associations.

In summary, we have described the more obvious as well as the subtle manifestations of the Chicanos' Indian past. Yet, what cannot be discerned is its influence on Chicano psychology—our thoughts, our reasoning, our logic, and our choice of values. In spite of all of the aforementioned manifestations, the Indianness of the Chicano is denied by many of *La Raza*, as is its very essence of *Chicanismo*.

One is reminded of the most apropos excerpt in José Anotonio Villarreal's *Pocho* which reflects so accurately the attitudes of two generations about the brown-white syndrome and Indian status, and the extent of denial of Indianness by mestizos born in the United States. Richard, the pocho, states to his Mexican-born father, Juan Rubio,

> "Do you think, Papa," he said, "that when we go to Mexico I could have a horse?"
> "That is understood."
> "A white one, and very big?"
> "If you want," said Juan Rubio. "But why do you want a white one?"

"Because I want the best."

"Who told you that? White horses are usually little more than useless."

"You are playing with me," said Richard. "Everyone knows that a white horse is the best horse there is."

Juan Rubio laughed. "Hoo, that shows how much you know. That is only in the motion pictures, but if you knew anything about horses you would know that a good horse is not chosen for his color...What is this obsession about the brown?" asked Juan Rubio.

"It is only—" Richard began.

"Enough! A horse is a horse!"

Richard asked, "Mama, was your great-grandfather a rich one?"

"No, but he was independent and worked for different people, because he was not a peon."

"He was Indian, was he not?"

"Yes, he was an Indian from the South country, but do not feel superior—you are Indian, too, as well as Spanish and probably even French."

"But my father told me I was not Spanish."...Richard had never understood that side of his father (Villarreal 1959, pp. 96-99).

Reading Chicano literature today, one sees obvious pride in the emerging Chicano cultural heritage—which is not yet clearly defined. The inconsistency is that the search tó reestablish or recapture the Chicano cultural heritage is frequently an attempt by Chicanos to return to their European or Spanish heritage. The emphasis is on the Spanish rather than the mestizo or the Indian aspects, yet Mexico's society is very definitely an Indian one.

It is not difficult to comprehend why *La Raza* consciously or unconsciously coveted a white image when one considers first the Mexican experience. It was the white Spanish European who violated the brown woman of Mexico, producing from that union the mestizo. The mestizo carried within his heart the seeds of conflict, being a bastard and part of neither of the two worlds around him. With time and numbers, however, he created his own world which he today dominates in the place of the colonial white European. Yet, there is a frustration. After throwing off the white world of the Spaniard and the Anglo, who continued the Spaniard's domination, some Mexican Americans yearn to be white. They are heard to say, "I have to wear a hat in the sun, because if I don't I'll get too dark;" other Mexican Americans romanticize both Chicanas with green eyes and fair complexions as well as white women. The reasons for this lie in the deep recesses of the Mexican American psyche, a psyche influenced by decades of relegation to an inferior racial and social status, and years of suffering from prejudice and discrimination which probably perpetrated irreparable harm in the hearts and minds of many Mexican Americans.

As pointed out before, one of the most important consequences of the Chicano Movement may be an alteration of this view. But we have, as yet, not reached that point. Some Mexican Americans, still caught up in the assimilation process, remain unmoved by the Chicano Movement and its call for cultural awareness, for we are a people caught in a paradox: Is assimilation into Anglo society to be resisted to the point of complete separation? To answer "yes" is being unrealistic. However, what has been started by the *Movimiento* is not about to die. There are signs that portend a change. The Indianness in our heritage will no longer be a source of embarrassment or something to ignore, but rather a source of pride and enrichment.

BIBLIOGRAPHY

Alport, Gordon. *The Nature of Prejudice*. Boston: Beacon Press, 1958.

Barrera, Mario; Muños C.; and Ornelas, C. 1972. "The Barrio as an Internal Colony." *Urban Affairs Annual Review* 6:465-98.

Calvin, Ross. *Sky Determines: An Interpretation of the Southwest*. Albuquerque: University of New Mexico Press, 1965.

Campa, Arthur. "The Mexican American in Historical Perspective." *Chicano: The Evolution of a People*. Edited by Renato Rosaldo. Minneapolis: Winston Press, 1973.

Casavantes, Edward J. *A New Look at the Attributes of the Mexican American*. Albuquerque: Southwestern Cooperative Educational Laboratory, 1969.

Cue Canovas, Agustín. *Los Estados Unidos y el México Olvidado*. México, D.F.: B. Costa-Amic, 1970.

450 años del pueblo chicano: 450 Years of Chicano History in Pictures. Albuquerque, N.M.: Chicano Communications Center, 1976.

Gamio, Manuel.*Mexican Immigration to the United States: A Study of Human Migration and Adjustment*. Chicago: University of Chicago Press, 1930.

López y Rivas, Gilberto. *Chicano; o, la explotación de "la raza."* México, D.F.: Editorial Imprenta Casa, 1969.

Mead, George H. *Mind, Self, and Society*. Chicago: University of Chicago Press, 1934.

Meier, Matt, and Rivera, Feliciano. *The Chicanos: A History of Mexican Americans*. New York: Hill and Wang, 1972.

Memmi, Albert. *The Colonizer and the Colonized*. Translated by Howard Greenfeld. New York: Orion Press, 1965.

Moore, Joan. "Colonialism: The Case of the Mexican American." *Social Problems* 17 (Spring 1970): 463-72.

Pitt, Leonard. *The Decline of the Californios: A Social History of the Spanish-Speaking Californians, 1846-1890*. Berkeley: University of California Press, 1966.

Samora, Julián, and Simon, Patricia V. *A History of the Mexican-American People*. South Bend, Indiana: University of Notre Dame Press, 1976.

Thomas, Jorge. "Influencia Azteca en la cultura y lenguaje de Nuevo Méjico," Unpublished M.A. thesis. Las Vegas, New Mexico: New Mexico Highlands University, 1974.

Toch, Hans. *The Social Psychology of Social Movements*. New York: Bobbs-Merrill, Co., 1965.

Twitchell, Ralph Emerson. *The Leading Facts of New Mexican History*, vol. 2. Cedar Rapids, Iowa: Torch Press, 1911-12.

Valdés, Daniel T. *Political History of New Mexico*, vol. 1. Unpublished manuscript, 1971.

Valdez, Luis and Steiner, Stan, eds. *Aztlán: An Anthology of Mexican American Literature*. New York: A.A. Knopf, 1972.

Villarreal, José Antonio. *Pocho*. Garden City, N.Y.: Doubleday and Co., 1959.

Weigle, Marta. *Brothers of Light, Brothers of Blood: The Penitentes of the Southwest*. Albuquerque: University of New Mexico Press, 1976.

Weiss, Frederick A. "Self-Alienation: Dynamics and Therapy," *Man Alone: Alienation in Modern Society*. Edited by Eric and Mary Josephson. New York: Dell Publishing Co., 1962.

Myth and Comparative Cultural Nationalism: The Ideological Uses of Aztlán

Genaro M. Padilla

> "...We are the fruit of the people who wandered from the mythical land of Aztlán, the first people of this land who wandered south in search of a sign."
>
> *Heart of Aztlán*

I

Much has been written about the pervasive presence of Aztec mythic elements, as well as about the theme of Aztlán as homeland in Chicano literature during the past two decades. Tomás Ybarra-Frausto's essay "Alurista's Poetics: The Oral, the Bilingual, the Pre-Columbian,"[1] is one of the early assessments of the indigenous mythic impulse in a writer and thinker who may, in large measure, be credited with generating the cultural nationalist call for a return to an indigenous spiritual homeland in the 1960's. In "From the Temple to the Arena: Teatro Chicano Today,"[2] Jorge Huerta offers useful remarks on the continuity between the "first indígena rituals" in Tenochtitlan and the theatrical ritual of groups like Teatro Campesino. Egla Morales Blouin describes the multiform uses of Aztec symbols and images in her informative article "Símbolos y motivos nahuas en la literatura chicano."[3] While Blouin's essay is mainly descriptive, she does comment upon the political, as well as the psychological, rationale for using the Nahuatl past in Chicano literature; she writes: "Como contraste a las repetidas humillaciones que brinda la realidad socio-económica, el constante recuerdo de una orgullosa ascendencia azteca sostiene el chicano."[4] Guillermo Lux and Maurilio Vigil expand upon the nationalistic impulse which turns humiliation about the Chicano's indigenous past into an intense retrieval of that past in "Return to Aztlán."[5] And tracing that return to Aztlán for the material of cultural and literary renewal, Tomás Vallejos has written an exhaustive and considerate dissertation exploring the various manifestations of ancient Indian myth in the fiction of Rudolfo Anaya, Tomás Rivera, Orlando Romero, Ron Arias and others.[6]

Yet, despite the relatively wide scholarship describing this Chicano appropriation of an indigenous past, rich in mythic power, little if anything has been written which would place the Chicano revitalization movement within a historical and comparative cultural context; that is, a context within which Chicano nativism is considered alongside cultural revitalization projects in other independence movements, many played out on a larger and much more violent stage. The association between political independence movements and the cultural nationalism that leads to a passionate rediscovery and recuperation of mythic origins has been so widespread that there are striking similarities between recent Chicano cultural nationalism, with its strong nativist impulse, and political liberation movements with their attendant nativism in, for example, eastern Europe during the mid-nineteenth century, Ireland, modern East India, China, and Africa.

The most recent example of a coincident nationalist movement occurred during the social and racial tumult of the 1960s when American ethnic groups attempted to resuscitate their cultural origins during a time when American social and cultural values were being challenged and often rejected. Imamu Baraka, Ron Karenga, Carolyn Gerald, to name only a few Black writers and cultural theorists, were among those bent upon reconstructing Black consciousness by challenging white cultural hegemonies and replacing them with neo-African symbols of blackness. As Gerald writes in "The Black Writer and His Role," "These [white] images must be mythically torn down, ritually destroyed...Our work at this stage is clearly to destroy the zero and negative image-myths of ourselves by turning them inside out."[7] Other American ethnic groups also sought to ward off the effects of white cultural hegemony by consciously revitalizing their own cultural sources with their sustaining legends and myths. What we see repeated again and again, whether it be in nineteenth-century Hungary or Czechoslovakia, the Irish nationalist movement, the African anti-colonial uprisings, or even the French Canadian autonomy drive (a social phenomenon which perhaps best parallels the recent linguistic and cultural concerns of the Chicano), is a close relationship between a people's desire to determine their own political fortunes and their passion to restore their own cultural mythos, a vital psychic component of national identity which gives energy and purpose to their political struggle.

In all of these examples, the relationship between political upheaval and the nativist artistic projects which seek to mend a people's threatened or even shattered cultural psyche bespeaks the lateral material and spiritual needs of a group. Discussing the process through which subjugated cultures reject the colonial structures that distort, devalue and seek to destroy their history, Franz Fanon, the Algerian intellectual who became a spokesman for African independence movements after World War II, points out the "dialectical significance" of restoring, even reinventing the native past, in spite of the persistent realities that seem to nullify such an antiquary undertaking. In *The Wretched of the Earth* Fanon writes:

> I am ready to concede that on the plane of factual being the past existence of an Aztec civilization does not change anything very much in the diet of the Mexican peasant of today. I admit that all of the proofs of a wonderful Songhai civilization will not change the fact that today the Songhais are underfed and illiterate...But it has been remarked several times that this passionate search for a national culture which existed before the colonial era finds its legitimate reason in the anxiety shared by native intellectuals to shrink away from that Western culture in which they all risk being swamped. Because they realize they are in danger of losing their lives and thus becoming lost to their people, these men, hotheaded and with anger in their hearts, relentlessly determine to renew contact once more with the oldest and most pre-colonial springs of life of their people...[8]

Fanon is careful to warn that the tendency to heroize the cultural self and to idealize the past must at crucial stages in the struggle be qualified; otherwise, the material aims of the group may indeed be led astray by idle dreams and empty symbols. Without heroic dreams and cultural symbols of mythic proportion, however, the material aims of a nationalist movement may lack the spiritual center which sustains struggle. The drive for a homeland, however tenuous, may be said to hinge upon the degree to which the group, inspired in part by its poets, is able to imagine its own mytho-historic identity. Even when the romanticizing of the past, as well as the present cultural identity,is exposed as a self-serving illusion and corrected by those social critics, historians, or political theorists whose view of social relations remains dispassionately fixed upon material forces in society, the mythic element that permeates the popular consciousness may not easily be exorcised as useless trivia since it has come to assume a life of its own in the group's imagination. It ceases, perhaps, to generate the fervor required for material political resistance, but it establishes another ground within the consciousness of the community as a genuinely recurring narrative that describes the genesis and the destiny of the culture. This appropriation of a legendary and heroic past establishes a storehouse of images and symbols which function as amulets, magical signifiers of self-preservation. The revived heroes and legends of the mythic past continue to inhabit the cultural imagination long after their service to the resistance movement has waned. In fact, these stories and legends now sustain a form of psychic resistance that remains intact well after the actual phase of physical resistance has ended. The role of the artist, then, proves to be a significant and often more continuous one than that of the political nationalist.

In this respect, Chicano artist-poets like the traditional *cantadores* (ballad-singers) or *cuentistas* (story-tellers) in the folk community, as well as writers like Alurista, Rudolfo Anaya, Luis Valdez, Tomás Rivera, as H. Ernest Lewald suggests, act as the "guardians of their people's culture and singers of its themes."[9] Or, to follow Bruce-Novoa's assessment of Alurista's assumed role as *tlamantini*, (Nahuatl, as Bruce-Novoa explains, for "philosopher or wise man"), who according to Miguel León-Portilla was "responsible for composing, painting, knowing, and teaching the songs and poems in which they [Aztecs] preserved their scientific knowledge."[10] This role as guardian and upholder of the group culture, it should be understood, increases in intensity and consequence in times of crisis. As Lewald points out in the introduction to *The Cry of Home: Cultural Nationalism and the Modern Writer*, these "guardians" or *tlamantinime* have at various times in history "worked and reworked myths and ritual that bound a group of people together with the aid of symbols and sounds, creating the magic spell which made men rush into battle, defy death, and accept an impending fate."[11] Their literature was one that "constantly kindled the folk imagination," one that gave people a common and shared identification as well as a common and shared destiny. The epic materials that we know as literature, frozen into text and taught today in the classroom as the Great Books, had in their originating historical moment an ideologically ethnocentric significance for their auditors. "Aeneas, Beowulf, or Roland," as Lewald says, "shouldered the heavy responsibility of carrying out their mission within a national framework. The *Iliad*, the *Eddas*, or the *Kalevala* constitute 'expressions of a profound sense of togetherness' in which human activity is energized into a spiritual force."[12] After serving an ethnocentrifying function, such cultural narratives assume a less politically balanced but equally privileged aesthetic function as the nation's literature. The symbols and sounds that made men rush into battle end-up outlasting the wars which, after all, recede into history as a series of stories that may, in due time, be reinvigorated with the heroic stature required by another generation of cultural guardians.

Such reworking of myths and recuperation of national epic narrative being the business of many poets in many nations and times, I would like to diagram a few of the cultural-nationalist literary projects that may be seen to correspond with the Chicano's archeological search for the mythic self. My purpose in all of this is to suggest, by way of both direct and implicit analogy, the manner in which nationalistically motivated reconstructions of cultural myths in other times and places illuminate the Chicano's appropriation and reinvention of the Mexican, and especially the pre-Columbian mythic and heroic past. That many such projects precede Chicano efforts does not in any way diminish the imaginative uses of the legendary past in Chicano literature. On the contrary, such knowledge gives historical context and socio-political warrant to the Chicano's myth-making enterprise. It indicates the extent to which the Chicano, threatened with cultural and spiritual extinction, has struggled to maintain group cohesion through myth and a heroized national past distinct from that of the United States. Moreover, we are urged to consider such issues as are at stake in the emergence of cultural-nationalist projects that the experiences of other groups may help us to clarify. When, for instance, does the appropriation of the heroic past lead to self-delusive political action, specifically to high-sounding but doomed battle against a superior military force? What happens when political activists mandate the work of the "guardians of culture?" When does myth become shrill propaganda? At what point should the past be challenged for its lies and deceits rather than idealized and accorded heroic dimensions for political purposes? The experiences of other groups may help us to answer some of these questions.

II

National liberation movements in mid-19th century eastern European countries, in Ireland at the end of the last century, and in Africa and French Quebec more recently, provide a small but significant field of examples upon which a discussion of such questions may be undertaken. The self-assumed mantle of cultural guardian, the nationalistic passion that often leads not only to recuperation but to outright invention of the mythic past, and the unavoidable tensions between the artistic imagination and the political mind all come into sharp relief when describing the cultural-nationalist projects in these countries. In every instance, the poet-intellectual-artist assumes a central role in the movement for a distinct cultural identity and national independence.

Before Alurista, Rodolfo Gonzales, Luis Valdez and Rudolfo Anaya consciously set about to reconstruct their peoples' indigenous sources through a literary discourse laden with culturally symbolic representations, artists and scholars in Czechoslovakia, Hungary and Poland, for example, were closely involved in the political efforts to revive, sustain, and direct national consciousness toward national independence from the Hapsburgs. In Czechoslovakia, while intellectuals and writers were paying lip service to the Viennese government during the day, they often secretly schemed at night to foment uprisings. The literature they produced during the first half of the nineteenth century was characterized by visitations into the Slavic past, usually in the form of nostalgic, often sentimental, but always highly patriotic history, anecdotal fiction, and poetry, especially ballads. Perhaps the best examples of Czech writers inspired by the nationalist impulse during that time are Frantisek Palacky (1798-1876) and Vaclav Hanka (1791-1861).

Palacky was a scholar whose *History of the Czech Nation in Bohemia and Moravia* (1836) ends with the accession of the Hapsburgs to the Czech throne in 1526. Ending with events that led to the demise of Czech political sovereignty, it is quite consciously a politicized history of a free Czech nation. Although exhaustive in its research on geography, diplomatic, legal and religious history, the narrative is ultimately a celebration of Czech life before the Germanic influence. According to Arne Novak, Palacky "idealized the Slavs and their early history, and contrasted the supposed democracy of the ancient Czechs and Slavs to the feudal order which was presumably typical of the Germanic spirit."[13] As national historian, Palacky was in a position of public importance that lent credibility to his work, even though "the picture it paints of the earliest history is a fiction, partly based on unauthentic sources and an over-idealization of an ancient Slavic past" (140). As a politically motivated revisionist history, then, it "reflects the author's desire to defend and extol the Czech past, and to serve a great mission of National Revival"[14] and restoration of the homeland.

During the 1960s, Chicanos freely engaged in this necessary archeological fabulation. By way of comparison, note this explanation offered by one Chicano about why the Spanish invaders were able to conquer the Aztecs so handily: "...according to the principles and philosophy of the Nahuas, aggression, warfare, private property, perfidy, treason, robbery, intoxication and adultery were virtually unknown since this was not in accord to the laws of nature or Tloke Nauake [humanity]."[15] One has to wonder just where this utopian tribe of Aztecas was residing when other tribes were being slaughtered by the militaristic Aztecs. This is an extreme example, but it indicates the extent which the nationalistic imagination may be driven to exalt the native past.

The story of Vaclav Hanka's part in the Czech national revival is equally fascinating. Hanka, a poet, Slavicist, and librarian at the Museum of the Bohemian Kingdom, was familiar with the Russian and Serbian folk epic, "considering it the equal of Homer and the nibelungenlied," Novak writes.[16] Regretting that nothing similar existed in the Czech national treasury, he, along with several scholar friends, decided to invent a national epic. They drew their material from Russian folk songs, Old Czech literature, and also from Homer, Tasso, Milton, and Ossian. They transformed the language into "archaic guise," "faked the paleographic transcription," and then set up the discovery of the "epic fragments." The result of this audacious project was first, the discovery (in an ancient Gothic vault nonetheless) of the *Rukopis Kralovedvorsky* (1817), a "13th century manuscript," and, in the next year, the mysterious find of an even older epic fragment, the *Rukopis Zelenohorsky*, which was dated from the 9th century. As Novak points out, in both of these supposedly rediscovered national epics, "Old Czech life and history, described in astonishing detail, shine with the glittering colors of a unique and highly developed culture. A two-fold virile ideal was placed at the pinnacle of national existence: the brave hero protecting the motherland and the mother-tongue from the attacks of foreigners, and the entrusted bard, beloved of the gods, who inspired the hero to great deeds..."[17]

Extremely popular because they assuaged "the self-esteem of a nation which had just begun to recover from long decline,"[18] the manuscripts were not positively exposed as forgeries until 1886, and even then against intense opposition from traditionalists who regarded the exposé as a betrayal of the country and its heroic past. As in Palacky's *History* and the nationalistically-purposive work of other poets and scholars, the impulse that led Hanka and his friends to invent an epic past sprang from their passion for national and cultural self-identity. Forgery notwithstanding, their enterprise itself may be seen as an epic endeavor undertaken on behalf of the Czech people.

The same drive for a distinct national identity fueled similar literary projects in other eastern European countries that were attempting to exorcise the debilitating influence of the German Hapsburgs. In Hungary, for example, literature has often been marked by a profound concern for cultural identity and the nation's political destiny. As Joseph Remenyi writes in *Hungarian Writers and Literature*,[19] prior to the war against Austria in 1848 there was a widespread cultural awakening that solidified the nation's will to survive. Again, the nation's poets and intellectuals were at the center of a movement to restore their racial epos and to celebrate "in the right spirit and manner the men and events of the heroic age of their forefathers."[20] Some writers did more than just fire the popular imagination with heroes from the legendary past as Mihaly Vorosmarty's (1800-1855) heroic epic *Zalan futasa* ("Zalan's Flight") had. Sandor Petofi (1823-1849), for instance, who wrote *Janos vitez* ("Hero John"), died on the battlefield as a common soldier in the futile fight for independence. Petofi believed poets had a calling beyond that of armchair revolutionaries producing inspirational patriotic verse. In his programmatic piece "Poets of the Nineteenth Century," Petofi wrote:

> Today the poets are ordained
> By God to be his guiding hand;
> They are the clouds of fire to lead
> The people to the promised land.[21]

As his Polish contemporary Adam Mickiewicz put it, this "cloud of fire," or *wiesczcz* (echos of *tlamantini* poet-prophet, seer, wise man, etc.), had a sacred duty not only to "lead his brothers, to show the road for the nations...[but] to shape one's spirit in such a way that inspiration should become a deed...[for] the resurrection of the Fatherland has come."[22] Petofi's own deed proved that his revolutionary philosophy was more than rhetorical drumbeating in verse.

These examples of countries in eastern Europe that have waged continuous struggle against foreign domination, as they do even to this day (Poland, for instance), indicate just how fiercely a group of people, united by a common threat, set about to sustain their cultural ethos. That the myths and legends are not only recuperated but even invented shows just how central a role they play in defining and establishing the spiritual identity of the nation.

However, since the national poet, the *tlamantini*, *wiesczcz*, or whatever the term used, plays a vital role in the movement for independence, the uses to which his work is put in the nationalist cause raises important questions. The greater the social responsibility he assumes for his work, the greater the artist's recognition of himself as a political, perhaps even a prophetic voice whose work not only reflects the experience of his people, but shapes and directs that experience. Herein lies a danger: the artist believes that, given his privileged position, he may genuinely shape some vital part of the cultural consciousness that leads to socio-political action, perhaps even to street battle and death. The stakes are large since, as Lewald observes, the "magic spell" which impels the populace to "rush into battle, defy death, and accept an impending fate" often marks the artist as a tool to be used in the worst way by political nationalists. The artist's responsibility may be measured in the number of lives sacrificed in a futile uprising or sacrificed for an uprising successfully commandeered by self-serving political nationalists.

Many are the writers who have lent their creative talents to a nationalist effort only to feel the sting of criticism from political extremists who dismissed their efforts as obfuscatory and trivial. As Lewald observes of William Butler Yeats' part in the Irish Nationalist Movement at the turn of the century, Yeats :

> best exemplified the ordeal of the artist forced to distinguish between a national vision and nationalistic means. His reluctance, after having written *Cathleen Ni Houlihan*, to produce further plays with a political texture for the Irish National Theatre shows the artist's awareness of the dangers in surrendering his craft to a non-artistic cause, in Yeats' case to put to use his world of myth, symbols, and language for a nationalistic purpose: a political solution for Ireland.[23]

Yeats' reluctance issued from the prescriptive political program certain nationalists demanded he build into his plays, as well as from his continual arguments with those nationalists whom, he felt, valued literature only when it was politically expedient. Their nationalist myopia had stunted their aesthetic sense, and the result, he feared, would be an Irish literature so transparently propagandistic and rhetorical that it would be the laughing stock of the English enemy.

Before he retreated from the nationalist cause, however, Yeats was instrumental in forming the Irish Literary Society of London (1891), the National Literary Society in Dublin (1892), and the Irish Literary Theatre in 1899. In all of these projects, the primary objective was to celebrate Irish literature, folklore and legend, and in the theatre to present topical political issues in the form of Celtic plays which, Yeats wrote to a friend, "would be far more effective than lectures and might do more than anything else we can do to make the Irish, Scotch and other Celts recognize their solidarity."[24] Yeats' own *Cathleen Ni Houlihan* (1902), among other pieces he contributed to the theatre, had an immediate impact in stirring nationalistic fervor. Like some of the *actos* and *mitos* produced by Luis Valdez's Teatro Campesino, Yeats' *Cathleen* was a "nationalist play which brought onto the stage an emblematic figure for Ireland, the Poor Old Woman who mourns her lost lands, who draws young men out to fight for her, and who, at the news of rebellion against the English, turns into a young girl, and she had the walk of a queen."[25]

Just as Yeats and his contemporaries set about to "create a sense of national identity they believed a necessary preamble to political action,"[26] so did Chicano playwrights like Luis Valdez, whose agit-prop teatro functioned as a consciousness raising vehicle for the farmworkers and for other budding activists who were being politicized. After the actos of the first years, the productions of El Teatro Campesino took on an increasingly dramatic complexity. Still socio-political at center, Valdez's mythic component gave the teatro a "stagey" effect that was extremely effective, if often perplexing to his audiences. His drama became increasingly esoteric and philosophical, a form of drama that required an audience schooled in pre-Columbian mythology, however much it had been adapted to the modern temper as well as to the iconographic needs of the political movement.

Like Yeats, Valdez was convinced that the Chicano cause would be served best by theater that synchronized the mystical and the political, or, put another way, the spiritual and the material. As Valdez stated it, El Teatro Campesino had to turn toward "religious theater" out of "political necessity." The cultural movement needed more than "exhortation or rhetoric," to quote Yeats. For Valdez this meant not a "teatro composed of actos or agit-prop but a teatro of ritual, of music, of beauty and spiritual sensitivity. A teatro of legends and myths."[27] And here, of course, he was referring to the ritual drama of the Aztecas and Mayas. Similarly, some 70 years earlier, Yeats wished also to recreate a theatre that would echo with Celtic ritual, that would be "like the drama acted of old times in the hidden places of temples."[28]

Both dramatists were put on the defensive by political nationalists who believed such ritual or mystical theater was too vaporous a way of dealing with the problems of the here and now. As Robert Tracy writes in "Ireland: The Patriot Game," "Yeats and the other Abbey Theater playwrights very quickly found themselves being denounced by the political nationalists for not being sufficiently positive and didactic."[29] In short, they wanted more drama like *Cathleen Ni Houlihan*, only more propagandistic. In Valdez's case, as Jorge Huerta points out, the attack came from "the emerging Chicano leftists who were making their presence felt in the Chicano movement and TENAZ [El Teatro Nacional de Aztlán]."[30] Their response was perhaps understandable given Valdez's statement that the Chicano must find "ultimate liberation in the Cosmic Vision of our Indio ancestors."[31] This "Indio Vision" was highly spiritual in its neo-Mayan philosophy of mystic love and harmony with the natural world. The reception to such a philosophy was predictable enough: "the leftist inclined groups could hardly be expected to applaud a message of 'In lak'ech' [neo-Mayan for 'You are my other self'] and 'Wait for Jesucristo-Quetzalcóatl.' 'What about the problems of today?' they asked, angered that the leading Chicano Theater company seemed to be losing its political perspective and proletarian origins."[32]

Yeats' response to similar criticism by the predecessors of today's Irish Republican Army was an increasing disillusionment with and detachment from the nationalist movement, whose leadership he regarded as stupidly narrow-minded in its disregard of things spiritual and aesthetic. Later, he would even blame his own early nationalist writing for the waste of young lives in a futile cause. In the poem "The Men and the Echo," written in 1939, he wondered, thinking of the abortive Easter Rising of 1919 when a few revolutionaries seized Dublin's General Post Office and proclaimed the Irish Republic from its steps only to be defeated and executed by the British, "Did that play of mine send out certain men the English shot?"[33] Pressed by guilt, Yeats surmised that given his earlier role of poet as social agent, or "cloud of fire," he had in some central, if mystic, way indeed been responsible.

Valdez has never expressed a similar sentiment, although one might argue that early Teatro Campesino material was measured for its effectiveness in sustaining the spirit of farmworkers who were striking the agribusiness giants, and later for its similar effect on consumers boycotting agricultural products, and that such actions often led to violence. Although César Chávez's philosophy of non-violence generally guided the national boycott, there was frequent violence in the fields and on the streets which may have been influenced by a guerilla theater that inflamed the emotions and identified an enemy against whom Chicanos might lash out. Valdez aside, however, there can be little doubt that at many rallies and demonstrations that turned into street battles, Chicanos had been provoked to anger, first, by police presence, and then, to an unrealistic militarism as the result of fiery political oratory coupled with verse and teatro celebrating the heroism of Aztec warriors like Cuauhtémoc or revolutionaries like Emiliano Zapata.

After Valdez turned away from what might be considered a directly confrontational political theater, the criticism leveled against him from the political nationalists became severe. Valdez's response was initially that of defending his theater's startling new philosophy by insisting that the Chicano must recreate an original relation with his indigenous past. Paradoxically, while this was a classic nativistic impulse, he also argued that such a return to the past required turning to a philosophy in which ethnicity and nationalism were to be regarded as superfluous concepts. Western linear history, with its attendant ethnocentric material concerns, was to be effaced in favor of a neo-Mayan concept of cyclical time, with "love" and "brotherhood" providing a cosmic center for the Chicano who had been displaced in modern American society.

It was perhaps the political contradiction rather than the acquiescent philosophy of brotherly love itself that troubled the activists. How could a drama that proceeded from a nativist orientation, that is, from a desire to restore an ethnocentrically indigenous consciousness, simultaneously eschew ethnicity and nationalism? The cultural nationalist argument hinged upon what appeared to be Valdez's betrayal of the vital objective of cultural maintenance, namely the reaffirmation of ethnicity. For those on the left, Valdez had simply turned his back upon history when he slipped into his cosmic robes.

Having more recently returned from the idealized ancient past to the stark historical present, Valdez's play *Zoot Suit* is an examination of the pachuco as a social rebel who was summarily brutalized for being willfully unique in a society that preaches individualism but enforces conformity, according to stifling white standards. Valdez's return to the mythical Aztlán, then, was aesthetically intriguing and widely influential on other writers, but it has not maintained a lasting presence on his stage. Still, one might argue that Valdez has simply constructed another mythic figure in the form of the pachuco anti-hero.

The scathing criticism by the political radicals, nevertheless, served a useful purpose since a danger in the nativist part of a cultural nationalist movement often lies in idealizing the past in a manner that may well deflect attention from socio-political and economic issues that require immediate action. Inventing a myth of a golden past can have the effect of lulling the group into inaction and a false understanding of its own history. It may lead to worship of ancestors who, in their own society, were as oppressive as the current enemy. Such was the case certainly for the Aztecs who built their great civilization in the Valley of Mexico on the toil and blood of those thousands of native compatriots they forced into slavery, and whose history and literature they also attempted to destroy. While, as Fanon suggests, it may have been necessary for Chicanos to "renew contact once more with the oldest and most pre-colonial springs of life of their people," it was also inimical to the social movement. And by his I mean to suggest that, instead of allowing the mythic past to generate re-empowering cultural narratives, what we often ended up with was shrill sloganeering that abused myth.

Although such renewed contact with the "pre-colonial springs of life" provides a "psycho-affective equilibrium...responsible for an important change in the native,"[34] one that presumably eventuates in communal rehabilitation, it also involves dangers which Fanon warns may well end in forms of exoticism and romantic idealizations of the past, which rather than furthering the material struggle; lead to its bogging down in dreams and delusions of a past grandeur. Such idealization and exoticism, as Ricardo Sánchez uncompromisingly charges in his comments on the Chicano use of the indigenous past, end up deflecting from the socio-political function of literature, especially when writers gloss over the present reality of, say, Native American reservation squalor in favor of what he terms a "pollyana indianness which never existed...; there are no pyramids nor fancy ideas at the Navajo nation, just as our barrios are not beautiful or edifying."[35] Much like Fanon, Sánchez warns against cultural exoticism in the form of literary tourists of the past, "such as the pyramid builders and their so-called jive of actionless indigenous [native Indians], roseated indios, and their perpetuation of quasimystical idiocies."[36] Sánchez's concerns have, of course, long been shared by writers and intellectuals from other cultures who have warned against the effects of deflecting from social realities via a mythmaking process which reduces history to simpleminded sloganeering. Some, however, share Sanchez's concerns, but do so with a difference–mythic literature is corrupted by all socio-political polemics.

Brendon Behan (1923-1964), an Irish writer who as a young member of the IRA spent some six years imprisoned for planting bombs in British shipping yards, savagely attacked the political use of national myths after his incarceration. A writer who came from a radical working-class family that had fought for the Revolution for nationalist reasons, Behan came to believe that nationalist causes were corrupted by those who trivialized the past and the national character. In his play *The Hostage* (1959), he dramatizes the way that "myths become weapons with which the old destroy the young" when naive revolutionaries are led off to battle by nationalist leaders who assume the role of "Brian Boru [a hero of ancient Ireland] in the battle of Clontarf leading his men to war and glory."[37]

More recently French Canadian writers, staunchly opposed though they might be to the assimilative coercion of the British majority in Canada, have sought to debunk their own impulses to romanticize the French past. Like the other writers we have surveyed thus far, French Canadian poets and novelists during the nineteenth and the first half of the twentieth centuries consciously set about creating a patriotic, even epic, literature based upon the history of their forefathers. "Faced with the English presence," Jacques Cotnam writes, "the French-Canadian writer, by the simple fact of writing in French, declared himself a militant; wholly devoted to the 'national cause,' he habitually turned to the past in his efforts to justify and to confirm his 'desire for survival.'"[38] The problem of course was that "there was far too great a tendency to flee from reality, seeking refuge in a mythical past that writers sought to resuscitate through a patriotic, moralizing literature, which reached its zenith in the praise of country life."[39] This nationalist literary project, moreover, leaned heavily upon a nostalgia for France itself as a model of civilization, intellect, and language, with the result that French Canadians developed a kind of "orphan's complex." Because the tie to French society was at best imagined, the literature has remained that of a people in exile; "exile in both the temporal and spatial sense," Cotnam notes.

After the long phase of nostalgic reminiscing that characterized French Canadian literature, their exile has in more recent years had the effect of hardening the will of Quebecois writers who have declared their intellectual and artistic independence from the Canadian cultural mainstream. Unlike their predecessors, however, the intellectuals and writers of the post-World War II era have been steadfastly self-critical in their reflections upon their historical reality on the continent. Instead of romanticizing the country life or exalting the virtues of the French rural populace, these writers have focused upon those elements of their isolated experience that have created a distinct cultural identity.

In this, the parallels between the French Canadian and the Mexican American, or to use the self-designated terms, Quebecois and Chicano, are astonishing. Chicano writers have also suffered from an "orphan complex" that led, in past generations, to an idealization of the Spanish forebearers, and more recently to a nostalgia for the Mexican homeland, especially as it has been imagined in that mythical realm of Aztlán. This impulse has manifested itself intensely in the last two decades, a period during which the Chicano, feeling deeply alienated from the foster parent United States, wished to maintain a vital spiritual link with Mexico, the model of language, culture and social behavior. This explains, in part, why Chicano cultural nationalists not only appropriated the pre-Columbian mythology of Mexico, but also its Revolutionary heroes–Benito Juárez, Emiliano Zapata, Pancho Villa–and affected a kinship with Mexico's common people and their history. These symbols of our relationship to Mexico as motherland, usually imagined in idealized rhetoric, provided a matrix of cultural identity that strengthened resistance against Anglo domination in this country. More recently, however, Chicanos, like their Quebecois counterparts, have found it necessary to exorcise or divest themselves of those elements of the Mexican mythos, ancient or modern, that deflect from the reality of their situation in this country.

Tomás Rivera, commenting upon the relationship of Chicanos to Mexican culture and literature, saliently summed up the issue:

I don't really feel that I have a strong relationship with it. I used to think I did at one time, but then I realized I had taught myself that I had that strong relationship. That is different than really having it. I read the Mexican Classics, became interested in Rulfo, Fuentes, Yáñez, Ramón Rubin, López y Fuentes, and the Mexican Revolution novel; read the ensayistas like Alfonso Reyes; all that. I tried to read as much as possible from the Mexican literary scene. Once I had read it, I felt a strong affinity to it. When I visited Mexico it reinforced that feeling. Then I began to realize that I'm not a Mexican. All of these things are a result of learning, not of growing up in Mexico with all its problems, its history, its beauty and all its affinities. I thought, "It's not really mine. I know it as mine, now, because I've learned it. I don't actually have it, nor have I lived it." After that I had to come back and say this is reality right here....The fact is that if I had not gotten a college education I would know very little about Mexico. O.K., I could go over and buy trinkets and look at the pyramids, but reality, ours, is not there; it's here.[40]

III

As Rivera suggested, the tie to the homeland, mythic or historic, ends up being more imagined than real. That is as it has to be, but it does not mean that the reconstituted idea of a homeland, a mythic origin, or a heroic ancestry serves as a facile means of escape from the realities of the present. On the contrary, such reconstitution must activate the spirit in the face of economic squalor, social alienation, and cultural dissolution. It does so always at the risk of falling into the mire of exoticism and an attendant retreat into inaction against which Sánchez and Fanon warn. The line between a mythic drama that helps to redeem people in the here and now, and one that simply lends to an opiated passiveness, is necessarily thin. Myths do kill time. When they do not, they do not endure as cultural property.

In the process of transporting the individual and the community onto an ahistoric plane of consciousness, however, myth and legend must also succeed in reinvigorating the material surface of history. Such a process requires an act of interpretation, or more precisely, an interpreter. Writers like Alurista in poetry, Valdez in drama, and Anaya in fiction act as the interpreters of the mythic past for Chicanos in much the same way that Vaclav Hanka, Sandor Petofi, and W.B. Yeats did for their respective people. The mythic texts of the culture are transcribed, as it were, through the texts these writers leave for us to interpret. If there is a falling back into sense-dulled exoticism, the fault may very well lie not in the transcriber's text, but in our inability to interpret the signs in the text. Or, to put it another way, the fault lies in our inability to reconcile history and myth. By bringing these two antipodes into conjunction, the spiritual and the material needs of the group also conjoin.

Rudolfo Anaya has repeatedly explored the relationship between myth and history, the spiritual and the material, the intuitive and the rational elements of culture. Many critics objected to *Bless Me, Ultima* (1972) on the grounds that it seemed non-referential even though it was set in a definable historical moment in a New Mexican village. Anaya's mythic concerns, however, seemed to overwhelm the social contexts of the novel while holding out the promise of reconciliation of troubling socio-historical issues through what may be identified as mythic consciousness. The one enduring dismissal of the book remains that of Joseph Sommers who remarked that it was a "harkening back in sadness and nostalgia for a forgotten, idealized, and unobtainable past."[41] Anaya's mythic enterprise, like-minded critics would have it, was an ideologically retrograde exercise in lyrical nonsense.

Undoubtedly affected by such negative criticism, in his second novel, *Heart of Aztlán*, (1976) Anaya attempted to invest the mythic component with direct political consequence by setting it squarely alongside a story in which a community is engaged in a bitter strike against railroad management. Myth, however, exists not merely as a reminder of a past grandeur or as political propaganda, but as a collective reservoir of the culture's intuitive understanding of itself and as a renewing force. In this novel myth leads to direct social action when a member of the cultural community, Clemente Chávez, learns how to follow, or read, the "signs" of his people's journey through history.

Encouraged by a "guardian of culture," or *tlamantini*, in this case

Crispín, keeper of the magical blue guitar, Chávez is able to move beyond
alienation and disbelief when he learns to read through the surface of history.
The *corridos* that Crispín sings carry the imaginations of these auditors out
of the time-locked present into a domain through which the mythic sources of
life avail themselves to men overwhelmed by the socio-economic exigencies
of the present:

> He sang the corridos of prior revolutions, he sang of ancient
> heroes, men of the people. The mystery of his melody and the
> magic of his words carried them out their present time and mis-
> ery to a time of legends and myths, and in that time he made them
> encounter the truth of their being.[42]

Although they have initially asked Crispín to "play of things as they
are," that directive is revoked when they ask him to play of "things as they
have been." Quick to seize upon the tradition of the *cantador*, Crispín turns
their attention away from the anger and despair of the present, not in order to
efface history (since corridos are composed of historic incident), but as a
means of bringing them back to themselves via a spiritual route. When
Crispín reminds them that they are "the fruit of the people who wandered
from the mythical land of Aztlán, the first people of this land who wandered
south in search of a sign" (p. 83), he challenges them to undertake their own
mythic quest, to interpret the signs of their own migration through history
just as the first people searched their migratory trail for signs that would
direct them to a new and permanent home, to a place when they might discover and sustain their communal destiny.

Crispín's end, like a corrido, is to encourage people, in this case the
people of Barelas who are locked in battle with the railroad bosses, to redis-
cover the sources of their own power and control, to know themselves by
knowing the songs and stories of their origins. Only by reinventing the past
may the present and especially the future be invented. Songs about the past
and ritual stories create a ground upon which time itself is neutralized, or to
put it another way, a ground upon which time is accorded manifold presence:
past, present, and future collapse into simultaneity. Relocating their own
spiritual center through the chant of magic words—a corrido, a cuento, or a
text—restores their clarity and understanding and ultimately renews the
group's social resolve. Hence, mythic thought precedes social action.

Or is this only so much escapist drivel? The realities of the material world refuse to bend to such fabulation and naive make-believe. The here and now cannot be broken, much less redirected to a social end through such simple-minded cant. So might ensue the argument of a political radical whose eye remains squarely fixed by historical materialism. As Clemente himself charges, "But the strike? The strike and the railroad? What do these stories have to do with that?" (p. 84) Indeed, the spell of the song is broken by such relentless questions. The men turn away from Crispín, back to their drinks and their disbelief. Relentless realities. After listening to the heroic legends of the past, the "grime and poverty of the barrio enveloped them again...[and] stories of the past didn't put beans and meat on the table for the family." They only "helped to pass the time and ease the despair of going jobless that winter, but that was all" (p. 85).

Anaya, however, like other ethnic writers before him, is engaging his critics in a dialectic here. The stories that the skeptical Clemente has heard continue to haunt him; he feels there is "something very true and very essential," something which "kept calling to him to find its meanings" (p. 85). Unable to rely upon Crispín for guidance, Clemente is left to interpret the signs for himself. He is forced to become an active auditor, a reader left to his own imagination and intellect. If he remains trapped in history, in socio-political facts alone, Crispín has suggested, he will cut himself off from the intuitive sources of knowledge that proceed beyond the pool of historical details. The myths and legends of the past are not static, neither shards nor fragile museum artifacts. "The legend renews itself with each generation," Crispín tells his people, but "the important thing is to know how to interpret the signs" (p. 84).

The function of the mythic imagination in what we call real life, Anaya suggests, must be more than a means of passing the time and easing the despair of joblessness, political disenfranchisement, and social alienation. The stories that our *tlamantinime* repeat to us contain the materials through which reality may be reconstituted. It is in seeing only the details of the story, its surfaces, that we fail to interpret the signs that lead to knowledge and the ultimate restoration of the cultural self. Anaya's stories, like those of Crispín, are meant to regenerate his readers' myth-making capacity. *Bless Me, Ultima, Heart of Aztlán* and *Tortuga* (1979) are important only in as much as they function as signs that must be interpreted and given meaning by his readers. The political function of such novels resides largely in the interpreters' ability to empower themselves by constructing a sense of themselves as much more than the mere material or political incidentals of a present historical moment.

Instead of evaporating into an idealized vision of the past, myth becomes socially powerful at the point where it intersects with history to provide a vision of the future which can be acted upon. The symbol of Aztlán as a mythic homeland provides a field of signs, some actual fragments from the cultural past reinvested with imaginative life, some images altogether invented for the psychic needs of a threatened culture, the interpretation of which may lead the Chicano out of the labyrinth of history into a future neither premised upon delusive fabulations of the past nor bled of the mythic capacity to sustain the story of the cultural self. Instead of battling each other, political theorists and poet-*tlamantinime* must reconcile history and myth, which after all are the materials of the same cultural story.

NOTES

1. Joseph Sommers and Tomás Ybarra-Frausto, eds., *Modern Chicano Writers: A Collection of Critical Essays* (Englewood Cliffs, NJ: Prentice-Hall, 1979), pp. 117-132.
2. Francisco Jiménez, ed. *The Identification and Analysis of Chicano Literature* (New York: Bilingual Press, 1979), pp. 90-116. In his recent book *Chicano Theater: Themes and Forms* (Ypsilanti, Michigan: Bilingual Press, 1982), Huerta provides a thorough and insightful discussion of the Teatro's evolution and its conscious appropriation of a neo-idigenous teatro of legends and myths.
3. *The Identification and Analysis of Chicano Literature*, pp. 178-190.
4. Blouin, p. 180: "In contrast to the repeated humiliations offered by their socio-economic reality, the persevering remembrance of a proud Aztec ascendency sustains the Chicano." (translation mine)
5. Arnulfo D. Trejo, ed., *The Chicanos: As We See Ourselves* (Tucson: University of Arizona Press, 1979), pp. 1-18.
6. "Mestizaje: The Transformation of Ancient Indian Religious Thought in Contemporary Chicano Fiction," Diss., University of Colorado, 1980.
7. Addison Gayle, *The Black Aesthetic* (Garden City, NY: Doubleday, 1971), ed., p. 376.
8. (New York: Grove Press, 1963), Constance Farrington, trans., pp. 209-210.
9. H. Ernest Lewald, ed., *The Cry of Home: Cultural Nationalism and the Modern Writer* (Knoxville: University of Tennessee Press, 1972), p. 11.
10. *Chicano Poetry: A Response to Chaos* (Austin: University of Texas Press, 1982) p. 71. Bruce-Novoa's study offers a close reading and imaginative explication of some ten poems from Alurista's *Floricanto en Aztlán* (1971). Central to my purpose here, he also offers reasoned commentary on Alurista's project of stripping the Chicano subject of its historically accumulated layers of Western consciousness through a poetry that "Posits the re-Indianization of America" (p. 85).

11. Lewald, p. 11.
12. Lewald, p. 11.
13. Arne Novak, *Czech Literature* (Ann Arbor, Michigan Slavic Publications, 1976), Peter Kussi, trans., p. 139.
14. Novak, p. 139.
15. Arnold C. Vento, "Myth, Legend, and History of Aztec Origins: The Oral Tradition," *Grito del Sol* 3 (July-September 1976), p. 103.
16. Novak, p. 142.
17. Novak, p. 143.
18. Novak, p. 143.
19. Published at New Brunswick, NJ by Rutgers University in 1964.
20. Remenyi, p. 17. Similar to the cultural reclaiming of the past, along with the necessary fabulations that took place in other countries, Novak writes that, a "distinct interest in ancient Hungarian poetry and in more recent folk poetry rose from the intensified political and cultural life of the nation...Hungarian poets and writers became conscious of their ancestral sagas, and for whatever information was missing concerning racial epos were substituted allusions and unique inventiveness..." (p. 17).
21. George Gomori, *Polish and Hungarian Poetry: 1945 to 1956* (Oxford: Clarendon Press, 1966), p. 21.
22. Gomori, p. 11. In the introduction, "The Poet's Historical and Social Role in Poland and Hungary," Gomori discusses the appropriation of the national mythic and legendary past as material to fuel Hungary's various independence struggles.
23. Lewald, P. 12.
24. Richard Ellmann, *Yeats: The Man and the Masks* (New York: E.P. Duton, 1958) p. 129.
25. Robert Tracy, "Ireland: The Patriotic Game," in *The Cry of Home* (Lewald, ed.) pp. 40-41.
26. Tracy, p. 40.
27. Luis Valdez, "Notes on Chicano Theater," *Chicano Theater One,* 1 (Spring 1973), p. 7.
28. Ellmann, p. 130.
29. Tracy, p. 43.

30. Huerta, *Chicano Theater: Themes and Forms,* p. 203.
31. Valdez, p. 7.
32. Huerta, p. 203.
33. Tracy, p. 41.
34. Fanon, p. 210.
35. Ricardo Sánchez in [Juan] Bruce-Novoa, *Chicano Authors: Inquiry by Interview* (Austin: University of Texas Press, 1980), p. 233.
36. Sánchez, pp. 232-33.
37. Tracy, p. 47.
38. Jacques Cotnam, "Cultural Nationalism and its Literary Expression in French-Canadian Fiction," (Noel Corbett, trans.), in *The Cry of Home*, p. 270.
39. Cotnam, p. 276.
40. Tomás Rivera in [Juan] Bruce-Novoa, *Chicano Authors,* pp. 152-153.
41. *Modern Chicano Writers*, p. 38.
42. Rudolfo A. Anaya, *Heart of Aztlán* (Berkeley: Justa Editorial, 1976), p. 83. All other references to this text will be by page number alone.

Aztlán, Borinquen and Hispanic
Nationalism in the United States

J. Jorge Klor de Alva

After eleven years of teaching at two universities in California, in 1982 I accepted an offer from the State University of New York at Albany. The shift to the East Coast introduced me to the complex world of Caribbean Latinos and the dramatic differences among the Hispanic cultures of the U.S. Immediately after my arrival I began to do research on and to write about these differences; one of my earliest efforts on the subject was the first draft of this essay. The text was presented in 1983 at the Latin American Studies Association meeting in Mexico City and the following year a second version was read at the annual meeting of the National Association of Chicano Studies held in Austin, Texas. Because of a long-time professional interest in Mesoamerican ethnohistory and Chicano intellectual history, prior to engaging in a reconsideration of the relevance of cultural nationalism among Latinos—the focus of the present article—I had already written several works concerned with the ideological uses of Aztlán made by Chicanos.[1] But through my Puerto Rican students and a summer of fieldwork in Puerto Rico (on the uses of music as a political tool), I discovered that Puerto Ricans had a concept analogous to the Aztlán of the Chicanos: Borinquen. This insight led me to write this essay. As something of a "period piece," I now present it as it was drafted in 1983 (with minor revisions), when the debate between cultural nationalism and historical materialism was still alive, Puerto Ricans were still new to me, and California was still fresh on my mind.[2]

With a population of [17 to 20 million], Hispanics, if erroneously seen as one cultural unit, are the second largest ethnic group in the United States and have transformed this predominantly English-speaking country into the [fifth] largest Latino nation in the world. Given their phenomenal rate of growth, many demographers expect them to be the largest minority early in the next century.[3] Their high density in many areas has already forced local politicians to take unprecedented notice of Latino demands. At the same time, although their percentage of the total U.S. population is relatively small [10%], their overwhelming concentration (63%) in the three critical states of New York, California and Texas, has given them a disproportionate national influence that presidential contenders are busily exploiting. With this potential thrust in mind, it is imperative that we come to grips with the fact that Hispanics have worked together very rarely on common political concerns and each group is appallingly ignorant of the others.[4] This essay is a contribution to the necessary dialogue demanded by the state of current Mexican/Chicano and Puerto Rican nationalism in the United States. It is a response to the critics of cultural nationalism as an organizing tool and it is a reevaluation of the roles played by the two key symbolic expressions of Hispanic cultural nationalism during the 1960s and 70s: Aztlán and Borinquen (the island of Puerto Rico).

It is clear from the 1980 census [and more recent demographic data[5]] that the War on Poverty failed Latinos, who in the company of Blacks and Native Americans continue to be trapped, for the most part, at the bottom of the American working class. The economic and historical causes that have kept exploited, working-class Hispanics in the U.S. from uniting in order to effectively advocate for the redress of their common grievances have been amply discussed in the relevant literature.[6] But one reason that is particularly salient for our discussion needs to be highlighted: divisions within the working class have not been reduced by the exclusivist theoretical and cognitive approaches of the Latino leaders and scholars. This point is not novel, but it continues to be ignored by many. In short, while generally sharing a working-class origin, these leaders have frequently been divided, beyond regional and partisan concerns, by the tendency to view reality through too narrowly deterministic or idealist perspectives.

This epistemological or, more precisely, cognitive problem of interpretation is everywhere evident at both the level of practice among organizers and in the writings of the intellectuals.[7] Obviously, the results of this situation at the level of mobilization are disorganization and political ineffectiveness. At the theoretical level the problems are not always so evident, though the consequences, as reflected in divisiveness and organizational disarray, certainly are.

For the purposes of our study I will briefly describe two of the most important opposing positions. On one side are leaders with a humanist bent, often schooled in literature or fine arts, who tend to focus on cultural concerns while emphasizing the cultural autonomy of the individual. Their naïve cultural nationalism is ultimately too chauvinistic to promote the unification efforts needed to overcome the divisive forces of monopoly capitalism and the seductiveness of modern fragmenting individualism. On the other side are those primarily trained in the social sciences, whose research is delimited by a preoccupation with economic and political issues, and whose eyes are fixed on social structures and the work force. The radicals among them disparage the importance of culture and nationalism while focusing primarily on the significance of class. To be sure, this dichotomy is deceiving in its simplicity and has become trite through repetition. I bring it up once more only to point out the following: the studies on the history of the Chicano and Puerto Rican struggles of the last two decades [the 1960s and 70s] have tended to confuse the shift in influence from one leadership sector to another for the progressive development of theory. That is, the loss of the vanguard position of early cultural nationalists and the subsequent rise to prominence of historical materialists and "socialists" have been interpreted primarily as an evolution in theoretical perspective while disregarding the possibility that what we have experienced may be "merely" a change in leadership.

The problem that attends this interpretation is not only the subsequent blunting of one of the most powerful tools for political organization (i.e., cultural nationalism), but the unfortunate distancing of these two valuable and necessary camps.[8] While there have always been those who can bridge the gap[9] and although the boundary between the two groups is porous, the screen that separates the hard extremes is always present. To address the significance of this screen it is useful to undertake a comparative study of Chicano and Puerto Rican cultural nationalism and the attacks against its various forms; but before doing this, we must turn briefly to the questions raised, first, by the meaning of culture and, second, by the uses of nationalism.

Culture

What is culture? The controversy triggered by this question is everywhere evident in the writings of Chicanos and Puerto Ricans. Except for those responses proffered by the more sophisticated (dialectical) scholars, the answers given tend to fall within one of two popular but simplistic categories: materialist or idealist. Both labels carry much politically significant semantic baggage, but in general the former suggests a materially determined basis for culture while the latter implies a certain autonomy for it.

Latino authors on the left agree that, in general, culture is class based; that is, since the distinct classes reflect different material conditions they necessarily express themselves as different cultures.[10] The implications of this position are substantial: (1) culture can be a tool for domination, if it is used to conceal reality, or liberation, if it helps to unmask the oppressor; and (2) culture is always changing, reflecting the transformations of the material base and the accompanying alterations resulting from the struggles between the classes.[11] Consequently, culture is not neutral. What counts as authentic culture is always a matter of class perspective; therefore, official and bourgeois claims concerning the supposed nonexistence of culture among Puerto Ricans or judgments about the "inferior" status of the culture of the ethnic communities in the U.S., as opposed to the "high" cultures of the motherlands, say more about the class origins and political ideology of the commentators than about the nature of the object of their studies.[12]

On the other hand, when vulgar (uncritical) class-oriented perspectives are applied to the analysis of culture, "national" or "ethnographic" categories, delimited by adjectives like "Puerto Rican," "Mexican," "Anglo" (-American), "syncretic," or "pure," lose their descriptive relevance. In their place we find labels like "bourgeois," "imperialist," and "proletarian" used to describe the significant cultural groupings. This shift in the categories of analysis makes complex cultural distinctions more difficult to understand. It betrays, once again, the materialists' tendency to downgrade what are considered ideal (false?) constructs (e.g., nation, ethnicity, or race). On the positive side, the search for the material bases of proletarian culture has led to an understanding of the false nature of some negative stereotypes. For instance, stereotypes that suggest the exploited masses are docile, inferior, or violent are either correctly assailed for being ahistorical and acritical or they have been identified as the result of the "colonized mentality" imposed by "imperialist" aggression.[13]

Unfortunately, the class-based categories of culture leave the question of identity up in the air. After all, being a proletarian is not quite the same thing as being a Chicano, although most Chicanos are proletarians. And while too much concern with identity "smacks of bourgeois individualism," the fact remains that the exlusive use of a class-based framework has done little to resolve the legitimate questions raised by the many Hispanics who suffer from being neither fish nor fowl, here or in their homeland. While I do not wish to suggest, as some have done, that "the most acute problem of the Puerto Rican in New York is that of the precariousness on which Puerto Rican identity is sustained,"[14] it is important to note that the issue of identity is critical both to the individual and to the task of political organization. Because materialists, as I have described them, assume culture is primarily determined by class, identity is likewise seen as the result of class membership.[15] The importance traditionally given to language, religion, and nationality (ethnic background) as determinants of identity is either denied or played down.[16]

Existentialist or optionalist postures that suggest the individual is the most critical force behind the formation of his or her identity are repeatedly assailed as idealist and lacking in historical perspective, since changes in identity are usually reduced by the critics to secondary responses following necessarily from the transformations in the material conditions. Paradoxically, although the role of personal choice as a psychological or social possibility is believed to be small, the political objective of the historical-materialist position depends precisely on the capacity of groups (necessarily made up of individuals) to overcome their oppression by *consciously* opting to struggle when the objective conditions promise success. This modern twist on the determinism versus free-will debate would be a trivial point, if Marxists and Existentialists had not continued debating it until the present, and if individual psychologies were not themselves even more complex than social structures.[17]

It makes sense that individuals cannot be fully aware of the multitude of forces acting to limit their options, particularly if their oppressors veil them, but to dismiss subjective preceptions as relatively insignificant is neither intellectually nor politically wise. However much material conditions set the stage for human action, it is individuals who must ultimately unravel the interpretations forced on them if they are to be mobilized to write their own social scripts. As a consequence, it sounds like an exaggeration when, for instance, an excellent scholar claims that with regard to the Caribbean peoples in New York today (or for that matter, with regard to Mexicans in Los Angeles) "we will never reach a comprehensive understanding of the implications of their presence here by asking particular individuals what they are doing in this city."[18] What particular individuals have to say on the subject is, in fact, absolutely necessary to know in order to reach a comprehensive understanding of the non-structural reasons for migration. After all, not all those similarly situated migrate, even when theoretically they could be expected to do so. Why some do and some do not, when both "should" have, is not a question that can be answered without inquiring into the nature of real lives. The countless interviews of Mexican immigrants, common in border studies today, provide invaluable data that is as necessary to put the structural dimensions of Mexican migration into the proper context as the structural dimensions are critical to understanding these data.[19]

In effect, culture and identity are obviously circumscribed by historical and material limitations; nonetheless, people do not live out their lives as abstract categories. Their primary reality is their individual consciousness, however precarious it might be in comparison to the solidity of their identity through group membership. A survey of the history and fate of ethnic labels is enough to make clear the importance that personal assessments of identity have in determining group solidarity and class-consciousness. Although it may be that for some "poco importa el nombre," the twentieth-century "dance" of ethnic designations suggests names matter to most.[20] Every label change, from Mexicano to Mexican American to Chicano, from Puertorriqueño to Hispano to Boricua or Nuyorican, or from Latin American to Hispanic to Latino, has been the result not only of changes in the material conditions, but of a dialectic between personal responses and the new historical situations.[21] The struggle among both Chicanos and Puerto Ricans to create a consensus around mutually acceptable labels indicates the importance and complexity of addressing identity and culture as organizing tools in the process of community building.[22]

Nationalism

Since "as a uniting force, nationalism is probably unparalleled in history,"[23] it is at the core of much of the political debate among both Chicanos and Puerto Ricans. This debate is suspended between two related poles: the link between class and nationalism, on one side, and the relation between culture and nationalism, on the other. Historical materialists emphasize the dependent nature of the former, while cultural nationalists stress the affinity of the latter. Once again, these two supposed extremes are opposed to each other only to draw out some salient distinctions pertinent to our study.

Nationalism as both an ideology and a material force can be either progressive or reactionary. In its progressive form it helps to clarify class contradictions, it leads the way to class solidarity, and it forms the catalyst by which subjective sentiments about exploitation can be transformed into social action. When the material conditions permit, progressive nationalism can result in socialism (which, barring imperialist forms of aggression, is ideally considered the authentic political expression of the state of the unexploited working class). Reactionary nationalism contributes to class oppression, is chauvinistic and divisive, leads to the idealization of the bourgeois state, and in its most extreme form results in fascism. The primacy of nationalism rests on the fact that "national consciousness often has been much more developed than class consciousness."[24] However, nationalism is not an autonomous force; it reflects class interests though it frequently cuts across them. This class-dependence has led some thinkers to argue that national struggle is class struggle (albeit of a distinctive form) or that nation and class do not contradict each other. Nonetheless, all agree that when overemphasized, nationalism not only negates class but serves to block the development of class consciousness.[25] Reduced to a nutshell, the above is representative of [1970s] Marxist Chicano and Puerto Rican thinking on the link between class and nationalism. Before we turn to a discussion of "the national question," a word on the relation between culture and nationalism would be useful.

To the extent that nationalism is class-based it cannot be stated categorically that it is defensive of culture. Class interests, especially in the age of transnational capital, often override nationalist sentiments, forcing so-called national culture to be demoted (by the promotion of foreign cultural elements) or destroyed (by denying its existence). Thus, nationalism is not always opposed to acculturation into a non-national culture. This is the case, for instance, in the Puerto Rico of Muñoz Marín and his followers, where cultural syncretism in the post-World War II period was promoted as official policy and arguments against the existence of Puerto Rican culture found official support. Furthermore, national culture in a class society is defined primarily by the cultural production of the dominant classes. Therefore, the merits of working-class culture are generally denied or attempts are made to empty them of their content by reducing "popular culture" to exotic or folkloric elements devoid of social significance.[26]

Except to the initiated, the relevance of nationalism to the study of ethnic minorities in the United States is not obvious. Laypersons naturally recognize nation and state as one, especially if they identify affirmatively with the latter. When ethnic concerns are considered "national" concerns what is usually meant is that they are widespread and in need of the federal government's attention. Ethnic groups are not assumed to be nations; thus nationalism is generally equated with patriotism and loyalty to the United States. On the other hand, some Chicano and Puerto Rican writers have claimed that their respective oppressed and unassimilated ethnic groups are nations that have been kept from being states solely by the political dominance and police powers of the U.S. government.[27] Most authors, however, identify the Chicano and Puerto Rican peoples in the

U.S. not as nations, but as oppressed national minorities forming part of a multinational state.[28] This controversy is a domestic version of the international debate on the right of peoples who consider themselves nations to struggle for liberation from oppressive states and, therefore, to struggle for political self-determination. To understand this important debate, which is at the center of the conflicts between native peoples and colonizers everywhere in the world, we must ask three key questions: What is a nation? What is nationalism? And who has the right to self-determination? Technically, this highly charged polemic has been labeled "the national question."[29]

In the United States national questions arise primarily from two quarters: Native American assertions of autonomy and sovereignty, against the claims of the federal and state governments; and from racial minorities who usually feel themselves united by other forces beyond class solidarity, especially since racism and uneven development have always fostered intraclass divisions that very frequently are as pervasive as those between the classes. Now, a result of these various divisions has been the retardation of class unity based on class consciousness. Furthermore, "racial" minorities—minorities physically (or socioracially) color-coded and thus distinguished from European-origin minorities—are less assimilated than their white "ethnic" counterparts. Therefore, these racial groups possess extensive non-Anglo American cultural traits, frequently feel alienated from the political institutions of the U.S., participate disproportionately in working-class cultural activities, and have been kept at a substantial social distance from the white majority. This segregation under conditions of superexploitation, coupled among some racial groups such as Latinos with the cultural reinforcement provided by continuous immigration from the homeland, have made racial minorities politically and socioeconomically different from ethnic groups like the Irish, Polish, or Italian-Americans. The distinction goes beyond mere "patterned differentiation" to actual group "coherence and solidarity," reaching, although rarely, institutional completeness and therefore socioeconomic autonomy.[30] This situation of segregation and oppression is what creates the context for debate and action on the national question by way of conscious resistance to assimilation and advocacy (or, at times, violent struggle) on behalf of socioeconomic, political, and cultural rights. In effect, racial ethnic groups such as those composed of Chicanos and Puerto Ricans have many of the characteristics of nations, though as fragments themselves of other nations they are arguably more like national minorities than "real" nations.

Because the United States is a multi-national state, whose nations are not all unified by the same criteria, the relevance of this analysis is limited to the Puerto Rican and Chicano communities. Many of the members of these communities feel themselves alienated and aggrieved, and if one believes they are separate nations, they have a legitimate right to make nationalist claims. Consequently, among Chicano and Puerto Rican activists, national questions are ultimately questions of political strategy. Most Hispanics are members of the working class and therefore the formation of class solidarity is one of their central political goals, but nationalism can be divisive so its use is often questioned. On the other hand, nationalism is the foremost organizational tool. Yet its effective use is dependent on how one responds to the questions of strategy necessarily raised by struggles for national liberation. What should be the goal of national liberation: Political autonomy? Effective political representation through electoral strategies? Or should the demand for self-determination be primarily a call for cultural autonomy, with local control of schools and bilingual-bicultural education? Chicano and Puerto Rican strategists are not in agreement as to what the right answers are. For those who do not apply mechanically Stalin's criteria for nationhood (common territory, language, psychology, and economy) or who accept with a critical eye Lenin's theories on the subject, nationalism can mean many things: it can be political, economic, or cultural.[31] But to what extent it truly can be of one sort without implying another is a crucial question; even though here—as in the case of the question concerning the right to self-determination—material, objective conditions, rather than theoretical expertise, ultimately determine the answer.[32]

CULTURAL NATIONALISM

Cultural nationalism is a complicated concept subject to varying interpretations, some of which are mutually exclusive and consequently the term is rarely defined when discussed. For at least one author, Tejano music is "the best example of Chicano cultural nationalism," for others it is at the center of racial identity and the political struggle for national liberation.[33] However defined, most writers correctly note that the romantic and parochial era of the cultural nationalist movement is now behind us, having been replaced by traditional or conservative ideologies, liberal concerns, or historical-materialist analyses. But because studies in the last category emphasize class, rather than race or culture, they are believed by progressive thinkers to be more likely to promote nationalist objectives by clarifying the real contradictions in capitalism.[34]

However, the theoretical problem of race or racism has plagued progressive, class-oriented scholarship for some time. Like the national question (or the issue of gender), the question of race is nowhere adequately analyzed in the classic Marxist literature.[35] With minor exceptions, white radical scholars, if they discuss race at all, continue to treat it as either an epiphenomenal variable that will disappear when society becomes classless, or as a form of false consciousness whose net effect is to divide the working class.[36] This theoretical bias on the side of class and the accompanying downgrading of race is evident also among some Hispanics and others thoroughly acquainted with the complexities of racism.[37]

An understanding of the relation between class and race, critical for a comprehension of cultural nationalism, has come about slowly and primarily through the development of various theoretical models that have yielded the dependency, internal colonial, class segmentation, racial dualism, and world-system approaches.[38] The best synthesis of a theory that takes into consideration the roles of race and class in society is that articulated by Mario Barrera, who argues that Chicanos (read also: Puerto Ricans) are made up of an "ascriptive class segment" defined as,

> a portion of a class which is set off from the rest of the class by
> some readily identifiable and relatively stable characteristics of
> the persons assigned to that segment, such as race, ethnicity, or
> sex, where the relationship of the members to the means and process of production is affected by that demarcation.[39]

It must be added that since most Chicanos and Puerto Ricans are at the bottom of all classes, especially the working class, they form "subordinate" ascriptive class segments. This definition only addresses the socioeconomic placement of working-class Hispanics in the political economy of the United States. But as noted earlier, since both culture and nationalism are at least in part class based, this principle can shed much light on Hispanic cultural nationalism. In particular, it limits the cultural content of this nationalism to the working-class version, and structurally explains its distinctions from other working-class cultures and Hispanic bourgeois cultures.

Puerto Rican and Chicano cultural nationalism were a response to both superexploitation (white labor has not had a parallel movement recently) and racism. As Barrera and others have pointed out, racism has served as a sieve, limiting social integration to only the most acculturated sectors, and has maintained the overwhelming majority of Latinos economically marginalized. Not only does racism provide extra profits for capitalism, but since it also has made cultural assimilation a slow process for first and frequently second generation Hispanics, it has helped to preserve separate ethnic cultures while promoting the creation of new ethnic-proletarian cultural expressions.[40]

Capitalism, then, has profited from racism and, in turn, racism has made possible the socioeconomic segregation necessary to give specific cultural content to the resistance efforts of Chicanos and Puerto Ricans. These Latino class segments have remained in possession of old and have conceived new cultural elements that are at the same time responses to subordinate class conditions, to specific cultural origins, and to *individual* creative forces. Therefore, the sociocultural coherence of these groups is to a great extent the result of the racially based circumscription of their position in the productive process. This unity on the basis of racial-ethnic-class identity has the potential to be honed into sharp cultural instruments useful in a nationalist class struggle. In the 1960s the potential of these weapons was well enough appreciated by some observers that it led them to speculate that racism was no longer useful to the dominant class. The expenses resulting from the social chaos and violence produced by racial minorities rioting under the banner of cultural nationalism was believed by these scholars to no longer be worth the profits made through racist mechanisms of exploitation.[41]

Despite the inevitability of cultural nationalism, its utility as a tool for political organization, and its importance as a flint with which to spark social agitation, it has been criticized by Chicano and Puerto Rican leaders and intellectuals representing the whole spectrum of political ideology. The conservative responses to it are obvious and not germane to our study; the responses from the left, however, need comment. One criticism frequently leveled at early cultural nationalist artists, paticularly poets, was that they were too focused on existentialist preoccupations. They were said to be too subjective, individualistic, and neither class nor revolution oriented since their solutions were personal rather than social.[42] In effect, this type of cultural nationalism was considered to be inspired by bourgeois rather than proletarian concerns and the resulting lack of proper political focus was severely assailed by many. Puerto Rican critics noted in 1974 that,

> Unfortunately, we frequently find among these poets the same dangers that stand as a barrier between the cultural and the political life of the whole community: the strained rhetoric of narrow, short-lived cultural rebellion, the anarchistic flair and utopian constructions, and the formalistic and private airs that hover out of reach of the people.
>
> • • •
>
> While it started in the cultural forefront of the political struggle, the...poetry as a whole has fallen behind...[and] has suffered from the lack of political direction, which has left wide open the road to a modish aestheticism and willful bohemianism.[43]

Beyond the assaults on the self-centered and politically ambiguous nature of the early works of cultural nationalists, other related complaints could be heard. I have already mentioned the potentially negative effects common to all forms of nationalism, especially chauvinistic divisiveness. However, the naïve, romantic version popular among early Hispanic cultural nationalists has been reproved for having yielded results particular to it that also exacerbated class schisms. First, these cultural nationalists are said to have placed too great an emphasis on race and racism and thus obscured the real sources of socioeconomic exploitation that victimize Latinos along with other oppressed groups.[44] Second, a tendency to reduce cultural poles to two, Latino and Anglo, has been criticized for having created a too rigid dichotomy that suggested the following: a static vision of culture, an absence of cultural elements common to other groups that if recognized could have been useful for community building, and a lack of ethnic cross-fertilization that could lead to new shared forms of resistance.[45] Third, because of the early cultural nationalists' proneness to visualize Chicano or Puerto Rican culture in an idealized fashion, accentuating its forms as unique, it is argued that there was a proclivity to aim at the preservation of culture rather than to aspire to transform it into an efficient tool for attacking capitalism by grounding this vision in a class analysis.[46] Fourth, the early absorption with the search in Mexico and Puerto Rico for the roots or essence of the culture and personality of Chicanos and Puerto Ricans is believed to have reduced the struggle for self-determination to a mere ahistorical and idealistic search for cultural identity. The error here was that this not only suggested that culture is static, but unwittingly disparaged proletarian cultural forms by putting too much stress on the cultural elements of the ruling classes in the motherlands, who claim for their "bourgeois" version of culture the status of national culture.[47] Lastly, cultural nationalists were believed to have at times limited their demands to mere reforms, stressing primarily the right to cultural autonomy. To one scholar this latter "reformist thrust" was such a perversion of goals that he declared: "Chicano cultural nationalism...is not a very important political factor in and of itself."[48] Indeed, the cultural pluralism frequently implied by old and current cultural nationalists has been a constant target for those opposed to its assimilationist assumptions, which argue that the same economic and political structures can serve as a base for dramatically different and contradictory cultural expressions.[49]

With this brief survey completed, we can now turn to the two most important symbolic forms of cultural nationalism developed by Latinos: Aztlán and Borinquen.

AZTLÁN

Aztlán, the legendary point of origin of the Aztecs, was believed by them to be located somewhere to the north of their capital, Mexico-Tenochtitlan.[50] For all the interest the notion of Aztlán has generated among both nonworking-class ethnohistorians in Mexico and primarily working-class-origin Chicanos, who identified it with the Southwest of the U.S., most Aztecs by the sixteenth century, shortly before and after the arrival of the Europeans, seemed generally indifferent to it. It seems that whatever orthodoxy existed on the subject was maintained only among those for whom the idea had political utility. In effect, Aztlán was a "class"-based symbol useful to the ruling elite as a part of their founding myth and charter of legitimacy; the nonprivileged sectors seemed to have derived little of value from this notion.[51]

Nonetheless, the appropriation from the elitelore of ancient Mexico of such a seminal emblematic device as Aztlán was the most brilliant political maneuver of the Chicano cultural nationalists. Nothing their critics have done has managed to surpass or equal this feat of organizational strategy. Under no other sign or concept, derived from the left, center, or right, were as many Chicanos mobilized and as much enthusiasm galvanized into political action—except for the concept of Chicanismo itself. For a movement hungry for symbols that could both distinguish it from other movements and unite it under one banner, Aztlán was perfect. So perfect, in fact, that almost two decades after it was unfurled it is still the single most distinguishing metaphor for Chicano activism. The term is ubiquitous: found in the strident political program called the *Plan Espiritual de Aztlán* and in the name of the most sober, scholarly Chicano journal, and it adorns the title of scores of poems, novels, paintings, and organizations, all of which display it both as a sign of their content and as a mark of their political ideology. Why?

It is well known that Aztlán, along with other symbols drawn from the mythology of the Aztecs, has been employed by Chicanos in many ways: in their search for a separate identity that can contrast with their Mexican heritage and Anglo environment; as a source of ethnic pride, by identifying with the well-known civilizations of ancient Mexico; and as a flag capable of uniting the heterogeneous Mexican communities of the United States, which are composed of members of all social classes, are geographically dispersed and therefore have divergent historical experiences, and whose political ideologies extend from ultra-right to extreme left.[52] These Aztec motifs, along with others extracted from the Mexican Revolution of 1910, have also been resorted to as arms in the class struggle.[53] All of this hints at the material basis of the cultural nationalists' preoccupation with Aztlán and related concepts.

As stated earlier, Chicano cultural nationalism was a response to racism and exploitation. Its florescence was made possible, as was well known to its proponents, by the social and political crises in which the United States found itself in the 1960s. From its first popular expression in the *Plan Espiritual de Aztlán*, Aztlán, a concept derived from mythical geography and political history, was associated with the issues of poverty, land, sovereignty, and political organization. Though clearly not socialist in orientation, it was politically motivated. It was nourished by the California agricultural labor strike initiated by César Chávez in 1965; by the Alianza land grant movement spearheaded by Reies López Tijerina, who during 1966-67 attempted to reclaim parts of the Carson National Forest in New Mexico for the local Hispanic community; and by the urban movements in Colorado and, especially, California, where students were organizing boycotts, "blowouts," and strikes.[54] Of course, the context of the ideological and organizational hegemony of the cultural nationalists was broader.

In the United States, the Black struggle for civil rights, the urban insurrections, the peace movement against the tragic Vietnam War, the widespread appeal of the anticapitalism espoused by the Neo-Marxists and the New Left, the ascent of feminist radicalism, and the anti-materialist challenge of the counterculture of college-age "baby boomers" all made the moment ripe for Chicano political protest. The domestic economic expansion produced by the war economy also contributed by making both the government and the society more willing than usual to underwrite ethnic-directed programs aimed at pacifying the indignant communities and coopting their radical leadership. Many whites and most non-whites believed, especially after Watergate in the early 1970s, that "America was systematically oppressive and immoral" and that "national confidence and self-respect were severely shaken" throughout.[55] It was a time for ethnic identities to be affirmed and aligned with the progressive sectors of the working class seeking to overcome their oppression. In the international scene, wars of liberation raged, students were rioting everywhere they could, and anti-Americanism was in full swing. In the midst of all these stimulations and opportunities for protest, the Chicano cultural nationalists were at the vanguard, particularly in the urban centers.

However romantic it may appear today, the *Plan Espiritual de Aztlán*, adopted by hundreds of young Chicanos and Chicanas during the 1969 Chicano Liberation Youth Conference in Denver, responded to the material conditions of the time and, although not class based, it articulated a program for the "liberation" of a national minority. The national question concerning the political status of Chicanos was hypothetically resolved with the affirmation: "We are a Nation, We are a union of free pueblos, We are Aztlán." They advocated for "social, economic, cultural, and political independence" as "the only road to total liberation from oppression, exploitation, and racism." By focusing on nationalism, instead of class, they created the potentially most inclusive organizational base possible. They sought control of lands "rightfully" theirs, economic autonomy, community control of education, self-defense, cultural affirmation, and political power through electoral strength. This "Plan," which set the stage for the mobilization and unification of a whole generation of Chicano youth, formed the ideological background for the popularity of Aztlán as the key symbol of El Movimiento (the Chicano sociopolitical movement).

In spite of the critics, it was not self-centered or divisive in intent; nationalism, after all, was a point of departure, unity with others fighting U.S. oppression and racism was a secondary, but important goal. It did not obscure socioeconomic issues, although it did underestimate the importance of class divisions. It sought to stimulate cultural creativity and did not hold a static view of culture; even though the full focus was on Chicano culture, and other working-class cultures were generally ignored, the "Plan" aimed at the transformation of elite, colonizing ideals and symbols through the production of a new "art that is appealing to our people *and relates to our revolutionary culture*." Thus it did not disparage proletarian culture while holding up a static version of elite Mexican culture as the model. It failed to develop a class analysis because it would not have been politically feasible at the time; unity, after all, had to precede everything else, especially since national consciousness was clearly more developed than class consciousness.[56]

The ideology surrounding Aztlán was only one aspect of Chicano cultural nationalism and it was primarily the product of only one sector of the community: the students. Turning to class analysis, much of the political confusion attributed to this ideology was the result of the race and class situation of the students that propagated it. Students, using the analysis of class structure by Erik Olin Wright, may be said to have "contradictory locations within class relations" and, therefore, "are not clear-cut members of the traditional classes, but occupy locations which are intermediate between two classes, in that they partake of some of the characteristics of both classes."[57] The political ambiguity resulting from this situation has already been analyzed;[58] in summary, students tended to be adventurist or reformist, failed to generate a mass movement, and though mostly of working-class origin, they were distanced from grass-roots elements. Furthermore, being more assimilated and assimilation-prone than the working-class Mexicans in the fields, restaurants, sweat-shops, or factories, the students were the group most concerned with questions of identity, ethnic affirmation, or radical (but alienating) nationalism. For the other sectors, less concerned with problems of identity or the need to underline their "Mexicanness" as a challenge to Anglo cultural domination, Aztlán and the indigenism it implied had little appeal.[59] While students were one of the most dynamic thrusts of the movement, they were destined to be replaced by the radical intellectuals (some of whom had been cultural nationalists), the working-class generated leadership, and the liberal bureaucrats spawned by the pacifying efforts of both the government and the private sector. The leftist theorists and working-class leaders had more clearly defined class-oriented goals, with the latter being more in touch with the oppression all rejected.

By 1973 the artists, students, and "lumpen" elements that had fostered cultural nationalism had lost the domestic and international historical contexts that had made widespread protest possible. Without that material base they were doomed to losing their hegemonic position to the reformist elements then in ascendancy and the socialist, historical-materialist theorists, whose intellectual acumen and radicalism, popular with the students, had caused to be turned over to them many of the new faculty positions created by the nationalist drive for Chicano Studies programs. At that point cultural nationalism lost its support within the Chicano academic community and outside of it reformist elements were soon to put it aside as impractical, simplistic, and un-American. The momentum of the old cultural nationalism was thus deflected in non-political directions before it could integrate a class-based analysis and a mature understanding of culture and race. With these advances it may have found a wider resonance within academia and among progressive Chicano activists, who would have welcomed its appealing organizational potential among Latinos and other working-class peoples.

Early Chicano cultural nationalism had its chauvinistic, individualistic, and ingenuous tendencies, but the specific ideology of Aztlán, espoused in the *Plan Espiritual de Aztlán*, was certainly liberationist. Despite its romantic utopianism and lack of a class analysis, it was the clear result of the class contradictions being reflected through racism, with its accompanying segregation and oppression, and the resulting Chicano working-class culture. But it took individuals with vision and imagination to interpret, articulate, and clarify, through the discourse of art and myth, the objective bases of the class struggle in a way that would be intelligible to the community.[60] In a sense, Chicano working-class culture, located metaphorically by the nationalist in the mythical geography of Aztlán, was the scene, however brief, where the most significant and effective political battles were fought, unity was forged, and a common purpose recognized. Presently, with leftist intellectuals and radical activists marginalized from the centers of power in the communities and with the cultural nationalists on the defense, advocacy for structural change or social action gets very little attention. Thus it is primarily demography applied to the electoral process that promises the greatest hope for meaningful political power in the future. But mobilizing the community for effective political change is a difficult task. Old-style cultural nationalists did it once under very propitious conditions that no longer exist.[61] But today a revamped, class-based cultural nationalism, which includes the positive aspects present in the old, may be what is called for as a mechanism by which to mobilize people to register, identify their interests, and vote in accordance with them.

BORINQUEN

Borinquen was the name given to the island of Puerto Rico by its original inhabitants. It is an island where all national questions are reduced to *the* national question: is Puerto Rico a nation? Its continuous existence as a colony, from the Spanish defeat and destruction of its population until the present day, forms one of the two main determinants of its socioeconomic, political, and cultural reality. The other critical factor is the massive emigration that has resulted from its colonial status: well over one third of all Puerto

Ricans live in the United States.[62] Puerto Rico is a colony of the United States, and in an age of neo-colonialism and socialist revolutions this status is, at best, anachronistic. The significance of these facts are debated by all Puerto Ricans, on or off the island. No subject is more passionately discussed, affirmed, or attacked than that of the political status of Puerto Rico. Nothing is believed to oppress more, promise more, or affect more aspects of everyday life than a change of status. It is the master symbol of every shade of Puerto Rican political ideology.[63]

The colonial status of Puerto Rico makes the relation between Puerto Ricans and the United States very different from the one that exists between Mexicans and the United States. All Puerto Ricans are citizens of the United States, thus immigration laws and officers are not a concern for them as they are for Mexicans. The U.S. presence is ubiquitous, affecting every institution on the island: from birth the islanders are intimately enmeshed in the political context of the U.S., from the postal service to the welfare system, from T.V. to the local naval bases. For all their class and culture-based similarities to Chicanos, Puerto Ricans in the United States are a unique Hispanic community.

Because of close air links with the island and the sharing of political experiences, the social, cultural, and political contacts between the mainland and island communities are extensive and intensive (though at times antagonistic), particularly when compared to those between U.S. born Chicanos and Mexicans in Mexico. Until the late 1970's boom in border and migration studies, most second generation Chicanos had paid little attention to the contemporary political reality of Mexico. When the early Chicano cultural nationalists turned their eyes toward Mexico it was usually to survey the mythology of the indigenous population, to study the results of the Mexican American War, or to be inspired by the lessons of the Revolution of 1910. On the other hand, among Puerto Rican nationalists in the U.S. (not to be confused with the followers of the Nationalist Party in Puerto Rico) the politics of Puerto Rico was/is *the* critical issue. The very close ties between continent and island lead Puerto Rican leaders from New York to campaign in Puerto Rico and, in turn, island leaders regularly campaign in the United States.[64] It is not surprising, therefore, that the Young Lords, once the most militant, widespread Puerto Rican nationalist group in the

United States, should have been so concerned with socialism and anti-imperialism since its early cultural nationalist phase.[65] For many Puerto Ricans their plight in the inner-city barrios was transparently connected to the political fate of Puerto Rico.

Since the 1898 Spanish American War, when Puerto Rico became a colony of the United States, the cultural identity of its inhabitants has been under siege. The extent of the resulting economic dependence that was imposed on the island has meant that no authentic national bourgeoisie capable of defending Puerto Rican culture has come into existence, and what could pass for such a sector has been pro-American in all but a token sense.[66] Ruling class culture in Puerto Rico, as is the case in capitalist societies everywhere, has been generally regarded as the national culture and consequently proletarian culture has been thoroughly discredited. Thus, except for the works of the leftist nationalists and socialists, working-class Puerto Ricans in the United States have had little from the island from which to draw in their efforts to assert a meaningful proletarian-oriented nationalism.[67] Their relatively small numbers, high concentration in a few large urban centers, and extensive exposure to U.S. culture before arrival, make it even more difficult for Puerto Ricans, in contrast to Chicanos, to resist the pressure to assimilate culturally. The resulting weakened sociocultural matrix found in the United States, particularly for the second and third generations, makes personal and collective identity an even more critical issue than it is for Chicanos. Wherever resistance has been possible, a heightened consciousness of identity and extreme and sustained nationalism have been a defense against this cultural assault.

Notwithstanding the difficulties inherent in relying on Puerto Rico for support, it was to Borinquen that the mainland Puerto Rican cultural nationalists of the late 1960s and early 70s first turned. Their literary production and political ideology reflected a romantic, idealized vision of the island. Like the mythical Aztlán, Borinquen was transformed in the ethnic mythology of the times into a lost tropical paradise, "all pregnant with sweetness."[68] It was the repository of all cherished values, the wellspring of resistance, and the object of nostalgic remembrances. In poems, novels, paintings, and pronouncements, Borinquen, like Aztlán, was held up as the promised land of hope.[69] This search for roots was not limited to the improvisation of a fanciful contemporary island, it also devised a fabulous Borinquen, graced by peaceful Taino inhabitants living in an idyllic pre-Hispanic setting. This indigenist strain complemented a sentimental longing for the spiritually rich and quiet life of the bygone peasants, the legendary *jíbaros*.[70]

These romantic myths were a call to action: Anglo-American imperialism was to be opposed by a nationalist cultural, social, and political program. And a pilgrimage to Borinquen to absorb the ancestral powers was a first step for many as they embarked on their resistance effort. Like first generation Mexicans in the United States, numerous Puerto Rican migrants live with the dream of returning to the homeland, and many in fact do. But for the second generation this need to return became a part of the personal and collective search for a cultural shield with which to protect their identity. Many were disappointed with what they saw and experienced on their arrival: Borinquen was not the paradise they imagined and fellow Puerto Ricans did not always greet them like long lost brothers and sisters.[71] Some disillusioned nationalist artists and political activists returned to their barrios in New York and elsewhere with a resolve to carry on their part of the class struggle at home, but they continued the battle for the independence of Puerto Rico.[72]

This shift signaled an important transformation in the politics and symbolism of activist Puerto Ricans in the U.S. Politically it implied a decrease in culture-based methods of organization and an increase in class-based techniques and aims: the Young Lords Party, for instance, became the Puerto Rican Revolutionary Workers Organization.[73] At the symbolic level the very real Borinquen, having failed to live up to its mythic image, was replaced by an emblematic Borinquen, one that was primarily "un estado de ánimo."[74] The metamorphosis of Borinquen, from an Edenic island in the Caribbean to a spiritual state within the heart of Puerto Ricans, parallels the transposition found in Rudolfo Anaya's *Heart of Aztlán*. In this novel the Chicano author creates an internal, psychological geography for Aztlán; this replaces its ancient mythical geography by a personal appropriation, but it also underlines the failure of the nation-building attempts of the stridently nationalistic *Plan Espiritual de Aztlán*.[75] Thus, before the mid 1970s the political organizational thrust of both of these symbols had lost its momentum: the cultural nationalists had gone from nation to notion, and in the process had lost their hegemonic position in their respective movements. But among mainland Puerto Rican cultural nationalists and socialists, concern with and agitation for the independence of the island continued to absorb their political energies.

Advocacy on behalf of the independence of Puerto Rico has a long history in the United States, dating at least to the nineteenth century. From the beginning of the modern diaspora, migrants had brought with them an ideology of nationalism and independence, and from the outset independence had both political and symbolic meanings. Puerto Ricans and non-Puerto Ricans in the 1930s showed their solidarity with the migrant community by expressing pro-independence sentiments. Many of those who arrived between the World Wars were socialists or supported the socialists' demands for independence; but even among those who did not, there was a constant interest in the political activities on the island and its status. However, after World War II, economic and political changes occurred in Puerto Rico that affected profoundly the political ideology of future emigrants. The post-War rise of a U.S. sponsored program (known as "Operation Bootstrap") focused on capital-intensive industrialization on the island, creating both the illusion of general prosperity and a very real increase in unemployment and dislocation as a consequence of the resulting uneven development. The socioeconomic transformation forced tens of thousands of displaced persons to emigrate to the United States, but the structural contradictions were veiled by the pro-American rhetoric of the new political administrations. Thus the emigrants translated their structurally constrained circumstances into subjective, personal motivations. Therefore, among the massive numbers of working-class migrants who arrived in the United States in the 1950s and early 60s, few were committed to the independence of the island.[76]

Still, the drive for independence among activists in the U.S. during the 1960s and 1970s, and to a great extent until the present, maintained the political and symbolic thrusts this crusade had for many of the early migrants. Before the 1950s the independence movement had always been symbolically important for the community-building efforts of the newly arrived. It was a nationalist banner under which most of the working class could unite in order to find the strength to resist and survive the racist and oppressive environment of the United States. The political end with regards to the island was, of course, its actual sovereign autonomy; however, after the 1950s this effort was attacked by many, particularly in Puerto Rico and among the conservative sectors in the United States. To most it seemed to be merely quixotic activism (particularly after the electoral defeats of the Independence Parties and the status plebiscites) or downright political and social thoughtlessness.[77] Although it soon began to represent a practically impossible goal for the near future, the pro-independence movement continued to be in the 1960s and 70s an important *symbol* for uniting the nationalist elements in the U.S. And it was a superb tool for political organization on behalf of local barrio concerns. Nonetheless, it did not overshadow, as one scholar has claimed,[78] the sociopolitical and economic goals of the early cultural nationalists, instead it helped to make mobilization for these goals possible.

Various early cultural nationalists, lacking a critical class analysis, naïvely tended to present the independence of Borinquen as a panacea guaranteed both to cure all the ills suffered by all Puerto Ricans and to unite them on the island. Progressive critics correctly assailed them for this, noting that even a socialist, autonomous Puerto Rico would neither solve the problems of Puerto Ricans in the U.S. nor would it attract back to the island the masses of second and third generation English-speaking Puerto Ricans.[79] Still, unlike the early concept of Aztlán that has now run its politically useful course, pro-independence mobilization in the U.S. continues to be a valuable symbolic weapon in the Puerto Rican "class struggle," both in the cultural and political planes.[80]

CONCLUSION

Unlike what Chicano cultural nationalists did when they made the symbol of Aztlán represent the Southwest (which made sense because the Southwest was formerly Mexican), Puerto Rican nationalists on the mainland never transformed their communities into a symbolic Borinquen; instead, their Borinquen remained anchored to the real island. Because the mainland Puerto Rican nationalists concerned themselves deeply with the political status of the island and because of their small number and close racial and residential proximity to the Black community, they integrated a materialist, class analysis into their work earlier and more extensively than happened among the more segregated and parochial Chicano nationalists. Consequently, after their disillusionment with the symbol of the mythical Borinquen, Puerto Ricans were able to transform it into a symbol of the real island's independence; that is, they replaced the symbolic Borinquen with pro-independence symbolism and activism. The shift from a deployment—for purposes of political organization—of romantic, naïve symbolic forms, to a reliance on a very real fervor for independence gave Puerto Rican cultural nationalists a continuous public forum. Whether this forum can ultimately become an effective one for political organizing in the U.S. depends on the fate of Puerto Rico, and the extent to which the interest in the island's independence can be transformed, through a class-based cultural nationalism, into an interest in pro-independentism electoral politics.

In the 1980s, liberals, the left, and progressive initiatives are under attack from the right and center. However, cultural nationalism—of the kind once found in the vanguard—could be a vibrant force for social change. But changed historic conditions demand different responses. Today a synthesis of old and class-based forms of Hispanic cultural nationalism may be the best mechanism for the successful channeling of the rising tides of Latinos toward political power and self-determination. But it remains to be seen whether today's Latino leaders can mobilize the communities as well as the cultural nationalists of the past. The call for a dialectical perspective on culture/nation and class is old, but this does not stop us from appealing to it again. We need leaders whose tactics are well grounded in the social sciences and whose strategies are informed by humanist concerns. In these times, more than ever in the recent past, much depends on this fusion of skills and interests.

NOTES

1. E.g., Klor de Alva 1981, 1986.
2. Substantive revisions in the text or endnotes will be found within brackets.
3. [E.g., Moore and Pachon 1985:52, 199; Davis et al. 1988:3.]
4. See Estades 1978:64, 73-77; Meyer Rogg and Santana Cooney 1980:passim; and the obvious exception, *Revista Chicano-Riqueña*.
5. [For up-to-date data see Moore and Pachon 1985; Brown, Oliver, and Klor de Alva 1985; Acosta-Belén and Sjostrom 1988.]
6. E.g., Acuña 1981; López 1980.
7. On the former see, e.g., García 1978, Almaguer 1978; on the latter see, e.g., Gómez-Quiñones 1971, Gómez-Quiñones and Arroyo 1976, Almaguer 1981:459-63, Ríos-Bustamante 1978, *Centro Taller de Cultura* 1976.
8. E.g., Gómez-Quiñones 1977:3-5, 1978:passim, 1982:75, 76; Muñoz 1974:120; Almaguer 1981:459-63; Mindiola 1977:179-85; *Centro Taller de Cultura* 1976:passim; Estades 1978:45-52.
9. E.g., Limón 1977; Flores 1979; Sánchez 1977, 1979.
10. E.g., Gómez-Quiñones 1977:6-7; Maldonado-Denis 1976:18; Ramírez 1976:109, 111, 114; Campos and Flores 1979:82, 143; Bonilla 1980:457; *Centro Taller de Cultura* 1976:2, 32-94; Muñoz 1974:120.
11. Gómez-Quiñones 1977:7-8; Campos and Flores 1979:135; *Centro Taller de Cultura* 1976:64-68.
12. Campos and Flores 1979:131-43; Bonilla 1980:464; *Centro Taller de Cultura* 1976:passim.
13. For examples of these critiques see Bonilla 1980:455-64; Barradas 1980:44; Seda Bonilla 1974:94-95; Vaca 1967.
14. Seda Bonilla 1972:458.
15. Gómez-Quiñones 1977:10; Campos and Flores 1979:145.
16. Bonilla 1973:226, 1974:68; Seda Bonilla 1980:passim.
17. E.g., Novack 1978.

18. Bonilla 1974:66.
19. E.g., Bustamante 1981:99.
20. Maldonado-Denis 1976:21; Gómez-Quiñones 1977:11.
21. Estades 1978:50; 73-75; Gómez-Quiñones 1977:11.
22. Barradas 1979:48, 53; Barradas and Rodríguez 1980:14; Seda Bonilla 1974:96-97, 1977:117.
23. Mindiola 1977:181.
24. Gómez-Quiñones 1982:75, 77, 80.
25. Gómez-Quiñones 1982:76, 79-80; Blaut 1982:22; Puerto Rican Socialist Party 1974:48; Pendás 1976; Mindiola 1977:181.
26. For affirmations of this critique see Campos and Flores 1979:129-134; Ramírez 1976:113; *Centro Taller de Cultura* 1976:70.
27. E.g., August 29th Movement 1976; Puerto Rican Socialist Party 1974:47-64; Blaut 1977:35.
28. E.g., Ríos-Bustamante 1978; Muñoz 1974:122; Cervantes 1977:132; *The Rican* 1974 and *Society and Culture* 1976.
29. Gómez-Quiñones 1982.
30. Peterson 1982:2.
31. Stalin 1942; Lenin 1968.
32. For a thorough review of this issue see Gómez-Quiñones 1982.
33. Reyna 1977:191; *El Plan Espiritual de Aztlán* 1972:402-406.
34. *Centro Taller de Cultura* 1976:142: Muñoz 1974:120-121.
35. For a discussion of the problem see Barrera 1979 [for a recent study see Omi and Winant 1986].
36. See Mindiola 1977:185; Almaguer 1975:72, 93.
37. See the discussion in Blaut 1977.
38. Bonilla and Girling 1973; Barrera, Muñoz, and Ornelas 1972; Almaguer 1975, 1981; García 1975; Barrera 1979; Montejano 1981.
39. Barrera 1979:212.
40. Bonilla 1973a:227; Maldonado-Denis 1976b:19; Seda Bonilla 1977:109, 1974:104; Ybarra-Frausto 1982:passim.
41. See Barrera 1979:207.
42. E.g., Campos and Flores 1979:136-39; Klor de Alva 1977:20-24.
43. *Centro Taller de Cultura 1976:146-48.*

44. E.g., Muñoz 1974:120.
45. E.g., Ybarra-Frausto 1978:92; *Centro Taller de Cultura* 1976:8, 55-56; cf. Gómez-Quiñones 1982:15.
46. E.g., *Centro Taller de Cultura* 1976:48; Bonilla 1974:69.
47. E.g., *Centro Taller de Cultura* 1976:58, 64-70, 186; Cervantes 1977:129; Campos and Flores 1979:131-35; Gómez-Quiñones 1978:passim; Leal 1977:118-23.
48. Cervantes 1977:131.
49. E.g., Bonilla 1973:229, 1974:68.
50. In general see Kirchhoff 1961:59-73; for its role among Chicanos see Klor de Alva 1981:28, [1986]; and Leal 1981:16-22.
51. E.g., Durán 1967:215-224; Chimalpahin 1965a:154 (for a Spanish version see Chimalpahin 1965b:123-125).
52. E.g., Elizondo 1978:24; Ortego y Gasca 1979:112; Ybarra-Frausto 1979:119; Leal 1979:28; Alurista 1977:49; Morales Blouin 1979: 179-80; Lux and Vigil 1979:15; Macías 1974:143; Segade 1973:4-5.
53. [E.g., Klor de Alva 1986.]
54. E.g., Matthiessen 1969; López Tijerina 1978; Gómez-Quiñones 1978.
55. Gleason 1982:133-35.
56. See *Plan Espiritual de Aztlán* 1972:402-406; Gómez-Quiñones 1978:28, 32, 1982:75.
57. In Barrera 1979:204.
58. Gómez-Quiñones 1978; Muñoz 1974.
59. See Gómez-Quiñones 1977:18.
60. E.g., Montoya 1980:126, 128-29; Alurista 1980:273-74, 276.
61. See Almaguer 1978:140-1.
62. *Puerto Ricans* 1976:4.
63. E.g., Bonilla 1973:224.
64. See Estades 1978.
65. Estades 1978:45-51; Abramson 1971; PRRWO 1974:70-79.
66. *Centro Taller de Cultura* 1976:72.
67. E.g., Campos and Flores 1979; *Taller de Formación Política* 1982.
68. Barradas 1979:51.

69. E.g., Barradas and Rodríguez 1980:16; Campos and Flores 1979:136; Barradas 1979:46-48, 1980:45; for an opposing view see *Centro Taller de Cultura* 1976:140.
70. Barradas 1979:50-51; Johnson 1980:110-23.
71. Merced Rosa 1974:57; Maldonado-Denis 1976:107; Seda Bonilla 1974:86, 1980:passim; López 1976:4; Barradas 1979:52.
72. E.g., Barradas 1979:53; Estades 1978:50.
73. Flores et al. 1981; PRRWO 1974:76-78; Estades 1978:50.
74. Barradas 1979:54.
75. Anaya 1976; Leal 1981:21-22.
76. See López 1980; Quintero Rivera, et al. 1981: *Taller de Formación Política* 1982; Maldonado-Denis 1976; Campos and Bonilla 1982a; *Centro Taller de Migración* 1975; Estades 1978; History Task Force 1979; Johnson 1980.
77. E.g., Johnson 1980:127-160; Maldonado 1983.
78. Estades 1978:78-79; Seda Bonilla 1972:455-456; cf. Silén 1974:19.
79. See López 1976:4-5; Ayala 1974:116.
80. E.g., Bonilla 1980:465.

BIBLIOGRAPHY

Abramson, Michael, ed. *Palante: Young Lords Party*. New York: McGraw Hill, 1971.

Acosta-Belén, Edna and Barbara R. Sjostrom, eds. *The Hispanic Experience in the United States*. New York: Praeger, 1988.

Acuña, Rodolfo. *Occupied America: A History of Chicanos*. 2nd ed. New York: Harper & Row, 1981.

Almaguer, Tomás. "Class, Race, and Chicano Oppression." *Socialist Revolution* 5 (July-September 1975): 71-99.

_____. "Chicano Politics in the Present Period: Comment on García." *Socialist Review* 8 (July-October 1978): 137-141.

_____. "Interpreting Chicano History: The World-System Approach to Nineteenth-Century California." *Review* 4 (Winter 1981): 459-507.

Alurista. "La estética indígena a través del Floricanto de Nezahualcóyotl." *Revista Chicano-Riqueña* 5 (Spring 1977): 48-62.

Anaya, Rudolfo. *Heart of Aztlán*. Berkeley: Editorial Justa, 1976.

August Twenty-Ninth Movement. *Fan the Flames: A Revolutionary Position on the Chicano National Question*. n.p., 1976.

Ayala, Dory. "On the National Question." *The Rican: Journal of Contemporary Puerto Rican Thought* 2 (1974): 114-116.

Barradas, Efraín. " 'De lejos en sueños verla...': Visión mítica de Puerto Rico en la poesía neoyorrican." *Revista Chicano-Riqueña* 7 (Verano 1979): 46-56.

_____. "Puerto Rico acá, Puerto Rico allá." *Revista Chicano-Riqueña* 8 (Primavera 1980): 43-49.

_____ and Rafael Rodríguez. *Herejes y mitificadores: muestra de poesía puertorriqueña en los Estados Unidos*. Río Piedras, P.R.: Ediciones Huracán, 1980.

Barrera, Mario. *Race and Class in the Southwest: A Theory of Racial Inequality*. Notre Dame and London: University of Notre Dame Press, 1979.

_____, Carlos Muñoz, and Charles Ornelas. "The Barrio as Internal Colony." In *People and Politics in Urban Society*. Edited by Harlan Hahn. Los Angeles: Sage Publications, 1972.

Blaut, James. "Are Puerto Ricans a National Minority?" *Monthly Review* (May 1977): 35-55.

_____. "Nationalism as an Autonomous Force." *Science and Society* 46 (Spring 1982): 1-23.

Bonilla, Frank. "Puerto Ricans in the United States and Puerto Ricans in Puerto Rico." *The Rican: Journal of Contemporary Puerto Rican Thought* 2 (1974): 65-69.

_____. "Beyond Survival: Por qué seguiremos siendo puertorriqueños." In *The Puerto Ricans*. Edited by Adalberto López. Cambridge, Mass: Schenkman, 1980.

_____ and Emilio González. "New Knowing, New Practice: Puerto Rican Studies." In *Structures of Dependency*. Edited by Frank Bonilla and Robert Girling. Stanford, Cal.: Stanford Institute of Politics, 1973 (a).

_____ and Robert Girling, eds. *Structures of Dependency*. Stanford, Cal.: Stanford Institute of Politics, 1973 (b).

Brown, Lester B., John Oliver, and J. Jorge Klor de Alva, eds. *Sociocultural and Service Issues in Working with Hispanic American Clients*. Albany: Rockefeller College Press, 1985.

Bruce-Novoa, Juan, ed. "Alurista." In *Chicano Authors: Inquiry by Interview*. Austin and London: University of Texas Press, 1980.

_____. "José Montoya." In *Chicano Authors: Inquiry by Interview*. Austin and London: University of Texas Press, 1980.

Bustamante, Jorge A. "The Immigrant Worker: A Social Problem or a Human Resource." In *Mexican Immigrant Workers in the U.S.* Edited by Antonio Ríos-Bustamante. Los Angeles: Chicano Studies Research Center, U.C.L.A., 1981.

Campos, Ricardo and Juan Flores. "Migración y cultura nacional puertorriqueñas: perspectivas proletarias." In *Puerto Rico: Identidad Nacional y Clases Sociales (Coloquio de Princeton)*. Edited by Angel G. Quintero Rivera, et al. Rio Piedras, P.R.: Ediciones Huracán, 1979.

_____ and Frank Bonilla. "Bootstraps and Enterprise Zones: The Underside of Late Capitalism in Puerto Rico and the United States." *Review* 5 (Spring 1982): 556-590.

Centro Taller de Cultura. New York: Centro de Estudios Puertorriqueños, C.U.N.Y., 1976.

Cervantes, Fred A. "Chicanos as a Post-Colonial Minority: Some Questions Concerning the Adequacy of the Paradigm of Internal Colonialism." In *Perspectivas en Chicano Studies*. Edited by Reynaldo Flores Macías. Los Angeles: Chicano Studies Research Center, U.C.L.A., 1977.

Chimalpahin Cuauhtlehuanitzin, Francisco de San Antón Muñoz. *Die Relationen Chimalpahin's zur Geschichte Mexico's*. Edited by Günter Zimmermann. Hamburg: Cram, de Gruyter, 1965 (a).

_____. *Relaciones originales de Chalco Amaquemecan*. Edited and translated by S. Rendón. México: Fondo de Cultura Económica, 1965 (b).

Cortés, F., A. Falcón, and J. Flores. "The Cultural Expression of Puerto Ricans in New York: A Theoretical Perspective and Critical Review." *Latin American Perspectives* 3 (1976): 117-150.

Davis, Cary, Carl Haub, and JoAnne L. Willette. "U.S. Hispanics: Changing the Face of America." In *The Hispanic Experience in the United States*. Edited by Edna Acosta-Belén and Barbara R. Sjostrom. New York: Praeger, 1988.

Durán, Fray Diego. *Historia de las Indias de Nueva España e Islas de la Tierra Firme*. 2 vols. Edited by Angel Ma. Garibay K. México: Editorial Porrúa, 1967.

El Plan Espiritual de Aztlán. In *Aztlán: An Anthology of Mexican American Literature*. Edited by Luis Valdez and Stan Steiner. New York: Vintage Books, 1972.

Elizondo, Sergio D. "Myth and Reality in Chicano Literature." *Latin American Literary Review* 5 (Spring-Summer, 1978): 23-31.

Estades, Rosa. *Patterns of Political Participation of Puerto Ricans in New York City*. Hato Rey: Editorial Universitaria, 1978.

Estrada, Leobardo. "The Demographics of the Latino Vote." *El Mirlo* 10 (Winter 1982): 1-2, 11-12.

Flores, Juan, et al. "La Carreta Made a U-Turn: Puerto Rican Language and Culture in the United States." *Daedalus* 110 (Spring 1981): 193-217.

García, Mario. "Racial Dualism in the El Paso Labor Market, 1880-1920." *Aztlán* 6 (Summer 1975): 197-218.

García, Richard A. "The Chicano Movement and the Mexican American Community, 1972-1978: An Interpretative Essay." *Socialist Review* 8 (July-October 1978): 117-136.

Gleason, Philip. "American Identity and Americanization." In *Concepts of Ethnicity*. Edited by Stephan Thernstrom. Cambridge: Belknap Press of Harvard University, 1982.

Gómez-Quiñones, Juan. "Critique on the National Question, Self-Determination and Nationalism." *Latin American Perspectives* 9 (Spring 1982): 62-83.

_____. *Mexican Students Por La Raza: The Chicano Student Movement in Southern California 1967-1977*. Santa Barbara: Editorial La Causa, 1978.

_____. *On Culture*. Los Angeles: Chicano Studies Research Center, U.C.L.A., 1977. (First published in *Revista Chicano-Riqueña* 5 [Spring 1977]: 29-47.)

"Toward a Perspective on Chicano History." *Aztlán* 2 (Fall 1971): 1-49.

_____ and Luis Leobardo Arroyo. "On the State of Chicano History: Observations on Its Development, Interpretations, and Theory, 1970-1974." *Western Historical Quarterly* 7 (April 1976): 155-185.

History Task Force (Centro de Estudios Puertorriqueños). *Labor Migration Under Capitalism: The Puerto Rican Experience*. New York: Monthly Review Press, 1979.

Johnson, Roberta Ann. *Puerto Rico: Commonwealth or Colony?* New York: Praeger, 1980.

Kirchhoff, Paul. "¿Se puede localizar Aztlán?" *Anuario de Historia* 1 (1961): 59-73.

Klor de Alva, J. Jorge. "California Chicano Literature and Pre-Columbian Motifs: Foil and Fetish." *Confluencia: Revista Hispánica de Cultura y Literatura* 1 (1986): 18-26.

_____. "Aztlán." In *Dictionary of Mexican American History*. Edited by Matt S. Meier and Feliciano Rivera. Westport, Connecticut: Greenwood Press, 1981.

_____."Critique of National Character Versus Universality in Chicana Poetry." *De Colores Journal* 3 (1977): 20-24.

Leal, Luis. "In Search of Aztlán." *Denver Quarterly* 16 (Fall 1981): 16-22.

_____. "Mexican American Literature: A Historical Perspective." In *Modern Chicano Writers*. Edited by Joseph Sommers and Tomás Ybarra-Frausto. Englewood Cliffs: Prentice-Hall, 1979.

_____. "Octavio Paz and the Chicano." *Latin American Literary Review* 10 (Spring-Summer, 1977): 115-123.

Lenin, V.I. *Selected Works*. 3 vols. New York: International Publishers, 1968.

Limón, José. "El folklore y los mexicanos en los Estados Unidos: una perspectiva cultural marxista." In *La otra cara de México: el pueblo chicano*. Edited by David R. Maciel. México: Ediciones "El Caballito," 1977.

López, Adalberto. "The Puerto Rican Struggle in the U.S." *Sociedad y Cultura* 1 (April 1976): 4-7.

_____, ed. *The Puerto Ricans: Their History, Culture, and Society*. Cambridge, Mass.: Schenkman, 1980.

López Tijerina, Reies. *Mi lucha por la tierra*. México: Fondo de Cultura Económica, 1978.

Lux, Guillermo and Maurilio E. Vigil. "Return to Aztlán: The Chicano Rediscovers His Indian Past." In *The Chicanos As We See Ourselves*. Edited by Arnulfo D. Trejo. Tucson: University of Arizona Press, 1979.

Macías, Ysidro Ramón. "Nuestros antepasados y el Movimiento." *Aztlán* 5 (Spring and Fall, 1974): 143-153.

Maldonado, A.W. "Against Puerto Rican Statehood." *New York Times*, 22 January 1983.

Maldonado-Denis, Manuel. "El problema de la asimilación cultural." *Sociedad y Cultura* 1 (April 1976): 18-27.

_____. *The Emigration Dialectic: Puerto Rico and the USA*. New York: International Publishers, 1980.

Matthiessen, Peter. *Sal Si Puedes: César Chávez and the New American Revolution*. New York: Dell, 1969.

Merced Rosa, Florencio. "One Nation, One Party." *The Rican: Journal of Contemporary Puerto Rican Thought* 2 (1974): 49-64.

Meyer Rogg, Eleanor and Rosemary Santana Cooney. *Adaptation and Adjustment of Cubans: West New York, New Jersey*. New York: Hispanic Research Center, Fordham University, 1980.

Mindiola, Tatcho. "Marxism and the Chicano Movement: Preliminary Remarks." *Perspectivas en Chicano Studies*. Edited by Reynaldo Flores Macías. Los Angeles: Chicano Studies Research Center, UCLA, 1977.

Montejano, David. "Is Texas Bigger than the World-System? A Critique from a Provincial Point of View." *Review: Journal of the Fernand Braudel Center* 4 (Winter 1981): 597-628.

Moore, Joan and Harry Pachon. *Hispanics in the United States.* Englewood Cliffs: Prentice-Hall, 1985.

Morales Blouin, Egla. "Símbolos y motivos nahuas en la literatura chicana." In *The Identification and Analysis of Chicano Literature*. Edited by Francisco Jiménez. New York: Bilingual Press, 1979.

Muñoz, Jr., Carlos. "The Politics of Protest and Chicano Liberation: A Case Study of Repression and Cooptation." *Aztlán* 5 (Spring and Fall 1974): 119-141.

Novack, George, ed. *Existentialism Versus Marxism: Conflicting Views on Humanism*. New York: Dell, 1978.

Omi, Michael and Howard Winant. *Racial Formation in the United States: From the 1960s to the 1980s.* New York: Routledge & Kegan Paul, 1986.

Ortego y Gasca, Felipe de. "An Introduction to Chicano Poetry." In *Modern Chicano Writers*. Edited by Joseph Sommers and Tomás Ybarra-Frausto. Englewood Cliffs: Prentice-Hall, 1979.

Pendás, Miguel. *Chicano Liberation and Socialism*. New York: Pathfinder Press, 1976.

Petersen, William. "Concepts of Ethnicity." In *Concepts of Ethnicity.* Edited by Stephan Thernstrom. Cambridge: Belknap Press of Harvard University, 1982.

PRRWO (Puerto Rican Revolutionary Workers Organization). "National Liberation of Puerto Rico and the Responsibilities of the U.S. Proletariat." *The Rican: Journal of Contemporary Puerto Rican Thought* 2 (1974): 70-80.

Puerto Rican Socialist Party. "The National Question." *The Rican: Journal of Contemporary Puerto Rican Thought* 2 (1974): 47-48.

Puerto Ricans in the Continental United States: An Uncertain Future. Washington D.C.: U.S. Commission on Civil Rights, 1976.

Quintero Rivera, Angel G., et al. *Puerto Rico; identidad nacional y clases sociales (Coloquio de Princeton)*. 2nd ed. Río Piedras, P.R.: Ediciones Huracán, 1981.

Ramírez, Rafael L. "National Culture in Puerto Rico." *Latin American Perspectives* 3 (1976): 109-116.

Research Institute Recommendations. August 10, 1979.

Reyna, José R. "Tejano Music as an Expression of Cultural Nationalism." In *Perspectivas en Chicano Studies*. Edited by Reynaldo Flores Macías. Los Angeles: Chicano Studies Research Center, U.C.L.A., 1977.

Ríos-Bustamante, Antonio. *Mexicans in the United States and the National Question: Current Polemics and Organizational Positions*. Santa Barbara: Editorial La Causa, 1978.

Sánchez, Rosaura. "The Chicana Labor Force." In *Essays on la Mujer*. Edited by Rosaura Sánchez and Rosa Martínez Cruz. Los Angeles: Chicano Studies Research Center, U.C.L.A., 1977.

Seda Bonilla, Eduardo. *Réquiem para una cultura*. 4th ed. Río Piedras, P.R.: Ediciones Bayoan, 1980.

_____. "Who is a Puerto Rican: Problems of Socio Cultural Identity in Puerto Rico." *Caribbean Studies* 17 (April-July, 1977): 105-121.

_____. "¿Qué somos: puertorriqueños, neorriqueños o nuyorriqueños?" *The Rican: Journal of Contemporary Puerto Rican Thought* 2 (1974): 81-107.

_____. "El problema de la identidad de los nuyorricans." *Revista de Ciencias Sociales* 16 (Diciembre, 1972): 453-462.

Segade, Gustavo. "Toward a Dialectic of Chicano Literature." *Mester* 4 (November, 1973): 4-5.

Silén, Angel Juan. "Aspectos sobresalientes del problema nacional puertorriqueño y la nueva lucha de independencia." *The Rican: Journal of Contemporary Puerto Rican Thought* 2 (1974): 14-20.

Stalin, Joseph. *Marxism and the National Question*. New York: International Publishers, 1942.

Taller de formación política. *La cuestión nacional: El Partido Nacionalista y el movimiento obrero puertorriqueño*: Río Piedras, P.R.: Ediciones Huracán, 1982.

Vaca, Nick. "Message to the People." *Mexican American Liberation Papers*. Berkeley, California, 1967.

Williams, Raymond. "Culture and Civilization." *The Encyclopedia of Philosophy*. New York: Macmillan, 1967.

Winick, Charles. *Dictionary of Anthropology*. New York: Philosophical Library, 1956.

Ybarra-Frausto, Tomás "Califas: California Chicano Art and Its Social Background." Santa Cruz, California, 1982. (Mimeographed.)

————. "Alurista's Poetics: The Oral, the Bilingual, the Pre-Columbian." In *Modern Chicano Writers*. Edited by Joseph Sommers and Tomás Ybarra-Frausto. Englewood Cliffs: Prentice-Hall, 1979.

————. "The Chicano Movement and the Emergence of a Chicano Poetic Consciousness." In *New Directions in Chicano Scholarship*. Edited by Ricardo Romo and Raymund Paredes. La Jolla, California: University of California, San Diego, Chicano Studies Monograph Series, 1978.

Aztlán, Montezuma, and New Mexico: The Political Uses of American Indian Mythology

Ramón A. Gutiérrez

In 1885, William G. Ritch, then Secretary of the Territory of New Mexico and the recently elected president of the New Mexico Bureau of Immigration, issued a promotional book on the resources of New Mexico entitled *Aztlán: The History, Resources and Attractions of New Mexico*, which was meant to attract immigrants to the territory. *Aztlán* had a press run of 27,000 copies in 1885, but previous editions of the book, published under the title *Illustrated New Mexico*, brought the total close to 100,000 copies.[1]

Aztlán was a handsomely produced case-bound book. Its brown cloth cover was intricately embossed with a gold foil engraving of Montezuma, the Aztec emperor (Figure 1), holding a sceptor in one hand and a ceremonial staff in the other, seated on an eagle with outstretched wings. Below Montezuma was the North American continent with two cities prominently marked—Mexico and Santa Fe. Ritch began the very first line of text in his

This article was written while the author was a Fellow at the Center for Advanced Study in the Behavioral Sciences in Stanford, California. The author gratefully acknowledges the support provided by the Andrew W. Mellon Foundation.

LEGEND OF MONTEZUMA.

Figure 1. Source: William G. Ritch, *Aztlán. The History, Resources and Attractions of New Mexico*, (Boston: D. Lothrop, 1885), p.4.

173

book by asking: "From whence came the tribes who founded and settled the City of Mexico?" "Aztlán," he answered. Ritch added that no one knew exactly where Aztlán actually was. Archaeologists had generally agreed that Aztlán was somewhere in Mexico's far north, "near the portion of New Mexico and Arizona bounded by the 35th and 37th parallel of latitude."[2] Ritch opined that this was probably the case. Otherwise, how could one explain the Pueblo Indian myths that told of Montezuma's life in New Mexico before he departed south to conquer the tribes of the Valley of Mexico?

The purpose of this essay is to explore why, in 1885, William G. Ritch wrote *Aztlán*. Why did he begin his promotional tract with the legend of Montezuma? What about this myth was particularly attractive to Anglo Americans contemplating a move to New Mexico? Why were parallels between the Aztec empire centered in Mexico City and the Pueblo Indians living near dusty Santa Fe being drawn in the promotional literature of the day? What fantasies of future development were being articulated in *Aztlán*? What does the publication of *Aztlán* tell us about the construction of myths and the political uses to which they are put?

These are the questions we will explore in this essay which is divided into three parts. In part one we will discuss the immediate history and politics of New Mexico that led to the creation of the territorial Bureau of Immigration in 1880, and particularly to the publication of *Aztlán* in 1885. In part two we will analyze the themes Ritch articulated in *Aztlán* to attract immigrants to New Mexico. Finally, in part three we will return to the "Legend of Montezuma" which was the centerpiece of Ritch's book, using it as a way of delving into the colonialist representations of New Mexico and its peoples that were being projected to the American reading public.

I. History

In 1850, only four years after territorial annexation by the United States, New Mexico had a population of roughly 60,000. Though the area was blessed with broad expanses of timber, arable land, sufficient water for irrigation, and abundant mineral deposits, these resources had remained largely unexploited. The only industries that had developed during Mexican rule were commercial livestock production destined for markets in

Chihuahua, México, and St. Louis, Missouri, fledgling textile mills, and small-scale mining. Most of New Mexico's citizens supported themselves by working the land, raising enough for subsistence and trading whatever surplus they produced to merchants for luxury items.

The land on which Hispanos toiled was inequitably distributed. The *ricos*, as the "rich" or large landholders were called, enjoyed the life of a comfortable regional gentry, engaged in mercantile activity, and lived by exploiting their retainers, their poorer kin, and their share-croppers (*partidarios*). The majority of New Mexico's *pobres*, or land "poor" farmers, eked out a living by working their small private plots and by grazing their livestock on land held in common by their communities as *mercedes*, or land grants.[3] A burgeoning working class of men and women sold their labor to others as miners, field hands, laundresses, and muleteers. The Pueblo Indians lived on their ancestral lands, working much as most Hispanos did. And the few Anglo immigrants who had entered the area as settlers came as lawyers, land speculators, merchants, soldiers, or yeoman farmers.

Since the end of the United States-Mexican War and the signing of the Treaty of Guadalupe-Hidalgo in 1848, the fate of the newly acquired American territory of New Mexico had been one of the hottest topics of national politics. From 1848 until 1912, when New Mexico finally became a state, various interest groups in the territory lobbied the American Congress to get their vision of the area's future encoded in law. Whatever faction one supported, sympathized with, or opposed, the issues at stake were clear. Who would control the development of New Mexico's lands, and therby dictate how its mineral wealth would be mined, how and where livestock would range, how its lands would be farmed, and when and where railroad lines would be laid? The resolution of all of these issues hinged on one: How and when would New Mexico became a state?[4]

For New Mexico's native Hispanos, the politics of statehood were clear. The sooner New Mexico became a state the better. So long as they were the numerically predominant population in the territory, they would control their own destinies. New Mexico would continue as an official bilingual state. The divinity of God would be taught in Roman Catholic schools. The communal land grants, which over the centuries the Spanish kings and the Mexican government had given them, would be held sacred. The profits from mining coal, iron, and other precious metals would be theirs. In short, there would be native home rule.[5]

The movement to delay statehood came primarily from Anglo settlers. They feared the creation of a state ruled and dominated by Hispanos. The anti-statists were a group composed of all those military officials, local prefects, lawyers, land speculators, and some Hispano allies to whom the territory had been administratively entrusted in 1846 after the Army of the West forcibly occupied New Mexico. This "territorial machine," as the historian Howard R. Lamar has called the coalition, wanted New Mexico to wait for its statehood until Americans were the numerically dominant group.[6]

Under Spanish, Mexican, and the early years of American rule, New Mexico had always been a marginal and insignificant area in national politics. The situation changed early in 1879 when the Santa Fe Railroad laid tracks across the territory. Instantly New Mexico was integrated into a complex transportation system leading to all the major manufacturing centers in the United States. Shortly thereafter the area's resources were made available to a larger market. With so much at stake, understandably, the statehood issue came to the fore again.

The Anglo proponents of statehood knew that they needed American immigrant bodies. But how could they attract others of their kind, given the fact that early Anglo travel accounts had depicted New Mexico as a wasteland inhabited by superstitious racial inferiors who lacked a strong work ethic?[7] Equally vexing, wrote Governor L. Bradford Prince in 1892, was the idea "prevalent outside of our own vicinity, that New Mexico is a land of dry and barren wastes, where there is little agriculture and no horticulture, where attempts at mining have been attended by failure and where nature had done almost nothing to attract or support a population."[8]

To create a new image for New Mexico, one which the territorial legislature hoped would attract American businessmen and farmers to the area, on February 15, 1880, the legislature created the New Mexico Bureau of Immigration. The Bureau's mission was "to prepare and disseminate accurate information as to the soil, climate, minerals, resources, production and business of New Mexico, with special reference to its opportunities for development, and the inducements and advantages which it presents to desirable immigration and for the investment of capital."[9] What was never mentioned in the Bureau's enabling legislation was the pivotal political role it ultimately would play in the statehood movement. If Anglos were to wrest control over New Mexico from the native Hispano elites, American immigrants were needed. Without them, writes Herbert H. Lang, what was deemed "an underdeveloped community of shepherds and subsistence farmers...[could not] evolve into a thriving, viable state in the American Union."[10]

From 1880 to 1912, when the activities of the Bureau essentially ceased—statehood for New Mexico having been accomplished—the Bureau published and distributed 124 known titles, totalling some 500,000 items.[11] The most popular of these promotional publications was William G. Ritch's book, *Aztlán: The History, Resources and Attractions of New Mexico*.

II. Aztlán

The bulk of *Aztlán: The History, Resources and Attractions of New Mexico* was devoted to a glorious description of all the resources and opportunities that awaited American immigrants. William G. Ritch listed the territory's mineral wealth, directions for reaching the various mining camps, and the exact railroad connections for the exportation of raw materials to manufacturing centers. "Rich mines are found in almost every direction...our mountains contain illimitable treasures, in the shape of lead, iron, copper, silver, mica and gold, and in the near future this beautiful country is destined to be known as the true El Dorado."[12]

Ritch promised capitalists and prospectors superb profits in New Mexico. He cited the case of the Sierra Grande Mining Company, which had begun with a small $10,000 investment and in less than two years had profited 5,000 percent, "or an annual return of thirty-fold" [sic].[13] "Incredible as it may appear," continued Ritch, other activities would yield comparable rates of profit. Anyone raising heifers could expect to make an annual average interest return of 62 percent, on stock cattle 43 percent, and on sheep 80 percent.[14] Those who believed in Ritch's solemn pronouncement, "Wealth seeks investment where there is profit, and is unerring in its judgment as no other representative of human intelligence can be," would truly realize their dreams in New Mexico.[15]

In addition to profits, New Mexico had two other inimitable resources:

its climate and its people. New Mexico's high altitudes, its dry atmosphere, its equable temperatures, and its generous sunshine made it a place where one's investment could be made to work "the year round."[16] Diseases that plagued workers in industrial centers were absent here. One found little heart disease, nervous trouble, rheumatism, asthma, or venereal disease. In fact, numerous men who once had suffered from consumption had regained their health quickly on breathing Santa Fe's air.[17]

New Mexico's salubrious climate had promoted the growth of a docile and industrious labor force. "The masses of the people are simple in their tastes and habits, peaceable and law abiding," wrote Ritch. The natives were a well-disposed, patriotic, and liberty-loving people who had always expressed warmth and friendship toward American immigrants. Those heinous crimes and domestic disorders for which New Mexico had become known in the 1880s were not the work of long-time local residents, Ritch maintained, but the activity of desperadoes from other areas who had "infested the Territory."[18]

Ritch, as president of the Historical Society of New Mexico, followed his inventory of New Mexico's resources with a truncated history of the area. This history was little more than an apologia for New Mexico's territorial annexation in 1848, and a particularly poignant exemplar of the Positivism that then had gripped Western intellectual life. Glorifying order and progress, Ritch reiterated the evolutionist theory of historical development that Henry L. Morgan had expounded in *Ancient Society* and that had been widely popularized in New Mexico by Morgan's assistant, Adolph F. Bandelier, as the Archaeological Institute of America's chief archaeologist at their Pueblo excavations.[19] According to them, New Mexico's history had progressed through four stages of evolution, culminating in "the magnetic wand of steam and iron," (i.e., the railroad) breaking down "the barriers of mountains, and join[ing] New Mexico with the world."[20] The first "epoch" of this history had been the settlement of the country by the Pueblo Indians' ancestral kin. "They constituted a people possessing...**many** of the characteristics, environments and habits of civilization."[21] For centuries the Puebloans had lived with "simple tastes, fixed habits, and habitations." They had toiled industriously and providently. They had been ruled by law and had developed an elaborate religious system, which, however "heterodox and idolatrous," had been sincerely believed by the people.[22]

The second epoch of New Mexico history had begun in the 1540s with the Spanish explorations of Francisco Vásquez de Coronado and with the area's colonization in 1598. These were years of "(ir)responsibility and dense isolation," wrote Ritch, "halcyon days of pooling for the few in peonage, peculiar contracts and bedeviled land grants, and upon the inseparable dry-rot arising from a thousand miles of isolation for centuries, and the attending monopoly of class interest."[23] This isolation had "stifled genius and killed enterprise." Paraphrasing comments made by Tranquilino Luna, the New Mexican U.S. Congressional delegate, regarding the deleterious effects of isolation, Ritch exclaimed, "the wonder is not, that they did not advance, but that they survived."[24]

Ritch's litany of social handicaps created and exacerbated by centuries of Spanish occupation was but a pretext for him to express his anti-Spanish and anti-Catholic sentiments. A particularly loathsome legacy of this period, he claimed, was the "land grant incubus" that had stifled the territory's free growth. Modernization awaited, but that did not come until the end of New Mexico's third epoch, its period of Mexican rule.[25]

The fourth, and according to Ritch, "the last" epoch of history, was ushered in by the "advent of the ever restless and irresistible American, to whom has been reserved the gigantic task of developing the illimitable resources of this most wonderful country, and by whom, eventually, the entire universe will be enriched in a most material manner."[26] Ritch explained that General Stephen Watts Kearney and the Army of the West had taken Santa Fe in 1846 peacefully, without force. Kearney came "with **the white-winged messenger of peace**, notwithstanding that he bore the insignia of war, and issued...his proclamation of good will and occupation in the name of the republic, offering the protection of a strong government, with stability and liberty to all the people."[27] Liberty had unfurled her banner in New Mexico, bringing with her the right to freedom of the press, of speech, and of person.

From 1846 to the early 1880s, hundreds of American immigrants had entered New Mexico who were "intelligent, patriotic, energetic, economical, honest and orderly."[28] Ritch maintained that "where hostile Indians roved a few years since, are now found prosperous mining and live stock camps, and flourishing cities and towns, and **an enlightened and enterprising population**."[29] In a short time these Americans had vastly improved the situation of the natives, bringing new ideas and new methods. They had advanced commerce, developed the mines, planted improved crops, and established public schools, all hallmarks of liberal progress.[30]

As an immigrant promotional tract, *Aztlán* was explicitly aimed at attracting "honest, industrious, and thrifty" men who were not afraid of hard work. Any person who was intelligent and had a small amount of capital, promised Ritch, could "become independent if not wealthy. There are many industries for him to take hold of."[31] For professional men, such as lawyers and doctors, there were many opportunities for them "*on top of the ladder.*" But if there were "not prepared to take their place *at the top*, it would have been better for them to have staid away."[32]

Men of means were important to New Mexico's economic development. But to prosper and to gain membership in the American union, the territory also had to attract yeoman farmers. As late as 1880, only nine percent of New Mexico's population had been born in the States. By this date too, only eighty-nine persons had requested public domain lands under the Homestead Act.[33] Thus much was made in *Aztlán* of the bountiful land to be had for a pittance in New Mexico.

Idyllic fertile valleys and grass-covered ranges awaited farmers willing to leave the Midwest, the South, and Northeast. Health, wealth, and happiness awaited them. Ritch told the yeomanry that their presence in New Mexico would be a civilizing agent. They would "plant free schools, conscience and toleration...[and] cultivate manly self-reliance and a healthy public sentiment."[34] For much of New Mexico's land was mired in Spanish and Mexican land grants, a system of communal landholding that "excluded the poor from the possession of landed property, and cursed so many countries."[35] If New Mexico was to prosper, individual will and initiative had to triumph. "Success or failure necessarily rests with the individual," wrote Ritch, and not with the moribund ideals of communalism.[36]

III. The Legend of Montezuma

Since so much of the message contained in the pages of *Aztlán* was a veneration of individualism, self-reliance, and the poor immigrant's dream of going from rags to riches, we return to the "Legend of Montezuma" we briefly mentioned earlier to see these same themes expressed, albeit in more disguised mythic form. In the opening pages of *Aztlán*, Ritch warned his readers that what he was presenting as a coherent Montezuma legend had in fact been "gathered from various sources and connected."[37] Ritch said that the Pueblo Indians of New Mexico and Arizona then believed that the great chief and emperor Montezuma had been born at the pueblo of Santa Fe[38] to a young virgin to whom the Great Spirit had given three pine nuts. The maiden ate one of the nuts and from it she conceived and bore a son named Montezuma. As a youth, Montezuma was not well regarded by his kindred. He was poor, led a vagabond's life, and was considered uncouth and rude.

But one day, the town's *cacique*, or chief priest, died. When the senior men, or *principales*, of the town failed to reach consensus on a successor, they surrendered the task to the village's young men. Quite by chance Montezuma was chosen for the post. Traditionally the *cacique* had been a man of great spiritual powers. Montezuma had none. And so it did not take long before the men started to ridicule him. Montezuma assured them that during the next hunt they would catch small game with their hands and that the large game would deliver themselves up. Near dawn on the day of the hunt, the Great Spirit encountered Montezuma, who was saddened because he knew that he lacked the magical powers to lead a successful hunt. "Do not despair, thou shalt be successful," said the Great Spirit. "Go to thy cabin and search for the blanket and moccasins thy mother left thee before she died." As Montezuma obeyed, the Great Spirit instantly washed and dressed him in proper ritual attire. He then gave the young man an animal-hoof rattle with which he would charm the animals to surrender. Montezuma used his rattle, and the town's men captured abundant game. As a result of these powers, not only was he revered as the town's *cacique*, but even people from adjacent provinces proclaimed him the greatest monarch.

The Great Spirit told Montezuma that one day a great eagle would lead him to his future capital and metropolis. When the prophesied day arrived Montezuma mounted the eagle, followed by numerous people. For many vernal blooms and numerous new moons they travelled, stopping here and there to form temporary towns, but never staying long. Finally, in A.D. 1325, they arrived at a lake. The guiding eagle immediately perched itself atop a prickly pear cactus plant and seized a serpent with its beak. This was the sign the Great Spirit had given Montezuma, by which he would know that he had reached Tenochtitlán, or Mexico. There Montezuma built a town and houses for the tribes that would form the Aztec empire.

William G. Ritch concluded the "Legend of Montezuma" by noting that the Aztec eagle perched on a prickly pear cactus with a serpent in its beak had become the Mexican Republic's coat of arms. This same image appeared on the New Mexican territorial seal, the only difference being, wrote Ritch, "that the Mexican eagle is nestled confidently under the shadowing wing of the emblem of our own nationality"[39] (see Figure 2).

Historically minded students of the southwestern United States will understandably wonder whether this myth of Montezuma's birth in Santa Fe bears even the slightest glimmer of truth. As Ritch himself admitted in 1885, no one then knew the exact birthplace of the Mexica or Aztecs. What was true at the end of the nineteenth century still holds today. Since it is often the habit of victors to rewrite their history to fit the political exigencies of the day, it should come as no surprise that even the Mexica themselves found it difficult to unravel their own mythologies to locate their place of origin. What the Mexica did assert unequivocally was that their ancestors had come from Aztlán. Where was this place Aztlán? Did it ever really exist?

Nigel Davis, the most prolific contemporary writer on Aztec origins, believes that Aztlán was more a concept than a place, and that if we are to interpret the concept correctly, we must delve into the Mexica's cultural development. For if, as it appears, the Mexica "possessed a modicum of civilization when they reached their ultimate habitat [in the Valley of Mexico], they could hardly have been living in the remotest wilds. If, on the contrary, they were nomads on their arrival,...the place of origin should be sought further afield, beyond the pale of Middle American civilization."[40]

The Mexica told the sixteenth-century friars, on whom we must rely for this information, that Aztlán was a place surrounded by water and that the Mexica had lived there as fisherman. After the Mexica left Aztlán, one of the first places they visited was Seven Caves. Since the legend of emergence from Seven Caves was not unique to the Mexica, but rather was a common myth of origin for many of the tribes in the Valley of Mexico, one can only surmise that it was a place where many tribes assembled after the collapse of the Toltec Empire in the twelfth century. Given the territorial limits of the Toltec Empire, archaeologists suspect that Seven Caves was rather close to Mexico City and that Aztlán was further off.[41]

We know quite well that shortly before they arrived in Mexico City the

COPYRIGHTED.

Figure 2. Source: William G. Ritch, *Aztlán. The History, Resources and Attractions of New Mexico*, (Boston: D. Lothrop, 1885), p.7.

183

Mexica were a heterogeneous tribe. Some spent their lives hunting and gathering, and others lived tilling the land—a combination that suggests the union of two very different groups. Wigberto Jiménez Moreno believes that the horticulturalists had probably originated as nomadic hunters in the Mexican state of Nayarit. They had entered the Toltec Empire sometime in the tenth century, and there had become semi-civilized. After the fall of Tula, around A.D. 1168, the Mexica returned to a nomadic life. Sometime between then and A.D. 1345, they temporarily settled at Seven Caves and there were joined by a group of nomadic hunters who were quite recent arrivals to the valley. Legend has it that the tribal god of these Aztecas, Huitzilopochtli, ordered them to change their name to Mexica, a change which suggests their absorption by the more civilized Mexica. Legend also has it that in conjunction with the name change the Aztecas obtained bows and arrows, a technological innovation for them.[42]

This brief survey of Mexica cultural development should lead us to conclude that the mythic Aztlán was probably not in New Mexico and that Montezuma was not born in Santa Fe. The existence of numerous trade links between the Valley of Mexico and the Rio Grande Valley during Toltec times, as well as the diffusion of Aztec ceremonialism and religious thought throughout vast portions of Mesoamerica, undoubtedly explains why so many northern Mexican Indian tribes told the Catholic missionaries and soldiers that Montezuma had originated in their villages; folk wisdom was simply being repeated over and over again.[43]

The question still remains, Why were American immigrants bound for New Mexico in the 1880s so fascinated by Montezuma and the legends of Aztlán? Several interrelated answers suggest themselves. The first explanation simply relies on the diffusion of the most current science at the time. It was noted earlier that the evolutionary scheme of history that William G. Ritch employed in *Aztlán* came largely from Lewis H. Morgan's book *Ancient Society*, through Adolph F. Bandelier's residence and research in New Mexico starting in 1882. Morgan's legacy in American anthropology was to supplant romantic representations of the Indians as Noble Savages, and instead to place Indians at the bottom of an evolutionary scale that led up toward European cultural dominance and superiority.

We see this concept excellently displayed in the evolutionary theories of Aztec social development. Morgan's reconstruction of Aztec society in

Ancient Society (the principal author and historical researcher for this book chapter was Adolph F. Bandelier) concluded the Montezuma had not been a mighty emperor, that he had not lived in an elaborate palace, and that Tenochtitlán had not been a bustling metropolis. Montezuma, Morgan claimed, had been a simple tribal war chief, living in modest communal dwellings, and Tenochtitlán had been a small town constructed much like the pueblos of New Mexico. The earliest Spanish chroniclers of Aztec society had grossly exaggerated what they saw, he declared. Notwithstanding his own racism, ethnocentrism, and total ignorance of Spanish documentary sources, Morgan and his assistant Bandelier asserted that they were best prepared to interpret what the Spanish *conquistadores* truly had seen.[44]

William G. Ritch took up this leveling of Aztec social complexity through comparisons with New Mexican pueblos in the introduction to *Aztlán*, a comparison made visually explicit in Figure 1: Montezuma sits looking over Santa Fe and Mexico City. Locating Aztlán in New Mexico, Ritch noted that the land was still occupied "by people of the same race and characteristics, except so far as changed by intervening centuries." Referring to New Mexico as a "pre-Columbian country" that had recently awakened "from centuries of abeyance, and the bursting of its bonds of isolation," he asserted that one found there "the seat of the antipodes of civilization upon the continent."[45] Here, then, using Morgan's evolutionary scheme, Ritch had reduced the Aztecs and the Pueblo Indians to the level of savagery.

One also sees in Ritch's Montezuma-Aztlán discussion a second theme, the rising importance of individualism to American culture as refracted through representations of the Indians. It seems likely that as the president of the New Mexico Historical Society, William G. Ritch was in the audience when Adolph F. Bandelier addressed the society in an 1882 lecture on "Kin and Clan." There Bandelier expressed his hostility toward communism, asserting that Indian clan organization "was the strongest, most efficacious, and most durable system of communism the earth has yet seen, and as such, the most powerful tyranny."[46]

Ritch reiterated very similar prejudices in the Montezuma legend he had pieced together for his readers. There Montezuma was not depicted as the leader of a larger clan-based society, but an individualist led by the Great Spirit to fantastic feats. Similarly motivated sentiments were again expressed, as we saw above, when Ritch discussed Spanish communal land grants. New Mexico's medieval conservatism would end, Ritch believed, only after the area was shorn, of its communal traditions, and became a state run by independent private landholders.

The whole discussion of the Montezuma legend and a New Mexican origin for the Aztecs, as articulated by Ritch in *Aztlán*, must also be placed in the larger cultural movement begun in the 1880s to construct out of the harsh realities of New Mexico a "Land of Enchantment" for investors, tourists, health seekers, alienated literati, and artists to exploit. Central to this movement, as T.C. McLuhan has splendidly illustrated in her book *Dream Tracks: The Railroad and the American Indian 1890-1930*,[47] was an alchemical marketing by the Santa Fe Railroad of a Southwestern Indian ceremonialism linked in unique spiritual harmony with the earth. Using illustrators, painters, and photographers, the Santa Fe Railroad's advertising department tried to recreate a lost world and a return to primitivism. In an America that in the 1880s was lamenting its spiritual impoverishment and searching for new inspiration in mythology and legends, the "Indian" of the Santa Fe Railroad was a prototype of a preindustrial society of simplicity, freedom, and nobility.[48]

Sylvia Rodríguez has brilliantly analyzed the contribution of the Santa Fe-Taos art colony to these developments. Anglo artists appropriated indigenous symbols and mystically projected them in art and literature, "with the individual ego cast large against the mythic, solitary landscape," disguising in their Indianist preservation politics their desire to keep New Mexico underdeveloped, but firmly under American rule.[49]

One has only to reexamine the triptych on page seven of *Aztlán*, which comes right at the end of the Legend of Montezuma (see Figure 2), to see the beginnings of the Indian primitivism and bohemian individualism that would blossom in New Mexico at the turn of the century, which McLuhan, Rodríguez, and others have documented and analyzed so meticulously. In the center portion of the Ritch triptych, a lone Indian, set before the sunrise, beholds the symbol of the United States, the American eagle, enveloping in an overwhelming, almost paternalistic fashion, Mexico's national symbol, the eagle perched on a cactus devouring a serpent. To the left of this scene is one depicting miners digging into the earth, and to the right a pastoral image of sheep and and cattle being tamed by a mounted cowboy brandishing a whip.

Aztlán, then, stands as a particularly poignant example of how a mythic complex was selectively appropriated, reinterpreted, and selectively transformed, in order to achieve concrete political gain. In 1885 William G. Ritch, as the territorial secretary, wanted to attract immigrants to New Mexico so that Anglos would outnumber Hispanos, his goal being an Anglo-dominated state. Ritch used all the energy and money he had, to project representations of an El Dorado that would appeal to capitalists and landless farmers, and to enlist the memories, hallucinations, and dreams of those spiritual refugees from industrial America who wanted to return to nature. Ritch and later witting and unwitting allies created their "Land of Enchantment," their caricatures of "Indians," and their quaint Hispano peasants, which the tourists still flock to New Mexico to see. And indeed, the myths became so powerful that now even the natives utter them as truth.

NOTES

1. The *National Union Catalogue Pre-1956 Imprints* lists only the third, fourth, and fifth editions of *Illustrated New Mexico*, noting that 11,000, 16,000, and 26,000 copies, respectively, of these editions had been published. If the first and second editions of *Illustrated New Mexico* each had a run of 10,000 copies, this would bring us to my 100,000 estimate. Ritch himself would report to the Bureau of Immigration's members in 1884 that during his first two years as president of the Bureau more than two million pages of promotional literature on New Mexico had been distributed. On this latter point see *Report of William G. Ritch to the Annual Meeting of the Bureau of Immigration* (Santa Fe, 1884), p. 6.

2. William G. Ritch, *Aztlán: The History, Resources and Attractions of New Mexico* (Boston: D. Lothrop & Co., 1885), p. 5.

3. Charles L. Briggs and John R. Van Ness, eds., *Land, Water, and Culture: New Perspectives on Hispanic Land Grants* (Albuquerque, 1987).

4. Howard R. Lamar, *The Far Southwest 1846-1912: A Territorial History* (New Haven, Conn., 1966), pp. 138-9.

5. Lamar, pp. 73-81.

6. Lamar, p. 73.

7. Raymund Paredes, "The Mexican Image in American Travel Literature 1831-1869," *New Mexico Historical Review 51*(1977), pp. 5-29, and "The Origin of Anti-Mexican Sentiment in the United States," *New Scholar 6*(1977), pp. 139-65; David J. Weber, "Scarce More than Apes: Historical Review of Anglo-American Stereotypes of Mexicans," in D. Weber, ed., *New Spain's Far Northern Frontier* (Albuquerque, 1979), pp. 293-307.

8. *Message of Governor L. Bradford Prince to the Thirtieth Legislative Assembly of New Mexico, December 28, 1892* (Santa Fe, 1892), p. xxxii.

9. Ireneo L. Chávez, *Compiled Laws of New Mexico, 1884* (Santa Fe, 1885), p. 628, as quoted in Herbert H. Lang, "The New Mexico Bureau of Immigration, 1880-1912," *New Mexico Historical Review 51*(1976), pp. 195-6.

10. Lang, p. 195.
11. Wilma Loy Shelton, *Checklist of New Mexico Publications, 1850-1953* (Albuquerque, 1954), pp. 22-9.
12. Ritch, p. 137. See also pp. 37, 40, 82.
13. Ritch, p. 47.
14. Ritch, pp. 58-61.
15. Ritch, p. 84.
16. Ritch, p. 41.
17. Ritch, pp. 41, 66-9.
18. Ritch, pp. 29-30.
19. Benjamin Keen, *The Aztec Image in Western Thought* (New Brunswick, New Jersey, 1971), pp. 380-410. Leslie A. White, ed., *Pioneers in American Anthropology: The Bandelier-Morgan Letters, 1873-1883*, 2 vols. (Albuquerque, 1940).
20. Ritch, p. 250. The four epochs of history are outlined on pages 135-36.
21. Ritch, p. 189. My emphasis.
22. Ritch, pp. 191-2.
23. Ritch, p. 8.
24. Ritch, p. 250.
25. Ritch, p. 81.
26. Ritch, pp. 135-36.
27. Ritch, p. 198, emphasis in the original.
28. Ritch, p. 30.
29. Ritch, pp. 198-99, emphasis in the original.
30. Ritch, p. 145.
31. Ritch, p. 116.
32. Ritch, p. 117, emphasis in the original.
33. Herbert H. Lang, "The New Mexico Bureau of Immigration, 1880-1912," *New Mexico Historical Review* 51(1976), p. 193.
34. Ritch, p. 8.
35. Ritch, p. 65.
36. Ritch, p. 8.
37. Ritch, p. 5.
38. Frank G. Applegate, in his book *Indian Stories from the Pueblos* (Philadelphia, 1929), pp. 171-78, essentially reprints the Montezuma legend William G. Ritch first published in *Aztlán*. The only difference

in the two stories is that the Tewa Indians of the San Juan area told Applegate that Montezuma had been born not in Santa Fe, but in Pose Uingge, a large prehistoric site about twenty miles north of San Juan Pueblo.

39. Ritch, p. 7.
40. Nigel Davis, *The Aztecs: A History* (London, 1973), p. 5.
41. Davis, p. 5.
42. Davis, pp. 2-25. Wigberto Jiménez Moreno et al., *Historia de México* (Mexico, 1967), pp. 115 et seq., as discussed in Friedrich Katz, *The Ancient American Civilizations* (New York, 1972), p. 134. See also Paul Kirchhoff, "Civilizing the Chichimecs," in *The Cultural History of Ancient Mexico* (Austin, 1948), pp. 134-35.
43. Nigel Davis, *The Toltec Heritage: From the Fall of Tula to the Rise of Tenochtitlán* (Norman, Oklahoma, 1980); Elsie Clews Parsons, "Some Aztec and Pueblo Parallels," *American Anthropologist* 35(1933), pp. 611-31; F. Mathien and R. McGuire, *Ripples in the Chichimec Sea: New Considerations of Southwestern-Mesoameri-can Interactions* (Carbondale, Ill., 1986); Frank Waters, *Book of the Hopi* (New York, 1963), esp. pp. 103-08.
44. Keen, pp. 380-91.
45. Ritch, pp. 21-22.
46. Bandelier quoted in Keen, p. 398.
47. T.C. McLuhan, *Dream Tracks: The Railroad and the American Indian 1890-1930* (New York, 1985).
48. McLuhan, pp. 1-19.
49. Sylvia Rodríguez, "Land, Water, and Ethnic Identity in Taos," in Charles L. Briggs and John R. Van Ness, eds., *Land, Water and Culture: New Perspectives on Hispanic Land Grants* (Albuquerque, 1987), pp. 313-403.

The Homeland, Aztlán/El Otro México

Gloria Anzaldúa

El otro México que acá hemos construido
el espacio es lo que ha sido
territorio nacional.
Es del esfuerzo de todos nuestros hermanos
y latinoamericanos que han sabido
progresar.
> —Los Tigres del Norte[1]

"The *Aztecas del norte*...compose the largest single tribe or nation of Anishinabeg (Indians) found in the United States today....Some call themselves Chicanos and see themselves as people whose true homeland is Aztlán [the U.S. Southwest]."[2]

Wind tugging at my sleeve
feet sinking into the sand
I stand at the edge where earth touches ocean
where the two overlap
a gentle coming together
at other times and places a violent clash.

Across the border in Mexico
   stark silhouette of houses gutted by waves,
    cliffs crumbling into the sea,
      silver waves marbled with spume
        gashing a hole under the border fence.

     Miro el mar atacar
    la cerca en Border Field Park
    con sus buchones de agua,
an Easter Sunday resurrection
of the brown blood in my veins.

Oigo el llorido del mar, el respiro del aire,
   my heart surges to the beat of the sea.
    In the gray haze of the sun
     the gulls' shrill cry of hunger,
       the tangy smell of the sea seeping into me.

     I walk through the hole in the fence
      to the other side.
   Under my fingers I feel the gritty wire
    rusted by 139 years
     of the salty breath of the sea.

Beneath the iron sky
Mexican children kick their soccer ball across,
run after it, entering the U.S.

    I press my hand to the steel curtain—
  chainlink fence crowned with rolled barbed wire—
rippling from the sea where Tijuana touches San Diego
   unrolling over mountains
     and plains
      and deserts,
this "Tortilla Curtain" turning into *el Río Grande*
   flowing down to the flatlands

of the Magic Valley of South Texas
its mouth emptying into the Gulf.

1,950 mile-long open wound
            dividing *a pueblo*, a culture,
            running down the length of my body,
                staking fence rods in my flesh,
                splits me   splits me
                    me raja   me raja

            This is my home
            this thin edge of
            barbwire.

            But the skin of the earth is seamless.
            The sea cannot be fenced,
        el mar does not stop at borders
    To show the white man what she thought of his
                        arrogance,
            Yemaya blew that wire fence down.

            This land was Mexican once,
                was Indian always
                    and is.
                And   will be again.

        Yo soy un puente tendido
            del mundo gabacho al del mojado.
        lo pasado me estirá pa' 'trás
            y lo presente pa' 'delante.
        Que la Virgen de Guadalupe me cuide
        Ay ay ay, soy mexicana de este lado.

The U.S.-Mexican border es una herida abierta where the Third World
grates against the first and bleeds. And before a scab forms it hemorrhages
again, the lifeblood of two worlds merging to form a third country—a border

culture. Borders are set up to define the places that are safe and unsafe, to distinguish *us* from *them*. A border is a dividing line, a narrow strip along a steep edge. A borderland is a vague and undetermined place created by the emotional residue of an unnatural boundary. It is in a constant state of transition. The prohibited and forbidden are its inhabitants. *Los atravesados* live here: the squint-eyed, the perverse, the queer, the troublesome, the mongrel, the mulato, the half-breed, the half dead; in short, those who cross over, pass over, or go through the confines of the "normal." Gringos in the U.S. Southwest consider the inhabitants of the borderlands transgressors, aliens—whether they possess documents or not, whether they're Chicanos, Indians or Blacks. Do not enter, trespassers will be raped, maimed, strangled, gassed, shot. The only "legitimate" inhabitants are those in power, the whites and those who align themselves with whites. Tension grips the inhabitants of the borderlands like a virus. Ambivalance and unrest reside there and death is no stranger.

> In the fields, *la migra*. My aunt saying, "*No corran*, don't run. They'll think you're *del otro lado*." In the confusion, Pedro ran, terrified of being caught. He couldn't speak English, couldn't tell them he was fifth generation American. *Sin papeles*—he did not carry his birth certificate to work in the fields. *La migra* took him away while we watched. *Se lo llevaron*. He tried to smile when he looked back at us, to raise his fist. But I saw the shame pushing his head down, I saw the terrible weight of shame hunch his shoulders. They deported him to Guadalajara by plane. The furthest he'd ever been to Mexico was Reynosa, a small border town opposite Hidalgo, Texas, not far from McAllen. Pedro walked all the way to the Valley. *Se lo llevaron sin un centavo al pobre. Se vino andando desde Guadalajara.*

During the original peopling of the Americas, the first inhabitants migrated across the Bering Straits and walked south across the continent. The oldest evidence of humankind in the U.S.—the Chicanos' ancient Indian ancestry—was found in Texas and has been dated to 35,000 B.C.[3] In the Southwest United States archeologists have found 20,000-year-old campsites of the Indians who migrated through, or permanently occupied, the Southwest, Aztlán—land of the herons, land of whiteness, the Edenic place of origin of the Azteca.

In 1000 B.C., descendants of the original Cochise people migrated into what is now Mexico and Central America and became the direct ancestors of many of the Mexican people. (The Cochise culture of the Southwest is the parent culture of the Aztecs. The Uto-Aztecan languages stemmed from the language of the Cochise people.)[4] The Aztecs (the Nahuatl word for people of Aztlán) left the Southwest in 1168 A.D.

> Now let us go.
> *Tihueque, tihueque,*
> *Vámonos, vámonos.*
> *Un pájaro cantó.*
> *Con sus ocho tribus salieron*
> *de la "cueva del origen."*
> *Los aztecas siguieron al dios*
> *Huitzilopochtli.*

Huitzilopochtli, the God of War, guided them to the place (that later became Mexico City) where an eagle with a writhing serpent in its beak perched on a cactus. The eagle symbolizes the spirit (as the sun, the father); the serpent symbolizes the soul (as the earth, the mother). Together, they symbolize the struggle between the spiritual/celestial/male and the underworld/earth/feminine. The symbolic sacrifice of the serpent to the "higher" masculine powers indicates that the patriarchal order had already vanquished the feminine and matriarchal order in pre-Columbian America.

At the beginning of the 16th century, the Spaniards and Hernán Cortés invaded Mexico and, with the help of tribes that the Aztecs had subjugated, conquered it. Before the Conquest, there were twenty-five million Indian people in Mexico and the Yucatán. Immediately after the Conquest, the Indian population had been reduced to under seven million. By 1650, only one-and-a-half-million pure-blooded Indians remained. The *mestizos* who were genetically equipped to survive small pox, measles, and typhus (Old

World diseases to which the natives had no immunity), founded a new hybrid race and inherited Central and South America.[5] *En 1521 nació una nueva raza, el mestizo, el mexicano* (people of mixed Indian and Spanish blood), a race that had never existed before. Chicanos, Mexican-Americans, are the offspring of those first matings.

Our Spanish, Indian, and *mestizo* ancestors explored and settled parts of the U.S. Southwest as early as the sixteenth century. For every gold-hungry *conquistador* and soul-hungry missionary who came north from Mexico, ten to twenty Indians and *mestizos* went along as porters or in other capacities.[6] For the Indians, this constituted a return to the place of orgin, Aztlán, thus making Chicanos originally and secondarily indigenous to the Southwest. Indians and *mestizos* from central Mexico intermarried with North American Indians. The continual intermarriage between Mexican and American Indians and Spaniards formed an even greater *mestizaje.*

El destierro/The Lost Land

Entonces corre la sangre
no sabe el indio que hacer,
le van a quitar su tierra,
la tiene que defender,
el indio se cae muerto,
y el afuerino de pie.
Levántate, Manquilef.

Arauco tiene una pena
más negra que su chamal,
ya no son los españoles
los que les hacen llorar,
hoy son los propios chilenos
los que les quitan su pan.
Levántate, Pailahuan.
                    —Violeta Parra, *"Arauco tiene una pena"*[7]

In the 1800s, Anglos migrated illegally into Texas, which was then part of Mexico, in greater and greater numbers and gradually drove the *tejanos* (native Texans of Mexican descent) from their lands, committing all manner of atrocities against them. Their illegal invasion forced Mexico to fight a war to keep its Texas territory. The Battle of the Alamo, in which the Mexican forces vanquished the whites, became, for the whites, the symbol for the cowardly and villainous character of the Mexicans. It became (and still is) a symbol that legitimized the white imperialist takeover. With the capture of Santa Anna later in 1836, Texas became a republic. *Tejanos* lost their land and, overnight, became the foreigners.

> *Y la mitad del terreno*
> *les vendió el traidor Santa Anna,*
> *con lo que se ha hecho muy rica*
> *la nación americana.*
>
> *¿Qué acaso no se conforman*
> *con el oro de las minas?*
> *Ustedes muy elegantes*
> *y aquí nosotros en ruinas.*
> —*from the Mexican corrido,*
> *"Del peligro de la Intervención"*[8]

In 1846, the U.S. incited Mexico to war. U.S. troops invaded and occupied Mexico, forcing her to give up almost half of her nation, what is now Texas, New Mexico, Arizona, Colorado and California.

With the victory of the U.S. forces over the Mexican in the U.S.-Mexican War, *los norteamericanos* pushed the Texas border down 100 miles from *el Río Nueces to el Río Grande*. South Texas ceased to be part of the Mexican state of Tamaulipas. Separated from Mexico, the Native Mexican-Texan no longer looked toward Mexico as home; the Southwest became our homeland once more. The border fence that divides the Mexican people was born on February 2, 1848 with the signing of the Treaty of Guadalupe Hidalgo. It left 100,000 Mexican citizens on this side, annexed by conquest along with the land. The land established by the treaty as belonging to Mexicans was soon swindled away from its owners. The treaty was never honored and restitution, to this day, has never been made.

The justice and benevolence of God
will forbid that...Texas should again
become a howling wilderness
trod only by savages, or...benighted
by the ignorance and superstition,
the anarchy and rapine of Mexican misrule
The Anglo-American race are destined
to be forever the proprietors of
this land of promise and fulfillment.
Their laws will govern it,
their learning will enlighten it,
their enterprise will improve it.
Their flocks range its boundless pastures,
for them its fertile lands will yield...
luxuriant harvests...
The wilderness of Texas has been redeemed
by Anglo-American blood & enterprise.
—William H. Wharton[9]

The Gringo, locked into the fiction of white superiority, seized complete political power, stripping Indians and Mexicans of their land while their feet were still rooted in it. *Con el destierro y el exilo fuimos desuñados, destron-cados, destripados*—we were jerked out by the roots, truncated, disemboweled, dispossessed, and separated from our identity and our history. Many, under the threat of Anglo terrorism, abandoned homes and ranches and went to Mexico. Some stayed and protested. But as the courts, law enforcement officials, and government officials not only ignored their pleas but penalized them for their efforts, *tejanos* had no other resource but armed retaliation.

After Mexican-American resisters robbed a train in Brownsville, Texas on October 18, 1915, Anglo vigilante groups began lynching Chicanos. Texas Rangers would take them into the brush and shoot them. One hundred Chicanos were killed in a matter of months, whole families lynched. Seven thousand fled to Mexico, leaving their small ranches and farms. The Anglos, afraid that the *mexicanos*[10] would seek independence from the U.S., brought in 20,000 army troops to put an end to the social protest movement in South

Texas. Race hatred had finally fomented into an all out war.[11]
My grandmother lost all her cattle,
they stole her land.

"Drought hit South Texas," my mother tells me. "*La tierra se puso bien
seca y los animales comenzaron a morirse de se*'. *Mi papá se murió de un*
heart attack dejando a mamá pregnant *y con ocho huercos*, with eight kids
and one on the way. *Yo fui la mayor, tenía diez años.* The next year the
drought continued *y el ganado* got hoof and mouth. *Se cayeron* in droves *en
las pastas y el* brushland, *panzas blancas* ballooning to the skies. *El
siguiente año* still no rain. *Mi pobre madre viuda perdió* two-thirds of her
ganado. A smart *gabacho* lawyer took the land away *mamá* hadn't paid
taxes. *No hablaba inglés*, she didn't know how to ask for time to raise the
money." My father's mother, Mama Locha, also lost her *terreno*. For a
while we got $12.50 a year for the "mineral rights" of six acres of cemetery,
all that was left of the ancestral lands. Mama Locha had asked that we bury
her there beside her husband. *El cementerio estaba cercado*. But there was a
fence around the cemetery, chained and padlocked by the ranch owners of
the surrounding land. We couldn't even get in to visit the graves, much less
bury her there. Today, it is still padlocked. The sign reads: "Keep out. Trespassers will be shot."

In the 1930s, after Anglo agribusiness corporations cheated the small
Chicano landowners of their land, the corporations hired gangs of *mexicanos* to pull out the brush, chaparral and cactus and to irrigate the desert.
The land they toiled over had once belonged to many of them, or had been
used communally by them. Later the Anglos brought in huge machines and
root plows and had the Mexicans scrape the land clean of natural vegetation.
In my childhood I saw the end of dryland farming. I witnessed the land
cleared; saw the huge pipes connected to underwater sources sticking up in
the air. As children, we'd go fishing in some of those canals when they were
full and hunt for snakes in them when they were dry. In the 1950s I saw the
land, cut up into thousands of neat rectangles and squares, constantly being
irrigated. In the 340-day growth season, the seeds of any kind of fruit or
vegetable had only to be stuck in the ground in order to grow. More big land
corporations came in and bought up the remaining land.

To make a living my father became a sharecropper. Rio Farms Incorporated loaned him seed money and living expenses. At harvest time, my father repaid the loan and forked over 40% of the earnings. Sometimes we earned less than we owed, but always the corporations fared well. Some had major holdings in vegetable trucking, livestock auctions and cotton gins. Altogether we lived on three successive Rio farms; the second was adjacent to the King Ranch and included a dairy farm; the third was a chicken farm. I remember the white feathers of three thousand Leghorn chickens blanketing the land for acres around. My sister, mother and I cleaned, weighed and packaged eggs. (For years afterwards I couldn't stomach the sight of an egg.) I remember my mother attending some of the meetings sponsored by well-meaning whites from Rio Farms. They talked about good nutrition, health, and held huge barbeques. The only thing salvaged for my family from those years are modern techniques of food canning and a food-stained book they printed made up of recipes from Rio Farms' Mexican women. How proud my mother was to have her recipe for *enchiladas coloradas* in a book.

El cruzar del mojado/Illegal Crossing

"Ahora sí ya tengo una tumba para llorar,"
dice Conchita, upon being reunited with
her unknown mother just before the mother dies
    —from Ismael Rodríguez' film,
      Nosotros los pobres[12]

La crisis. Los gringos had not stopped at the border. By the end of the nineteenth century, powerful landowners in Mexico, in partnership with U.S. colonizing companies, had dispossessed millions of Indians of their lands. Currently, Mexico and her eighty million citizens are almost completely dependent on the U.S. market. The Mexican government and wealthy growers are in partnership with such American conglomerates as American Motors, IT&T and Du Pont which own factories called *maquiladoras*. One-fourth of all Mexicans work at *maquiladoras*; most are young women. Next to oil, *maquiladoras* are Mexico's second greatest source of U.S. dollars. Working eight to twelve hours a day to wire in backup lights of U.S. autos or solder miniscule wires in TV sets is not the Mexican way. While the women are in the *maquiladoras*, the children are left on their own. Many roam the street, become part of *cholo* gangs. The infusion of the values of the white culture, coupled with the exploitation by that culture, is changing the Mexican way of life.

The devaluation of the *peso* and Mexico's dependency on the U.S. have brought on what the Mexicans call *la crisis. No hay trabajo.* Half of the Mexican people are unemployed. In the U.S. a man or woman can make eight times what they can in Mexico. By March, 1987, 1,088 pesos were worth one U.S. dollar. I remember when I was growing up in Texas how we'd cross the border at Reynosa or Progreso to buy sugar or medicines when the dollar was worth eight *pesos* and fifty *centavos*.

La travesía. For many *mexicanos del otro lado*, the choice to stay in Mexico and starve or move north and live. *Dicen que cada mexicano siempre sueña de la conquista en los brazos de cuatro gringas rubias, la conquista del país poderoso del norte, los Estados Unidos. En cada Chicano y mexicano vive el mito del tesoro territorial perdido.* North Americans call this return to the homeland the silent invasion.

> *"A la cueva volverán"*
> —El Puma *en la canción "Amalia"*

South of the border, called North America's rubbish dump by Chicanos, *mexicanos* congregate in the plazas to talk about the best way to cross. Smugglers, *coyotes, pasadores, enganchadores* approach these people or are sought out by them. *"¿Qué dicen muchachos a echársela de mojado?"*
> "Now among the alien gods with
> weapons of magic am I."
> —Navajo protection song,
> sung when going into battle.[13]

We have a tradition of migration, a tradition of long walks. Today we are witnessing *la migración de los pueblos mexicanos*, the return odyssey to the historical/mythological Aztlán. This time, the traffic is from south to north.

El retorno to the promised land first began with the Indians from the interior of Mexico and the *mestizos* that came with the *conquistadores* in the 1500s. Immigration continued in the next three centuries, and, in this century, it continued with the *braceros* who helped to build our railroads and who picked our fruit. Today thousands of Mexicans are crossing the border legally and illegally; ten million people without documents have returned to the Southwest.

Faceless, nameless, invisible, taunted with "Hey cucaracho" (cockroach). Trembling with fear, yet filled with courage, a courage born of desperation. Barefoot and uneducated, Mexicans with hands like boot soles gather at night by the river where two worlds merge creating what Reagan calls a frontline, a war zone. The convergence has created a shock culture, a border culture, a third country, a closed country.

Without benefit of bridges, the *"mojados"* (wetbacks) float on inflatable rafts across *el Río Grande*, or wade or swim across naked, clutching their clothes over their heads. Holding onto the grass, they pull themselves along the banks with a prayer to *Virgen de Guadalupe* on their lips: *Ay virgencita morena, mi madrecita, dame tu bendición.*

The Border Patrol hides behind the local McDonalds on the outskirts of Brownsville, Texas or some other border town. They set traps around the river beds beneath the bridge.[14] Hunters in army-green uniforms stalk and track these economic refugees by the powerful nightvision of electronic sensing devices planted in the ground or mounted on Border Patrol vans. Cornered by flashlights, frisked while their arms stretch over their heads, *los mojados* are handcuffed, locked in jeeps, and then kicked back across the border.

One out of every three is caught. Some return to enact their rite of passage as many as three times a day. Some of those who make it across undetected fall prey to Mexican robbers such as those in Smugglers' Canyon on the American side of the border near Tijuana. As refugees in a homeland that does not want them, many find a welcome hand holding out only suffering, pain, and ignoble death.

Those who make it past the checking points of the Border Patrol find themselves in the midst of 150 years of racism in Chicano *barrios* in the Southwest and in big northern cities. Living in a no-man's-borderland, caught between being treated as criminals and being able to eat, between resistance and deportation, the illegal refugees are some of the poorest and the most exploited of any people in the U.S. It is illegal for Mexicans to work without green cards. But big farming combines, farm bosses and smugglers who bring them in make money off the "wetbacks"' labor—they don't have to pay federal minimum wages, or ensure adequate housing or sanitary conditions.

The Mexican woman is especially at risk. Often the *coyote* (smuggler) doesn't feed her for days or let her go to the bathroom. Often he rapes her or sells her into prostitution. She cannot call on county or state health or economic resources because she doesn't know English and she fears deportation. American employers are quick to take advantage of her helplessness. She can't go home. She's sold her house, her furniture, borrowed from friends in order to pay the *coyote* who charges her four or five thousand dollars to smuggle her to Chicago. She may work as a live-in maid for white, Chicano or Latino households for as little as $15 a week. Or work in the garment industry, do hotel work. Isolated and worried about her family back home, afraid of getting caught and deported, living with as many as fifteen people in one room, the *mexicana* suffers serious health problems. *Se enferma de los nervios, de alta presión.*[15]

La mojada, la mujer indocumentada, is doubly threatened in this country. Not only does she have to contend with sexual violence, but like all women, she is prey to a sense of physical helplessness. As a refugee, she leaves the familiar and safe homeground to venture into unknown and possibly dangerous terrain.

> This is her home
> this thin edge of
> barbwire.

NOTES

1. Los Tigres del Norte is a *conjunto* band.
2. Jack D. Forbes, *Aztecas del Norte: The Chicanos of Aztlán*. (Greenwich, CT: Fawcett Publications, Premier Books, 1973), 13, 183; Eric R. Wolf, *Sons of Shaking Earth* (Chicago, IL: University of Chicago Press, Phoenix books, 1959), 32.

3. John R. Chávez, *The Lost Land: The Chicano Images of the Southwest* (Albuquerque, NM: University of New Mexico Press, 1984), 9.

4. Chávez, 9. Besides the Aztecs, the Ute, Gabrillino of California, Pima of Arizona, some Pueblo of New Mexico, Comanche of Texas, Opata of Sonora, Tarahumara of Sinaloa and Durango, and the Huichol of Jalisco speak Uto-Aztecan languages and are descended from the Cochise people.

5. Reay Tannahill, *Sex In History* (Briarcliff Manor, NY: Stein and Day/ Publishers/Scarborough House, 1980), 308.

6. Chávez, 21.

7. Isabel Parra, *El Libro Mayor de Violeta Parra* (Madrid, España: Ediciones Michay, S.A., 1985), 156-7.

8. From the Mexican *corrido, "Del peligro de la intervención,"* Vicente T. Mendoza, *El Corrido Mexicano* (México. D.F.: Fondo De Cultura Económica, 1954), 42.

9. Arnoldo De León, *They Called Them Greasers: Anglo Attitudes Toward Mexicans in Texas, 1821-1900* (Austin, TX: University of Texas Press, 1983), 2-3.

10. The Plan of San Diego, Texas, drawn up on January 6, 1915, called for the independence and segregation of the states bordering Mexico: Texas, New Mexico, Arizona, Colorado, and California. Indians would get their land back, Blacks would get six states from the south and form their own independent republic. Chávez, 79.

11. Jesús Mena, "Violence in the Rio Grande Valley," *Nuestro* (Jan./Feb. 1983), 41-42.

12. *Nosotros los pobres* was the first Mexican film that was truly Mexican and not an imitation European film. It stressed the devotion and love that children should have for their mother and how its lack would lead to the dissipation of their character. This film spawned a generation of mother-devotion/ungrateful-sons films.

13. From the Navajo "Protection Song" (to be sung upon going into battle). George W. Gronyn, ed., *American Indian Poetry: The Standard Anthology of Songs and Chants* (New York, NY: Liveright, 1934), 97.

14. Grace Halsell, *Los ilegales*, trans. Mayo Antonio Sánchez (Editorial Diana Mexica, 1979).

15. Margarita B. Melville, "Mexican Women Adapt to Migration," *International Migration Review*, 1978.

ABC: Aztlán, the Borderlands, and Chicago

Sergio D. Elizondo

Some day, when an accurate, well-documented sociohistory of the Chicano is written, when historiographers have a poetic view of our past, it is hoped that scholars and writers will become more metaphorical so that the term *Aztlán* can take on a more complete meaning than it seems to have currently.

It is likewise hoped that at that auspicious time, we shall not be as fearful of ourselves to speak the truth in public more forcefully than we are at the present. At that time it would be more pleasurable to deal with the whole concept of the abode of our Hispanic and Amerindian ancestors. At that time, poetry, sociohistory, philosophy and indeed our very presence may be more wholly integrated as the *persona chicana* that many dream that we have become. For now, we hope for a more universal union of minds such as we hoped for two decades ago. Dreamers of a brilliant future free of ignorance and superstition would do well to anticipate more fulfilled lives for our descendants and possibly some respect from those who presently, as testimony of their decadence, continue to oppress us and many others in this land.

We have needed to know and understand our history better. We understand now the Border between the United States of America and the Estados Unidos Mexicanos; now we would do well to consider that Borderlands might be a more appropriate term to designate the entire area over which the Chicano people are spread in this country. In so doing, we would come also to understand that the mere physical extension between the U.S.-Mexico border and, let us say, Chicago, is a fact of human dispersion, and *not* a diaspora of the Chicano people. It is not static for us, but rather it has always been a dynamic and natural motion motivated by laws and processes common to all cultures. Our migrations north of the old historical border have extended the geography and social fabric of Aztlán northward in all directions; we have been able to expand our communal life and fantasies. Our Chicano society today has been able to function better communally because we share much knowledge about ourselves and use it more efficiently than in the past.

The term Borderlands carries an added meaning beyond the traditional term *border*. It connotes that we, as Chicanos, shall forever in our lives carry values that identify us as descendants of the modern and ancient cultures of Indian America, Mexico, and Spain.

The border between the United States and México is one of the longest between any two countries; it is some 3,000 kilometers long from Tijuana–San Ysidro to Brownsville–Matamoros. This line that divides the two countries was fixed after 1848 following the Angloamerican war of conquest of México; an adjustment was made upon the purchase of the Mesilla territory in 1852.

In our generation, however, there has been a series of events, changes, and a renewed interest in the interpretation of the culture of the area of this borderland.

It seems that for a proper view of this phenomenon one ought to recall the historical events that shaped the concept of the borderland in the past leading us to the present reality as seen by many writers: the latter period is the principal thrust of this proposition.

Moved by physical vigor and a well-motivated nationalistic and religious zeal, the Spanish, in the first half of the sixteenth century, have recently conquered and destroyed the material majesty of the *Mexica* "empire," and sought to extend their hegemony north of the borderlands of Mesoamerica. They entered the most physically forbidding land of the desert north. It was a feat that befitted Spanish daring and sense of mission for God, king, and personal fame at a time when Spain also was at the peak of its political, military, and cultural renaissance. Traveling from the translucent valley of Mexico City to the cool and beauty-filled highlands of the present day Santa Fe was a journey that exceeded the distance between the royal city of Toledo in Castilla La Vieja to the kingdom of Naples (annexed by the Spaniards in 1504). It has now been nearly four hundred and fifty years since Francisco Vásquez de Coronado entered the dry lands north of the Río Grande del Norte. And it was along the elongated basin of this river that the Spanish conquerors, with the assistance of Tlaxcalteca natives from the environs of Tenochtitlan, founded their physical and symbolic settlements such as missions, *presidios, ayuntamientos* and laid out a traditional square plaza that imitated the urban plan of their possessions in Mexico and in Old Spain.

The Spanish and their Mexican subjects moved into Alta California and Texas; two centuries later the Spanish settlements and influence all along the Río Grande, the Gila, and the sparsely-populated California territory became a fact. The Spanish-Mexican people did not grow much numerically, but their national language and forms of culture were firm. Native Indian customs did not really influence the strangers' own cultural fabric as happened in the more populated Mesoamerican lands with Mexico City as their center. While the people of the northern provinces were far from being culturally homogeneous, their social, economic and national reality was not as diversified as that of their southern Mesoamerican relatives. We think that society on these extensive Borderlands was purely rural and idyllic where the *ricos* were the privileged few who would enjoy more of the finer stuff of life, a situation that might not differ much from that which prevailed in the wealthier south where the seat of real power developed figuratively upon the rubble and ashes of the former *Mexica* empire. One could well surmise that the quality of life generally did not improve during the early Mexican period of independence.

The loss of the northern borderlands was due in part to the failure of centralized power to populate, strengthen, and develop it. Also, a very probable cause was the vision of the more 'ambitious,' 'aggressive,' 'materialistic,' 'zealous' Anglo-Americans who could so easily invade the borderlands. The 'idyllic' life came to an end owing to the defeat and humiliation of México in 1847 and the ineptitude of its leadership.

The new master's arrogance is well documented in the text of the *Treaty of Guadalupe Hidalgo*. This arrogance was well reflected in the messianic attitude of expansion that extended all the way to the Pacific Ocean. This has become so great a social and philosophical problem that it has affected negatively the behavior of some Chicanos and that of some American nativists who seem to believe that the entire goodness of the American nation was reserved for the ruling descendants of the ex-Europeans. It is not an exclusive Angloamerican prerogative, for it appears to occur wherever two contrasting cultural systems come into contact; a clash between adversaries decides the winner who imposes his dominance. He first destroys the very foundations of the conquered people, such as the power base, and then imposes his cultural apparatus through dominance of the autochthonous primary values, such as language, religion, and the economic means of support. While the *Treaty of Guadalupe Hidalgo* guaranteed specifically the freedom of religion, it promised nothing concerning the integrity of language use or the control of the roots of power, i.e., the economy. The Treaty set the stage for another phase of white Angloamerican imperialism that had been occurring during its movement west of the original national American territory after independence.

One ought to remember again that what is being said here is not new. The point stressed is that these are the foundations of cultural conflict involving the national, material, and ideological makeup of the Borderlands especially after 1848. This assumption becomes necessary in this view in order to point out the fact of the preservation of Chicano cultural values and dynamics precisely within the dominating process that has attempted to impose its nationalistic determinism for six generations; it then redounds in the increasingly greater importance of the so-called Chicano Movement of the decade of the 1960s.

It is a known fact that the southwestern region of the U.S.A. bears the strong social and cultural characteristics of its Mexican Mestizo multicultural background, containing a plethora of values that have been filtered from the many different tribes of ancient and modern México. The Spanish peninsular background, through its language as base and the Roman Catholic religion as the catalyst, has given the Chicano a pluralistic identity of a biological, linguistic, and atavistic variety. One could say that those are reasons our skin coloration is varied and our multiglossae of Mexican Spanish appear in many variants wherever Chicanos live. The vast territory of the southwestern Borderlands appeared to separate us politically and economically to the detriment of group unity; not so in the more lasting, transcendental customs and values. Religion has remained strongly Roman Catholic. The family, regardless of its extension, is an important factor for self-identity. And while language takes on many expressive forms regionally, it is still a source of relevant affective comfort.

The Borderlands in our day are still the mythical expanse of earth from eastern Texas to California, holding the treasured geological beauty that has been a factor in shaping the process of cultural development from the sixteenth century, a phenomenon that afforded Chicanos in former times the opportunity to identify differently with the physical varieties in the immediate areas where we live, but without affecting the continuity of cultural recognition. The affinities among the Chicanos are now communally more recognized among ourselves than in the past.

Provincial attitudes aside, the Spanish Americans of New Mexico seem to be more like anyone else from the Aztlán Borderlands than the Franco-Americans of the northeastern U.S.A., or the Swedish-Americans of Minnesota, to cite only two general examples. We have spoken Spanish continuously since the middle of the sixteenth century.

The Borderlands we have known impressionistically through official frontier outpost reports, the literary images of non-natives, even early Spanish narratives, are here today. But the Chicanos no longer live in their "traditional" places along the Río Grande, as riparians along *arroyos* and other streams, nor in the *barrio*, the segregated enclave, nor on the streets leading out from the *plaza*. The population of the Spanish-Mexican American Mestizo no longer is a footnote, officially or otherwise, recalled by the uninformed. We are now a nation of at least fifteen million people in the American nation, not counting an unknown number of undocumented Mexicans (and very recently Central Americans). This realization ought to be sobering to skeptics, and it should prompt us to ask for a new description of our actual physical presence, the extent of our cultural dimension, the atlas of our language use, and the limits of the Borderlands in view of the present concentration of more than five hundred thousand *Raza* in Chicago.

The presence of the Spanish in New Mexico since about 1540, the natural growth of its population for the next two centuries, the settlement of Texas and Alta California and the Pimería, the heavy immigration during and following the Mexican Revolution, and the apparent and continuing stream of workers from Mexico from the early forties to the millions at the present; all such factors become of primary importance in an analysis of the Mexican-Chicano presence in the Borderlands today. That Mexico now has a population of some 75 million might remind us that millions of its unemployed migrate north in search of work, in other words, it's a veritable humanitarian form of foreign aid.

Just as the Spanish and the Mexicans moved in as uninvited guests into the territories north from Mexico, so did the Anglo-Americans in the Southwest.

Armed conflicts between the natives and the Spanish Mexicans ended more than one hundred years ago, except for the resistance of the Apaches who battled both the Mexicans and the Anglos until late in the last century. The frontier Borderlands have been free of armed clashes in this century. Struggles between the three cultural groups having ended, the people settled down peacefully to the task of developing the land, and a private, racial and cultural consciousness became a natural course.

With the Spanish presence and its hegemony gone, the culture of the various regions began to look more Mexicanized beginning with the preservation of the many variants of Mexican Spanish, a family-centered Mexican Catholic religion with its Christ-Guadalupe bivalent form of official and familiar worship dating back more than four hundred and fifty years to the present (since December 12, 1531); the traditional close-bound-family life, a plethora of affective gratification and sentiment, remains probably one of the most unshakable social factors of ethnic identification on all social-typological levels. We remember this aspect of our civilizaiton, if we are to understand the causal determinations of our intellectual and aesthetic forms of expression in all modes within the group. Chicanos, regardless of our feelings of personal self-identification as Tejanos, Mexicanos, Mexican Americans, Spanish, Spanish Americans, Americans or Latinos, have the same cultural refuge.

Out of the ancient cultures of Spain and Mexico a new and distinct *persona* has been formed, being neither "pure" Spanish nor Mexican, but *Mestizo*. One must understand this about us in order to comprehend the mythos of today's Chicano and Mestizo lifestyles in the present concept of Aztlán. Aztlán, the mythical abode of the ancient Nahoa tribes which wandered the south to Mesoamerica to establish various kingdoms and cultures. After

Mexican independence and the withdrawal of direct Spanish influence, the Mexican-Mestizo cultural hegemony was confronted for the first time by the new presence of the Anglo-Saxon people. In the new political and social systems, the Mestizo became a weak adversary facing the better-armed and greedier newcomer.

We could expect to see in future generations a greater influx of people from south of the Borderlands, a steady stream of immigrants divided into the documented and those who decide just to go north disregarding political boundaries, acts of legislation, and the vicissitudes encountered in a land that still does not readily accept "colored" people. But if numbers are not that important, one must reckon with the cultural influx that seems to revitalize language use as an immediate determinant in a culture, not to mention other equally imperative cultural baggage brought along by the newly-arrived *Mestizos*. Whether the person comes from Mexico or Central America, it is all the same as far as the *Mestizo* culture is concerned.

Although the physical border has been Mexicanized for four centuries, what can we say of the further physical and moral Latinization of the Borderlands as far north as Chicago?

While we as Mexican-Chicano-Mestizos become more adept at understanding and publicly expressing our Latin American origins, we also now seem to understand much better those factors, moral and social, as Americans. We can now see in this decade of greater social and economic mobility that our destiny is inexorably tied to the past. It has been attempted here to demonstrate that there need not be a constant, forced state of aversion toward Chicanos, especially if they are ethnically-culturally secure and included in the greater and dominant sector of American society, thanks to the mind-opening events of the past twenty years.

It can be affirmed that there have always been forms of cultural consciousness from the beginning of the Latinization process for more than four centuries. A motion that has not abated through the generations, but which has grown to accommodate, to integrate, to assimilate and to acculturate, less for reasons of survival than for natural forms of reformation in contact with an equally strong national social unit.

It could be argued that none were more surprised than ourselves as Chicanos when in the 1960s we confronted the established powers to realize how politically and educationally unprepared we were to face and to challenge one of the most monolithic and nativist modern nations in this century. Education, as one of the most critical issues of the struggle, quickly became the cause of our tactical failures precisely at a time when we needed it as a weapon of social liberation and economic advancement. But that aside, our primordial zeal filling us with pride and strength carried us from office to office to dress down, cajole, threaten, force, and shame the very fellow Americans who for *their* eight generations had been parroting the principles that guarantee equality for all. The so-called Chicano Movement fizzled out in less than a decade, but more transcendent aspects of human understanding prevailed as in the past, the most widespread being racial and cultural consciousness. This time those involved in it wanted more than the tokenism that establishment Americans had practiced for generations. The Chicanos demanded more of the good things for all *Raza*, and the Anglos gave, though grudgingly and never enough. It is evident that cultural consciousness is a relative fact of life wherever there are Chicanos today, and it could well be the most valuable piece of identification that has come out of the heroic period of Chicano activism in the sixties. Now we can expect all sorts of emergent opinions from social scientists and humanists in new research which will probably reveal more scientifically than ever the merits and demerits of our social and economic mobility. These people who have been denied their opportunity for sustained progress by three powers— Spaniards, Mexicans, and Anglo Americans, at least since 1960–have been able to express the joy of gratification.

While the Chicanos are still a dispersed cultural, social, and political group, it is clear at this writing that the old seeds of resistance sown in the last century, the cowboys' and miners' strikes during the first half of the present, the surge of ethnic consciousness from the Second World War, the courageous contribution and integrity of César Chávez and the beleaguered farm workers, the angry revolt during the Chicano Movement, has given the Chicano-Latino-Mestizo the strength to mature as a collective *persona* and the strategies to hold what we have earned in contact with a racist, greedy, and xenophobic dominant society. It seems more certain now than ever that there is no turning back from the present. It is a good period of time to survive and live well despite the moral and social decadence of the patronizing cultural group.

Our ancient tools of survival, language, religion, and family, continue to sustain us. Our linguistic atlas is not any longer the discredited form of personal expression of former generations, for it is larger and more extensive than ever in our efforts to codify, define, and clarify it scientifically. We have also learned to be more tolerant of one another's dialectical variables, thanks to greater awareness of our multicultural diversity and more formal education.

We watch with some degree of satisfaction as the English-speaking monolinguals approach our group to partake of our traditional foods and even our language resources, albeit for commercial purposes. The Anglo is becoming Latinized.

While a progress report on attitudes by our own older generation still shows traces of nativist cultural conservatism, the vigor of our new generations overshadows the darkened mantle of ignorance that had been only too common among our ancestors. It is the idea of progress that has by now become more powerful than the doctrine of docility that has traditionally been promoted by the clergy, benign as their intentions might have been; nevertheless, such superstition and paternalism seem to affect us less than formerly. Though there is still a perceptible line of political, moral, and social conservatism among many, the impact of greater formal educational achievement carries more of the weight of progress than ignorance and superstition. This has brought degrees of mutual cordiality between Anglos and Mestizos, and we all gain much from it.

It seems that various results from the quiet after the storm of militant activism have contributed toward the emergence of spiritual, if not economic, cordiality. One of the most outstanding of these fruits is the phenomenal rise of artistic production and expression. The most serious and evident of these is the resurgence of literature since the publication of *Pocho*, a novel by José Antonio Villarreal in 1959. The publication of such a novel initiated a prolific period of literary production in English and Spanish. Such best-selling works as Rudy Anaya's *Bless Me, Ultima* became a piece of written art that Anglos enjoyed and praised, thus promoting greater rapprochement between Anglos and Chicanos. It would seem that not enough is known about Chicano creative writers, or about our many young social scientists, humanists, and educators; their numbers, however, reveal a new presence in the nation. This is not to say that it really matters whether the established society accepts our scientific credentials, for the work of our learned *Mestizos* benefits our group immediately more than the dominant sector. However, our accomplishments belong to the entire nation.

There is not enough space here to enumerate all the progress the Chicano-Mestizo has made over two decades. Neither can we look back to the first half of the sixteenth century and give a detailed balance of all things of lasting value that have been produced. Let it suffice that a significant step forward has been taken by scholars recently as they propose that early Spanish narratives of exploration such as that of Alvar Núñez Cabeza de Vaca, among others, are now considered as part of Chicano literature because their subject matter is *Aztlanense*. Its particular rhetoric becomes more Chicano and less Spanish due to the impact of the new images on the intellect and the sensitivity of the writer-perceiver. The concept of Aztlán as myth gathers depth of meaning, if one accepts the proposition given above, and the worth of such a cultural concept gains in reality for all of us, the contemporary and living descendants of all other *Aztlanenses* throughout the entire dynamic process of our history.

Every day we meet many different people in the community, and as it happens, we see ourselves in the many ways we are changing socially and linguistically, but the greater impact of institutions such as the Spanish language media immediately reminds us with the influences that we might not be as fragmented as we often lament. More so, the communications media in Spanish are growing and improving though slowly. The lag in the development of the television and screen industries as pertains to the Spanish speaking people is due more to the marketing shyness of the moguls that control it than due to their social need. It may be a matter of time when the Chicanos themselves, probably with the support of the financially powerful, will see a greater presence in this important industry. This matter is brought up at this time in the belief that the media, when finally integrated to our social image, will serve to strengthen our cultural consciousness.

But in order to realize our wish we shall have to exert an extra effort such as we have been able to put forth in many other sectors. The time for it is more propitious than ever, for we see a factual attenuation of conflict between our two cultures, probably more for reasons of private economic interest on the part of the powerful in the national culture than a lessening of subconscious fears of a "Mexican peril" in the minds of the Anglo people. At least this is what can be perceived at the present, but as Chicanos we would have a good reason to reserve final judgment with the awareness that a people's psychic defenses might reawaken, let us say, in a time of economic or military crisis. American national dogma exists to this day in the dark corners of racists and others who would want the U.S.A. reserved for white, Anglo-Saxon Christians of all denominations. A note of optimism, however, may have already sounded in this decade of the eighties as someone out there has proclaimed that this is the decade of the "Hispanic." But substantial progress in *all* areas of human concern is, frankly, not seriously evident, except for the presence of *Raza* in the armed forces. That in itself is of no transcendent value except for those among us who still believe that militarism is a promising avenue to follow toward social and economic liberation. *Todo se vale*, there is a degree of value in everything we do, even through our large presence in the military.

While we have little power to influence national policy and social custom, we could agree, that as an established cultural minority within the dominant majority, forms of aquiescence could be tacitly adopted as many Chicanos, during the heroic period of the movement, did philosophically. We may still fear that during our generation, and a few more to come, the U.S.A. as a whole will not be ready to live up to the commitment of the constitution nor the eternal, universal presence of full and unequivocal enjoyment of human rights for Chicanos and other American minorities. Many believe that this realization is fair, neither offensive nor defensive, but communally present in our private existence. This proposition has been our primary and lasting source of personal integrity and strength as a culturally different group considering our regional differences in superficial modes of deportment, our multiglossae and changing socioeconomic condition for the time being. This is what our mythical condition as people of Aztlán may come to mean more clearly as time passes. Intellectual and emotional factors shape our personalities as we are rapidly becoming more *publicly* productive intellectually, and as we appear more frequently in the realm of the national scene, a quantum jump from the days of "The Sleeping Giant." Emotionally and aesthetically, we have arrived, having developed our arts as best as we have been able with literature clearly ahead of all other forms of artistic expression. Apparently we have done this in a way that no other group has been able to do to this day, that is, in an ethnic language as well as in English.

Our small efforts in artistic expression, firm and disciplined as they are, are quite meager as compared to the commercial power of the established national corporations. For instance, our literary production is published almost exclusively by small presses, brave enterprises that manage to survive in a nation that does not eagerly tolerate small scale efforts in an industry that has been taken over by faceless multinational businesses whose human decision-makers care little for the ethics of fairness to all, or the aesthetics which is the central object of literary art. Our art has survived in the worst of times despite financial poverty, early years in the business, and a rather weak Chicano reading market. No one can tell what the future holds for writers, but it would be hazardous to assume that Chicanos will not be writing for generations to come. If Hinojosa and Anaya are now being read in West Germany, can we not assume that others are in line for distribution in countries outside the U.S.A.? Again, time and the merits of artistic sense and discipline are sure to be factors which determine the durability of the art. Judging from the steady production of such consummate masters as Hinojosa, Anaya, Méndez, and Gary Soto, then there ought to be little fear that our most developed art will be with us for a long time. Treated as an internal colony, relatively uneducated and facing formidable odds, we are distinguished as a permanent nation within a nation, with a collective subconscious that has remained under public scrutiny. Now our artisans and scientists show our truer face before the world through a more correct reinterpretation of all aspects of our cultural character.

There is a new pace, a new determination to unveil a more complete image of our society. As it occurs, we may see ourselves in a new mirror and what we see of ourselves indeed is more gratifying than formerly. As a surprise to the world here and beyond, we might well be satisfied that our progress has been achieved with little or no loss of the primary values of a profound faith in our religious background, an aesthetic sensibility, our adherence to family bonds and a commonly held *simpatía* through which we recognize ourselves as *Raza*. The historical process has bloomed after generations of dark images that threatened the suppression of all forms of our culture. We were able to take the worst this nation's sinister weapons could inspire.

To conclude this essay is to reiterate the obvious: it can only end on a note of optimism for us all as we take stock and summarize the factors that suggest strongly the imminence of our presence and expectation of times to come.

Despite satanic efforts of the powerful and privileged few in our society at the present, one can still perceive that our American community is more educated than ever to the point that a totalitarian government may not be established. Our language, Spanish, has not only survived but it perdures quite well. We have a growing *Raza* population. Formal education is on the rise as there is a perceptible attenuation of social and economic dominance. We are the owners of an innovative, serious, and disciplined literature; our provincialism has been preserved but not at the expense of the universaliza- tion of our cultural consciousness. This consciousness seems to be on the rise, or at least we know that "the lights changed back in the sixties," and while we still entertain degrees of local self-identification, we know that all of those names we call ourselves find solace under the same benign umbrella of brotherhood. The U.S.A. seems to understand us somewhat better now, as an attitude of increasing tolerance seems to be overshadowing the xenophobia and racism of earlier years. At least this particular social dis- ease seems not to be as prevalent and unchecked as before. There is more cultural understanding now than only a generation ago as we, ourselves, understand, and reaffirm our own multicultural character and show less pre- occupation than formerly with how white or Spanish we are. Only the most uninformed, insecure or vain among us hold onto such cultural fantasies of a purer Caucasion background. There is a continuous heavy immigration, the undocumented being the predominant sector, and this historical fact of the social mobility of our population may well be assumed to be tantamount to a continuing process that nurtures our Mexican-Mestizo culture. To ignore this reality is to negate that Mexico, with its population now at 75 million, is static. The rise of our artistic expression in so many forms is only the begin- ning of an outpouring of our ancient aesthetic sense which formerly had been frustrated more by oppression and disenfranchisement than for lack of will or talent. Our resolve on this matter was initially rekindled during the 1960s, and we are still at it and improving with discipline and tenacity. We might momentarily reconsider the matter of Spanish-speaking immigration as an objective factor determining a greater degree of language use in all strata of our society, a phenomenon of flux and constant mobility that surely affects the permanent maintenance of the Spanish language. The greatest efforts to detain the tide of undocumented immigrants has been shown to be unwork-able. There are signs that short, rash or inhumane measures to interdict the millions of Mexicans and other Latinos from coming to the source of their prehistorical birthplace–an unthinkable occurrence, an unlikely thought–shall continue to have a strong current of cultural nourishment for generations to come, probably forever. If our cultural values have survived the worst forms of oppression, who are we not to dream that this country has yet to see the best of our cultural impact, a presence that is indeed a joy to conceive?

For dreamers and scientists of today, for all of us, regardless of the degree of information we have on hand, it is true, that the concept of the mythical Aztlán is very much alive in our minds and hearts. The mythical source of our *Nahoa* ancestors at the present still resides in the subconscious of all who proudly accept our nonwestern cultural background. We may see it in the present state of life more than ever. The concept of Aztlán as myth is the legendary and real component of our system of primary values that lay veiled, until recently, underneath the dust of our lack of awareness; it still is there, only now it glows.

Myth, Identity and Struggle in Three Chicano Novels:

Aztlán...Anaya, Méndez and Acosta

history remains
a silent poet
and class struggle
its verb on earth

Alurista

Mexicans became de facto U.S. citizens through the Guadalupe Hidalgo Treaty which ceded half of northern Mexico to the United States in 1848. Such an event in no way diminished the relationship which these people maintained with Mexico and things Mexican.[1] In fact, if one could speak of their steady acculturation and assimilation into North American culture, one could, on the other hand, readily point out the innumerable ways through which Mexicans in the U.S. tried–often successfully–to preserve their cultural integrity.[2] The history of the "American Southwest" between 1848 and 1969 reveals the indelible contributions to the culture and the industrial coming of age of the territory which Mexicans once called their homeland. It also reveals the methodical exploitation and mistreatment of generations of Mexicans–both native and immigrated–to the point of forcing them into anomic behavior, a self-defeating identity crisis, and the social alienation predicated on a state founded on racial, sexual, ethnic and class oppression.

While the subordination of Mexican workers escalated immediately following the American occupation of northern Mexico, now referred to as "the southwestern United States," one should note that numerous revolts sought to regain some of the dignity the loss of land, language and culture had occasioned. Some political and material gains were sometimes achieved, and Chicano sociologists and labor historians have contributed significantly in this research area.[3] This paper will also focus on "struggle," but of a very different nature—though inextricably connected with material, dialectical, class struggle—and that is: the desire and struggle of U.S. Mexicans, of Chicanos, to think or, better yet, *rethink* themselves as one, as whole, and as a meaningful people on earth. *How* this struggle and desire is manifest in three contemporary Chicano narratives which make use of myth as the unifying force in the psyche of the Chicano characters in their novelistic production constitutes the primary and central concern of this critical inquiry. The myth, common to all three novels, which this study will unveil, is *Aztlán.* The novels to be examined are: 1) *Peregrinos de Aztlán (Pilgrims of Aztlán)* by Miguel Méndez; 2) *The Revolt of the Cockroach People* by Oscar Z. Acosta; and, 3) *Heart of Aztlán* by Rudolfo Anaya.

Before proceeding to an analysis of each text it may be appropriate to discuss briefly "myth," particularly as it is to be distinguished from "fantasy." Fantasy is, more often than not, the product of an individual mind that chooses to see the world, the real, through a non-ordinary set of manufactured, that is to say, made-up conditions. Fantasy artificially constructs a world which in fact becomes a form, a way of escaping the real one. Fantasy may project itself into the future and, in fact, predict possible developments in the concrete world (such is the case of Jules Verne's science fiction) so that what is clearly false and non-existent at a given point in historical timespace can, with the inevitable passage of time in the same or different space, become a reality, a palpable and verifiable event or thing.

Myth, on the other hand, is always the product of not only more than one mind, but, in fact, of several generations who share a particular space over a significant period of time. Myth has, if obscure more often than not, a historical consensus. Functionally, it differs from fantasy in that myth connects a people more solidly with their timespace; instead of distancing one from the real, myth explains and gives significance to the individual's life within a larger, often cosmic, always generationally social, context. Myth has historically been the fabric with which civilizations, that is to say, large social formations, were bound together as in a covenant. Consensus, collective consensus, is the key to the understanding of myth. At the very core of both fantasy and myth resides desire. Desire in fantasy results in the fulfillment, vicarious of symbolic, of otherwise, in the real world, impossible objectives and it often leads to the development of new options or ideas that may be practicable in the future. In myth, desire results in the reunion of the individual with the collective species being as well as the natural and cosmic world within which one lives; the terms religion and yoga, for example, mean just that: to reunite, to be one with the otherness.[4]

The myth upon which the three novels, here to be examined, are based is a myth of origin. The myth of Aztlán has at least three traditions in distant historical periods. For the purposes of this study, I will call the first "The Pre-Mexica" version.

The Pre-Mexica version dates back to the arrival of the first settlers of what is today known as Mexico, which could be as far back as 19,000 B.C.[5] In this version of the myth, Aztlán is situated east of the present day peninsula of Yucatan and the Gulf of Mexico. It is thought to be an island, now lost in the Atlantic Ocean, where an advanced civilization, the Chanes (which means the "people of the snake" in Mayan) established the center of their civilization, which extended itself east to India and Egypt and west to Mexico, Yucatan and Central America.

The second version, the Mexica's Aztlán, was the product of the theocratic militarism which Tlacaelel, an advisor to three Aztec/Mexica rulers, crafted to be the motherland of the Mexica. It was crafted for only the Mexica, and not the whole of the people populating Mexico at the time of their arrival to Mesoamerica and the central valley of Mexico during the later quarter of the first millenium after Christ and a half century before the arrival of the Spaniards.[6] Motecuhzoma Ilhuicamina actually sent an expedition to the north of Tenochtitlan (present day Mexico City) searching for vestiges of the Mexica motherland: Aztlán. This version would have located the center of the geographical Aztlán somewhere around the four corners area in the southwestern United States. The purpose of the journey was, clearly, to legitimize the power which the Mexicas had come to wield by the fourteenth century A.D. This Aztlán was also believed to be the source, the origin of the Mexica lineage.

The third version of reference to Aztlán, the Chicano version, is elaborated in "The Spiritual Plan of Aztlán" drafted and legitimized by the delegates to the first national Chicano youth conference held in Denver, Colorado, during March of 1969. Here, again, we find that Aztlán is used as a metaphor which unifies the various delegations from all over the United States into one nationalist body. Aztlán, in this case, is referred to as being more than a geographical location when the plan states at its closure: "We are Aztlán."[7] Here the myth assumes a different role. Aztlán is no longer just an origin, a source, a motherland, a testimony to an ancient heritage and tradition. Aztlán has become a mission and a state of mind, a way of facing contemporary reality and social conditions. The plan speaks of reclaiming that which once belonged to its original inhabitants: the fruits and the wealth of the land which its heirs still work to date. Rightful ownership is not established, however, on the basis of lineage, but rather on the basis of "those who work it." "Borders," geographical boundaries, are not to be drawn so that Aztlán in this case may be the actual equivalent to the American continent and its inhabitants.[8] The novels which this study proposes to examine were all written after 1969, and all three of them make reference to both the Mexica and the Chicano version of the myth; none of them address the legendary *Aztlán Aztatlán (Atlantis)* of the Pre-Mexica, Mayan version. At this point we shall focus on the work of Rudolfo Anaya: *Heart of Aztlán* (1976). We shall then proceed with Miguel Méndez: *Peregrinos de Aztlán*, (1974), then to finalize this inquiry with Oscar Z. Acosta's work: *The Revolt of the Cockroach People* (1973).

Heart of Aztlán is a novel set in the forties. The story is linear and simple: a Chicano family leaves their rural home in Guadalupe, New Mexico, to search for work and a new lease on life in Albuquerque. This move is the cause of great pain to the father, principally, who has to sell his land in order to make the move. Without land, Clemente Chávez (the protagonist of the novel), feels alienated, rootless and without a clear identity or destiny. The work that he finds with the Santa Fe railroad soon turns sour because of a much-needed strike for better wages and working conditions. The family itself begins to suffer the disintegrating influence of the city; his children begin to lose the traditional respect accorded parents in a Chicano, New Mexican rural setting. Crispín, a blind poet who possesses a "magical blue guitar," along with a witch who possesses a "magical black stone," become the sources of new hope for Clemente, his family and his people by rekindling the myth of Aztlán as an original source of power and new faith.

Anaya, more so than the other two authors examined here, uses myth as a healing power capable of restoring self-respect, self-worth, and self-determination. When Clemente finds himself at the end of his wits and faces the total destruction of his self concept, Crispín rescues him from a frozen death in an alley and introduces him to the legend of Aztlán. The workers on strike find themselves hopeless and without a leader. Crispín feels that Clemente is the chosen one to receive the power of the myth and then to transfer it, convert it into strength for his people. Clemente speaks:

> "Por Dios Santo...that is what I need to live! I will search for those signs, I will find that magic heart of our land about which you whisper [the heart of Aztlán], and I will wrestle from it the holy power to help my people...I don't know if this is an insanity that possesses me, but at least it has a purpose, I feel that purpose!" (*Heart*: 122-23)

Myth, in this context, is magical and can help Clemente in his struggle to rethink, to redefine himself and his people. The myth of Aztlán is a powerful source for the development of a new, self-affirming identity. Clemente is told that the "heart of Aztlán" was located somewhere around Albuquerque and the Sandia mountains. The founders of the legendary Aztlán were asked to leave it in order to journey south to establish a great civilization (that of the Mexicas) but were told that they would journey back in the future in order to reclaim its original splendor. Reference is made here to the Mexica and the Chicano version of the myth where Aztlán is an original motherland, a mission to be accomplished and a power to be harnessed. Anaya has captured in this novel the most positive aspects that a myth can present to a people in need of rediscovering their worth and a reason to live and struggle for. While it is clear that the material conditions suffered by the striking workers is sufficient cause for their material struggle, it is also clear that a spiritual vacuum has to be filled by something other than the traditional Catholic faith which promises the Kingdom of Heaven for the poor and the meek. Aztlán is the myth, the force, the psychic construct that can and, at least in the novel, indeed, fill the spiritual (i.e., psychological) void experienced by Clemente, his family, and the striking workers. This myth offers some relief on earth and it calls for social and political struggle as opposed to calling for penance, patience and blind faith for a better world in the afterlife. At one point Clemente exclaims, "I am Aztlán" so that the mythical place is transformed into a state of being, after which he accepts the leading role amongst the strikers. At the end of the novel the people have resolved to struggle and Clemente leads them:

> Crispín strummed a tune of liberation on the blue guitar. The people began to move, marching to a *new* step, singing the songs of the revolution which would *create their destiny*. Around the perimeter of the shops armed guards fingered their rifles nervously. The dogs they held on leashes growled uneasily. They could smell fear, but they were not trained to deal with the burning force that came singing up the barrio street. In the dark, cold night the blaring sirens announced the mobilization of another force at the barricades, but the people did not hesitate. "Adelante!" they shouted without fear. (*Heart*: 208-9)

The rekindling of an old myth, at least in this novel, results in a new faith, in a new self concept and courage to be, bridging the 1930's with the 50's and the 70's.

Méndez addresses Aztlán as a land to which the ancestors of the ancient Mexicas now return, as undocumented workers.

> Del sur iban, a la inversa de sus antepasados, en una peregrinación sin sacerdotes ni profetas, arrastrando una historia sin ningún mérito para el que llegara a contarla, por lo vulgar y repetido de su tragedia. Sin embargo, un episodio de la vida de Ramagacha, mucho tiempo después de sucedido, sirvió de cita a un hombre que conversaba en grupo, palmoteando los zancudos

enrabiados, que en centenares sembraban de ronchas y comezón las pieles sudorosas. (*Peregrinos*: 64)

Aztlán for Méndez is not mythical utopia or even the new society that the heirs of the ancients are to bring to its traditional glory. Aztlán is the territory occupied by the norteamericanos *and* the capitalist Mexicanos on the borderland between the U.S. and Mexico; it is a place of toil and misery for those who have recently returned. And, for those who have been in the territory for generations, it is a place where their labor is exploited and their dignity stripped away on the basis of cultural, racial and economic differences. The novelistic production of Méndez focuses on the alienation which abounds in a land of wealth, a wealth that, even though produced by a majority working class, is enjoyed only by a handful. The silent poet, history, is not silent in the Méndez novel at all, but is in fact ever present. Dialogical class discourse in *Peregrinos de Aztlán* is most deliberately codified through the meticulous characterization of the various personages which populate his novel. Myth, here, conversely becomes the absent cause, the origin lost which history and concrete social conditions will *not* allow its protagonist to retrieve as a source of hope, or even traditional pride. There is no narrative space allotted to the myth of Aztlán becoming a state of mind or a source of consciousness. Aztlán, for Méndez, is at best a nationalist ideal to be sought and fought for by a new generation yet to come, a generation that, in his own terms, will not be willing to tolerate the kind of institutionalized ethnocentrism, racism and class oppression to which Mexicans, Native Americans, *and* other Third World people are subjected to in the United States. At worst, Aztlán is a long lost legend that has become a nightmare embodied and disguised in the so-called "American Dream."

The Revolt of the Cockroach People by Oscar Z. Acosta was the first novel to be published which made reference to the myth. If for Anaya Aztlán is a healing myth and for Méndez a future ideal, Aztlán is a contemporary war cry for Acosta.

Christmas Day, seven hours after the arrest of the St. Basil Twenty-One, we returned, this time without picket signs or candles. I am still numb, grim from my conversation with Stonewall.

While the Faithful inside pray and count their beads, we march silently in front of the church and demand the release of our prisoners.

The media turn out in full force. Chicanos have not fought inside a temple since the Spanish conquistadores invaded the shrines of Huitzilopochtli in the Valley of Mexico. We make headlines without the assistance of Stonewall and his liberal white connections. McIntyre heaps it on us. We are the rabble at the foot of the cross, calling for the death of Christ. We are agents of the devil and communists to boot.

'Actually, we're Jewish underground,' I say with a straight face. The man taping the conversation has told me he is from the biggest newspaper in Tel Aviv. He doesn't smile.

A team with cameras tells us they are making a film in America. They are from Berlin and want me to explain the purpose of our demonstration. I tell them that the Church and government have combined to exterminate us. 'We are the Jews of Nazi America,' I tell the people of Berlin.

A reporter from LIFE wants to know if any of our members are affiliated with radicals. How do I answer the charges of the Cardinal and the Chief of Police?

'Well...yes, I belong to some violent organizations,' I say.

'Is this for publication?'

'You can tell the whole world, mister.'

'Well...?'

'I'm an American citizen....Nixon is my leader.' (*Revolt*: 78-79)

Acosta's novel best exemplifies the "Chicano version" of the myth though he makes no specific reference to it. The "revolt" which he addresses in his narrative clearly implies it. Here, again as with Méndez, we find a narrative where class discourse and history, far from being an absent cause—the silent presence which speaks between the lines—is the central dialogical strategy of his literary production. His novel is written in what has come to be called a "gonzo" style where the author is a participant observer in the world of events which he narrates. Acosta focuses on the Chicano revolt in Los Angeles, California, between 1968-70, a period during which thousands of Chicanos mobilized publicly to assert their self-determinant presence in the U.S. It is during this period that Aztlán becomes *the* metaphor which best codifies the nationalist Chicano fervor of the sixties. Acosta mediates the alienation of the days of the "revolt" through mythic, nonordinary mental states and a stark and cynical irony. Aztlán, in Acosta's narrative code, though not enunciated significantly, is evoked as a force, the force of history and class, sexual and cultural contradictions that prevail during the social space between the sixties and the eighties.

Anaya uses myth as a "healer," whereas Méndez sees myth as a restructuring agent, and Acosta renders myth as a revolutionary war cry. All three codify Aztlán as borderless and belonging to those who work, who toil for the wealth that, presently, others who own the means of production enjoy. Aztlán is a cry for struggle, redefinition, and self-determination; it abhors war, misery and the total annihilation of the human species in any of the novels here examined. Aztlán is positioned as an origin and the promise of a future possibility for a more humane social formation.

> P.S. I was just one of a bunch of Cockroaches that helped start a revolution to burn down a stinking world. And no matter what kind of end this is, I'll still play with matches. (*Revolt*: 257-58)

NOTES

1. While there are many works on the subject I would recommend two general works for a panoramic introduction of the history and relationship of the "borderland" Chicano/Mexican connection, *North of Mexico* by Carey McWilliams and *Occupied America* by Rudy Acuña.

2. Here again the work of numerous scholars in the history and sociology of Mexicans in the U.S. should be examined for a thorough discussion on the subject. A brief listing follows: *The Mexican-American People* by Grebler, More and Guzmán; *A Documentary History of Mexican-Americans* by Wayne Moquin; *Mexican-Americans in the U.S.* by John H. Burma; *Introduction to Chicano Studies* by Durán and Bernard (First and Second Editions/ Articles vary); *Chicano Manifesto* by Armando Rendón; *La otra cara de México* by Carlos Monsiváis and David Maciel.

3. The work of professor Dr. Juan Gómez-Quiñones, precursor and "father" of Chicano labor history research, is a must (many of his students have contributed significantly as well: Luis Arroyo, David Weber, Emilio Zamora, Víctor N. Cisneros, et al). *Orígenes del movimiento obrero chicano* by Juan Gómez-Quiñones and Luis Leobardo Arroyo as well as *Las ideas políticas de Ricardo Flores Magón* by Juan Gómez-Quiñones. Also look up *Race and Class in the Southwest* by Mario Barrera.

4. The discourse on myth to be found throughout the works of Mircea Eliade and Claude Levi-Straus are particularly relevant to our discussion of the role and function of myth in the development of large social formations and what they consider to be their "civilized" concensus.

5. While the antiquity of the Maya-Itzae (The "old" Maya), the Olmecs and the Toltecs is far from being irrevocably settled by anthropologists or archaeologists, do look up *Queen Moo, the Maya and Atlantis* for a linguist's approach to the question of antiquity and transatlantic contact; this book is authored by Augustus Le Plongeon.

6. *Los antiguos mexicanos* and *Aztec Thought and Culture* by Miguel
    León-Portilla are essential works for an introduction to the study of the
    theocratic militarism of the Mexicas/Aztecs.
7. Armando Rendón, in his *Chicano Manifesto*, includes a number of
    "declarations of independence" in an appendix to his text. "El Plan
    Espiritual de Aztlán" is included there and a discussion of it is found in
    chapters 1-15.
8. Rendón, Armando. Ibid. Appendix

Aztlán: A Homeland Without Boundaries

Rudolfo A. Anaya

The ceremony of naming, or of self-definition, is one of the most important acts a community performs. To particularize the group with a name is a
fundamental step of awareness in the evolution of tribes as well as nations.
The naming coalesces the history and values of the group, provides an identification necessary for its relationship to other groups or nations, and most
important, the naming ceremony restores pride and infuses renewed energy
which manifests itself in creative ways.

I have reflected often during the last fifteen years on the naming
ceremony that took place in the southwestern United States when the
Chicano community named Aztlán as its homeland in the late 1960s. This
communal event and the new consciousness and consequent creative
activity which was generated within the Chicano community during this
period marked an important historical time for our people.

The naming ceremony creates a real sense of nation, for it fuses the
spiritual and political aspirations of a group and provides a vision of the
group's role in history. These aspirations are voiced by the artists who recreate the language and symbols which are used in the naming ceremony.
The politicians of the group may describe political relationships and symbols, but it is the artist who gives deeper and long-lasting expression to a

people's sense of nation and destiny. The artists, like the priests and shamans of other tribes, express spiritual awareness and potential, and it is the "expression" of the group's history, identity, and purpose which I label the "naming ceremony." In the ancient world this expression of identity and purpose was contained in the epic; thus, we read Homer to understand the character of the Greeks.

Various circumstances create the need for national or tribal definition and unity. The group may acquire cohesion and a feeling of nationhood in times of threat, whether the threat be physical (war or exploitation) or a perceived loss of tribal unity. Group existence may also be threatened by assimilationist tendencies, which were a real threat experienced by the Chicano community in the 1960s. A time of adventure and conquest, or the alliance of political interests may also bring nations to self-definition. Most notably, times of heightened spiritual awareness of the group's relationship to the gods create this sense of purpose and destiny in the community. Usually these times are marked by a renaissance in the arts, because the artists provide the symbols and metaphors which describe the spiritual relationship.

So it was for *la raza*, the Mexican-American community of this country in the 1960s. This cultural group underwent an important change in their awareness of self and that change brought about the need for self-definition. The naming ceremony not only helped to bond the group, it created a new vision of the group's potential.

Where did the Chicanos turn for the content needed in the naming ceremony? Quite naturally the community turned to its history and found many of its heroes in the recent epoch of the Mexican Revolution. Some of us explored the deeper stratum of Mexican history, "myth" and "legend." It was in the mythology of the Aztecs that the Chicano cultural nationalists found the myth of Aztlán. How did the content of that myth become part of the new consciousness of our community? That is the question which our philosophers have tackled from various perspectives, and it has been part of my preoccupation.

The naming ceremony, or redefinition of the group, occurred within the ranks of the Indohispanos of the Southwest in the 1960s. Leaders within the Hispanic community–educators, poets, writers, artists, activists–rose up against the majority presence of Anglo-America to defend the right of the

Hispanic community to exist as a national entity within the United States. Two crucial decisions were made during this period by these guardians of the culture: one was the naming of the Chicano community and the second was the declaration of Aztlán as the ancestral homeland. "Somos Chicanos," we are Chicanos, declared the leaders of the nationalistic movement, and thus christened the Mexican-American community with a name which had archaic roots. By using this term the Chicano community consciously and publicly acknowledged its Native American heritage, and thus opened new avenues of exploration by which we could more clearly define the mestizo who is the synthesis of European and Indian ancestry.

"Aztlán is our homeland" was the second declaration, and this assertion defined the "national" status for the group. Aztlán was the place of origin of the Aztecs of Mesoamerica, the place of the seven caves recorded in their legends. The Chicanos had returned to Native American legend to find the psychological and spiritual birthplace of their ancestors.

These declarations were of momentous, historical significance. An identity and a homeland were designated once again on the northern borders of Hispanic America. The naming of Aztlán was a spontaneous act which took place throughout the Southwest, and the feat was given authenticity in a meeting that was held in Denver in 1969 to draft *El Plan Espiritual de Aztlán*. The naming of the homeland created a Chicano spiritual awareness which reverberated throughout the Southwest, and the naming ceremony was reenacted wherever Chicanos met to discuss their common destiny. I believe that no other activity of the Chicano Movement was as important as this declaration. It is now time to explore why such an event took place, and to examine closely the possibilities which were inherent in that event.

The threat to the Chicano community was most often defined by the leaders of the Chicano Movement of the 1960s as a political and economic threat, an exploitation of the Mexican-American population. Finding solutions to economic and political exploitation was of paramount importance, but within the movement were also heard the voices of cultural nationalists who insisted that the definition of the homeland, Aztlán, and the reconstitution of the old tribal history and heritage were just as vital for the Chicano community. In fact, the two issues went hand in hand, and in retrospect we can see that the leaders of the two factions of the movement should have worked closer together. The cultural nationalists created the symbol of national unity for the community; the political activists should have seen its potential and used the symbol to provide access into the mainstream political structure. The two areas of endeavor should have combined efforts, but often that was not the case.

The context of the Chicano Movement was broad, and the struggles for definition of goals and leadership within the movement still need more historical analysis. I leave that review of the broader picture of the movement to other disciplines; my focus is the naming of Aztlán. What indeed took place when the Chicanos defined their homeland? How did the momentous act serve the Chicanos then and today? Why had we returned to Aztec legend to name the homeland, and how did that return to legend create "rights (to homeland) by legend?" Would this "right by legend" be as powerful a binding force for Chicanos as "right by treaty?" We knew we could turn to the Treaty of Guadalupe Hidalgo, a historical treaty between nations, to define ourselves as Mexicans with certain rights within the borders of the United States, but that political definition had never been enough. A group defines itself not only politically but it also defines its character, that is, its soul. To define ourselves we turned to Native American legend, and there we found a meaningful part of our ethos.

My thoughts lead me to believe that the tribes of our species arrive at new stages of communal awareness as they evolve. During these historical moments of illumination, the group creates the context of its destiny in time, and so the group becomes master of its own time, or as Miguel León-Portilla, the renowned Mexican philosopher, would say, the group becomes the "señores of their own time." Did we indeed become the "señores of our own time" during the 1960s? Did we take charge of the time and create the epic literature which would define us?

Let us review the historical setting for the Indohispanos of the Southwest when we celebrated the naming ceremony. It was a time when we saw our community assaulted by poverty and oppression; the denigrating effects of racism ate away at our pride and stamina. Assimilation, on the other hand, only raised false hopes for our people, so it was a time of crisis, a time that begged for the "señores of the communal time" to once again insist on our right to our values and history. If this didn't happen our community was doomed to existence as a tourist commodity, admired for its quaint folkways but not taken seriously by the world of nations.

For too long the Indohispano community had projected only its Spanish history and heritage, for that projection suited the powers that dealt with this community as a tourist commodity and as a community that could do service work for the society in power. That identity left out the reality of our mestizo heritage. Part of the Movement's work was to revive our connection with our Indian past, and to seek a truer definition of that past. This meant reviving the history, myths, spiritual thought, legends, and symbols from Native America which were part of the Chicano's collective history. The search found the umbilical cord which led to Indian Mesoamerica and the Pueblos of the Río Grande; that is, in the act of declaring our identity and nationality, we acknowledged our Indian American parentage.

It was in Mesoamerica that we rediscovered the legend of Aztlán, a story of mythic proportions, rooted as it was in the tribal memory of the Aztecs. Why was the legend not readily available to us, say in the legends of the Pueblos of the Río Grande? Perhaps it was, but by the middle of the twentieth century we as "Hispanos" were separated from the Pueblo Indian world of our ancestors. A color consciousness which has been such a negative element in the history of the Americas affected our own people, and, falling prey to the pressure, the large mestizo population moved to identify with that which was Hispanic. Indian thought, once accessible to our ancestors, was withdrawn to the inner circle of the Pueblo, and the myths of the Americas were revealed only to those of us who delved into the symbolic meanings in the collective memory.

In 1848 there was the continued sense of separation when the United States annexed what is now the Southwest from Mexico. Separation from roots created vulnerability because our worldview was centered in community and its relationship to the earth. Even in the endeavor of education where democracy promised equality and access, we felt denied. Thus our search for Chicano roots led to Mesoamerica and Aztec legend, and there we found Aztlán; put another way, Aztlán was waiting for us.

In Aztlán, the legend said, the seven tribes emerged from the seven caves of a mountain, a descriptive and archetypal metaphor which expresses the coming into a new age of consciousness from a prior time. They left Aztlán because they had received the prophecy to migrate south in search of Tenochtitlan, there to establish their new civilization. How may we interpret this? Was this archetypal expulsion from the place of origin (Aztlán) like an expulsion from the Garden of Eden, the motif of an archetype in myth repeating itself? Or was leaving the place of origin a challenge to humanity, a challenge of evolution?

The ancestors of the Aztecs named their homeland Aztlán, and legend placed it north of Mexico. Aztlán was the place of origin, the sipapu, the Eden of those tribes. There they came to a new relationship with their god of war, Huitzilopochtli, and he promised to lead them in their migration out of Aztlán. This was spiritual yearning and evolution working hand in hand. They figuratively and literally emerged into the present world, their present time, and they became the "señores of their own time." More literal interpretations have suggested the seven tribes were seven clans who broke the covenant of Aztlán and were expelled; I choose to interpret the legend in the context of world mythology. Leaving the caves of Aztlán was paramount to being born, and with birth came suffering and the migration out of Aztlán to the land promised by their war god. Spiritual aspiration had moved them to form a new covenant with Huitzilopochtli which would sustain them during the long years of migration southward, eventually to found the civilization of Tenochtitlan, present day Mexico City.

The migration and quest of the original inhabitants of Aztlán can be viewed in the context of world mythology: like the Jews migrating from Egypt in the time of their Exodus to settle in the promised land, the Aztecs migrated south to establish the new nation of Tenochtitlan. These elements of the saga are the stuff of great drama and tragedy. In 1521 Cortes and his Spaniards were to lay siege to the Aztec kingdom and destroy it. But good drama and tragedy rise from the archetypal content of myth, and the time of myth is continuous. For me, the most interesting element in that history is the often-hidden fact that it was those Mesoamerican Indians who later journeyed up the Río Grande with the Spanish conquistadores; they were returning to their original homeland.

Chicano writers interested in the old legends which revealed our Native American past were drawn to the legend of Aztlán and its meaning. In it we saw a definition of our homeland from a Native American point of view, and we explored that area of history. What and where was the mythic Aztlán? Could the old legends of indigenous America serve a useful purpose in the Chicano Movement? Why did this legend of the indigenous homeland have such an influence on our thinking? We knew that the absorption of the

Chicano into the mainstream American culture was occurring so quickly that unless we re-established the covenants of our ancestors our culture was threatened with extinction. In fact, some suggested that the Chicano community should assimilate into the Anglo-American mainstream and forget its history and language. The concept of a bilingual, bi-cultural group within the United States was seen as a threat, and in many quarters that view is still held today. The time of crisis for our community demanded a new definition of national unity.

For me, part of the answer lies in an interpretation of human nature and its relationship to myth. Myth is our umbilical connection to the past, to the shared collective memory. After long years spent in the realm of imagination and creativity, I came to understand that many of the symbols which welled up from my subconscious were not learned, they were part of my ethos, symbols from the archetypal memory residing in the blood. Another question intrigued me: our communal relationship with time. The ancestors of the Aztecs had lived through a period of heightened awareness. Were we the Chicanos living through a similar period of time in the 1960s?

I believe the essence of the Chicano Movement was the naming ceremony I have described, and the creation of a cultural nationalist consciousness which brought together our community. This coming together in the naming ceremony duplicated the earlier time in the history of our ancestors. Yes, there was a real Aztlán, but there was also the spiritual Aztlán, the place of the covenant with the gods, the psychological center of our Indian history. During the period of awareness, the collective soul of the group renewed itself through myth; it is what the tribes of humankind have done throughout history.

The communal activity was crucial to the scenario, for myth is a communal response to spiritual crisis. The new consciousness created in the 1960s was a psychological centering, and the possibility of being in touch with our real history was available to each individual. We had become the "señores and the señoras of our own time" in the ceremony of naming, and it is important to stress the role of the Chicana, for the women of our community played a pivotal role in creating the Movement. One only has to look at the literature of the period to read the celebration of Aztlán which we created.

We took a new look at the history of the Indohispano community in the

Southwest, a group whose traditions dated back to the sixteenth century and the entry of the Hispanos and Mexicanos into the pueblos of the Río Grande. A unique Indohispano culture had evolved along the northern Río Grande, a product of the process of synthesis which was already at work in Mexico as the Old World and the New World met and merged. The most interesting development of that process was the evolution of the "New World person," the person in touch with the mythology of the Americas which I have explored in my writing.

The same synthesis would not take place when the Anglo-American came to the Southwest in the mid-nineteenth century. The Hispano and Anglo worlds remained apart, meeting to conduct business in an ethnic mosaic, but seldom creating a personal commingling. The genetic pools have not mixed in a significant way, and only in a small way is it occurring in contemporary times. Still, the issue of ethnicity is not static and it is one we need to face creatively.

The established Indohispano culture was based in the villages, but by the 1960s the community was largely an urban group, and so to reconstitute our history during this time of crisis some returned to the villages to look for origins. Another meaningful return was into the history of the Americas where we examined our Indian roots, the soul of the Americas. There we found not only indigenous historical time, but mythical time which is continuous; that discovery was to have a tremendous impact on the healing of our social fabric. In Mesoamerica we encountered the pre-Columbian thought of Mexico. That return to the legends and myths of the New World led the Chicano to Aztlán. In the process of returning to our myths and legends we were not short-sighted idealists that thought the oppression our community suffered would disappear. We knew better, but our search was spiritual in nature, and our community desperately needed the reaffirmation. We had faith that by bringing to light our history, even the esoteric history of myth and legend, we could bring to fruition a cultural renaissance and create a new time of hermandad. That new era of brotherhood would not only unify us, it would unleash the creative potential of the Chicano community.

In the 1960s the same spiritual yearnings and crisis that had concerned the original inhabitants of Aztlán now concerned the Chicanos. A cycle of Chicano history was repeating itself. Our poets and writers became the leaders of the Chicano Movement, and as they brought to focus the aspirations of the people they took upon themselves a role common to our culture, the role of older, wiser leaders or ancianos, the role of those señores and señoras who dare to be aware of the burden of time and act to alleviate the burden for the communal good of the people. Needless to say, those same leaders would be criticized when the ambitious goals of the Movement were not fully realized.

A new quesiton arose: Would the promise of continuity and self-actualization inherent in our myths and legends bring with it the fruition of potential and freedom? Could we save our history and community from obliteration within the confines of Anglo-America by reincorporating the old legends into our worldview? Some said no. Myth was ephemeral, it had no substance, it distorted reality. What the Chicanos needed was direct political mobilization, perhaps revolution. They did not need to arm themselves with ancient stories.

Those of us who saw the potential of myth as truth, or myth as self-knowledge, argued that it was indigenous America that held the tap root of our history; its mythology was the mirror by which to know ourselves. Chicanos had to experience a new awareness of self, just as our Native American ancestors had come to that new plane of consciousness eight centuries before in Aztlán, and coming to this knowledge of our historical continuity was a means toward community action.

Aztlán is real because myth is real, we argued. Aztlán was potential because it was a place of prophecy. Migrating groups of Asians, in the process of becoming indigenous Americans, had settled in Aztlán. There they evolved new levels of spiritual orientation to cosmos, earth, and community. Isn't this the process of spiritual and psychological evolution? Isn't this how our human potential evolves? So it happened to these tribes of Native Americans. Somewhere in the deserts and mountains of what we now call the Southwest, they created a covenant with their gods and from there they moved south to Mexico to complete the prophecy.

Of course they did not arrive at full potential, no one ever does. They were still heir to human failure, but we know their later artistic achievements were of a grand scale. Even their warring society would incorporate the religion of peace of Quetzalcóatl. All of Mesoameric and the tributaries as far north as Chaco and Mesa Verde were, I suspect, renewed during that era.

A new age of spiritual illumination had come to the Americas, and the journey from Aztlán to Mexico was part of that tremendous change. From the Pueblos of the Río Grande to Mesoamerica and neighboring tribes, the people of the Americas were evolving into new realms of consciousness.

The need for a homeland is inherent in the collective memory of any group, it is a covenant with the tribal gods. The spiritual yearning for homeland is encompassing, but because the geography of the earth is limited, homelands rub against each other and create friction. We have not yet moved to a new consciousness where the Earth truly becomes the homeland of everyone. Perhaps that is our next step in evolution, and perhaps there are already signs that this is happening. Do we as heirs and inhabitants of Aztlán dare to take this next step and consider our homeland without boundaries? Do we dare to reach out and encompass the true spiritual relationship inherent in homeland with every other group who dreams of homeland?

The Indohispano of the Southwest was influenced by the spirituality of the pueblos of the Río Grande, even though the Catholic faith was imposed on the indigenous faith. There were elements of brutality in the Spanish conquest, this is documented, but the synthesis which was taking place in Mexico between the Old World and the New World was accelerated in Aztlán after the 1680 Pueblo Revolt. The Indohispano religious sensibility was influenced by the Pueblos, and so respect for the earth became an important ingredient in the unique worldview being formed in Aztlán. The recognition of the Earth as mother (la sagrada tierra) permeated the spiritual life of the Hispanic villages, and the process of synthesis fused Spanish Catholicism with Native American thought. The clearest symbol of this process of syncretism was the merging of the Virgin Mary with the Indian Goddess (Tonantzin) to give form to the brown madonna of Mexico, La Virgen de Guadalupe. Truly, an original blend of American spirituality was evolving.

What did all this mean to the real world of politics which the Chicano struggled to enter and influence in the 1960s? Unfortunately, the historical assessment made thus far weighs heavily on a materialistic interpretation. I am convinced that a history of that era and of our culture must take both the sacred and the profane into account. To understand our culture only through a materialistic account will not provide a true picture of the nature of our community. For me, the Chicano Movement succeeded because it changed part of our social and political role within the society, but also because it created a cultural renaissance in the Chicano community. The release of creative energy in which the artists defined self and community was the hallmark of the Movement. The spiritual energy which once filled the consciousness of the original inhabitants of Aztlán and propelled them south to Mexico to fulfill their destiny led us to proclaim our existence and found our nation.

A spirit of liberation swept over our people, releasing a chain reaction of new energy, initiative and originality. The Movement gave birth to the term Chicano, the bold new image born of Hispanic and Indian synthesis. To some extent that image penetrated the Anglo-American consciousness, and to some degree it moved unto a world stage. But the image was really for our community, the naming was to renew identity and awareness of our history. The changes wrought in the psyche of the Hispanos of the Southwest by the use of the word Chicano were enormous. True, some in our community resisted the naming and to this day do not identify with Chicano, but one cannot deny the positive benefits of reinvigorated pride, especially in artistic creativity, which swept across the land.

The true guardians of Aztlán have been the Río Grande Pueblo people, and the knowledge and love for their homeland has kept their spiritual thought alive in the face of overwhelming odds. They have kept themselves centered with the earth, and that has provided their communities a spiritual and psychological center. The Chicano, the new *raza* of the Americas, is heir to the same earth and a legacy of spiritual thought which can help center the individual. In a world so in need of ecological and spiritual awareness which would allow us to save the earth and practice democratic principles of love and sharing, these ties to the earth and the care we must give to this area we call Aztlán still provide hope for our community. We have within us the inner resources to become new guardians of the earth and of peace.

We have seen the blossoming of this potential in our generation. Chicano art, music and literature have gained a foothold and are shaping new perceptions. Within the arts lie reflections of our values, not only the cultural trappings of the day to day world, but the old values which spring from our mythologies. Respect for the earth of Aztlán is one of these values, and if we are truly living in an era of a new consciousness, we must reach further into our human potential and consider Aztlán a homeland without boundaries.

This is a most difficult proposal, the idea that we can move beyond our ethnocentric boundaries, that we can envision the limitations of ethnicity even as we extol our self pride. The argument of survival in our modern world seems to urge us towards the common center of our humanity. When we established our rights to the homeland of Aztlán, we understood that that right belongs to every group or nation, and we understood how we share in all the homelands of world mythology. The children of Aztlán are citizens of the world. We must move beyond the limitations of ethnicity to create a world without borders. Each community rising to its new level of awareness creates respect for self and for others, and we are in need of this awareness before we destroy the Earth and each other.

An idealistic, utopian thought? Perhaps, but one we need to dare to consider. Those who deal in competition and the selfishness of the modern nation-state are in control, and they have falsely named competition and material gain as the true values of the world. Perhaps it's time to think of unity. Aztlán can become the nation that mediates between Anglo-America and Latin America. We can be the leaders who propose human answers to the human problems of the Americas. The real problem of border regions when addressed from a world perspective should be dealt with in human terms, in terms of families and neighbors, not terms of profit or ideology. Unity and human potential should guide us, not market values and the gross national product. This, after all, is the challenge of our generation, to create a consciousness which fosters the flowering of the human spirit, not its exploitation. We need healing in our world community; it can start here.

This is the legacy of Aztlán: it is a place where seven tribes of humankind came to a new awareness of their potential, a new sensitivity in their relationship to earth and cosmos. Here those first inhabitants of Aztlán took their destiny into their own hands, they were born into a new prophecy, and they moved to complete it. Can we do less?

That illumination and leap of faith for those people did not make for perfection. History moves us toward perfection through small epiphanies. The tribes moved out of Aztlán as Adam and Eve moved out of Eden, to challenge the future and to fulfill their potential. Our nature moves us forward, groping for illumination, yearning for a truer knowledge of our spiritual and human relationships. We know within that we can create a more fulfilling and harmonious future. For me, this is the promise of Aztlán.

Contributors

Luis Leal was born in Mexico and received his education in the United States (B.S. Northwestern University; M.A. and Ph.D. University of Chicago). He has taught at the University of Mississippi, Emory University, and the University of Illinois at Champaign-Urbana. He retired from Illinois as a Professor Emeritus in 1976 and accepted a Visiting Professorship at the University of California, Santa Barbara, where he now teaches in the Department of Chicano Studies. He has published several books, among them *Mariano Azuela, vida y obra* (1961), *Breve historia de la literatura hispanoamericana* (1971), *A Decade of Chicano Literature* (edited in cooperation with members of UCSB Chicano faculty and staff), *Juan Rulfo* (1983), *Aztlán y México* (1985). *Luis Leal: A Bibliography with Interpretative and Critical Essays* was published in 1988 by the Chicano Studies Library, University of California, Berkeley. His reputation is world renown in the areas of the Spanish American short story, Mexican literature in general, Chicano literary history, and in the area of cultural studies from Latin America.

Michael Pina studied at the University of California at Santa Barbara in the department of Religious Studies. He has an abiding interest in Mesoamerican cultural ways and religious thought. His interest in Aztlán grew out of his contact with this myth in Chicano literature, art, and political thought. His article seeks to penetrate the romantic veneer which has surrounded Aztlán and allow people to view the myth with respect to broader "historical," cultural, and theoretical contexts. He is currently studying law at Santa Clara University.

John R. Chávez, Associate Professor of History at Southern Methodist University, received his Ph.D. from the University of Michigan and did his undergraduate work at California State University, Los Angeles. Before joining the faculty at SMU, he taught at several other institutions, including Cal State—Long Beach, Michigan, and Texas A&M. His major research interest is the symbolism of land, space in general, and its relationship to Mexican-American identity. He is currently working on a history of the East Los Angeles Community Union. The following is a list of his publications: Book: *The Lost Land: The Chicano Image of the Southwest*. Albuquerque: University of New Mexico Press, 1984. Articles: "Aztlán, Cíbola, and Frontier New Spain." *Campo Libre* 1 (Summer 1981): 193-211. "The Image of the Southwest in the Chicano Novel, 1970-1979." *Bilingual Review*, forthcoming. Book chapter: "John Francisco Rechy." In *Chicano Literature: A Reference Guide*, pp. 323-32. Edited by Julio A. Martínez and Francisco A. Lomelí. Westport, Conn.: Greenwood Press, 1985.

Cosme M. Zaragoza, born in Irapuato, Guanajuato, Mexico, earned a degree in law from the Universidad de Guanajuato, Mexico. He later received a master's degree in Latin American Literature and a Ph.D. in Spanish and Bilingual Education from the University of Arizona, where he taught until 1984. He also held an appointment at Pima Community College at Tucson, Arizona. He has also been named to the editorial board of *Saguaro* (1984-85), published by the Mexican American Studies and Research Center, University of Arizona. He is now associate professor of Foreign Languages and Literature at the California State University, Fresno, President of the Consortium of Universities Mexico-United States, and former director of the California State University Summer Study in Guanajuato, Mexico. He has presented numerous papers and published several articles on Chicano Literature, including "Historia del pueblo de origen mexicano y movimiento chicano," *Inventario*, 66 (1987). "La función del prólogo en la novela chicana." *Inventario*, 90 (1987).

Guillermo Lux, a native New Mexican, took his undergraduate degree from the University of New Mexico where he graduated with honors. His graduate degrees were in political science, history, and literature at Stanford University and the University of Southern California, where he studied under Professor Manuel Servin. He has had numerous research grants and fellowships. Since 1970, he has been a professor of Southwestern and Latin American History at New Mexico Highlands University. He has published over thirty-five articles and reports. Recent chapters on the Southwest in books are: "Return to Aztlán: The Chicano Rediscovers His Indian Past," (co-authored with Maurilio Vigil), in *As We See Ourselves*; "Ancient Aspirations: A Mexican-American View of Land Reform," in *Land Reform, American Style*. His books include *Politics and Education in Hispanic New Mexico*; *Historical Dictionary of the British Caribbean*. His forthcoming books are: *Paso Por Aqui; The Hispanic Experience in New Mexico Since 1846* and *Politics and Education in New Mexico*.

Maurilio E. Vigil, a professor of political science at New Mexico Highlands University was born in Las Vegas, New Mexico. He received his B.A. (1964) and M.A. (1966) in political science from New Mexico Highlands University and his Ph.D. (1974) in political science from the University of New Mexico. He is a former Danforth Associate and has served as an evaluation panelist for the National Science Foundation Graduate Fellowship and Minority Graduate Fellowship programs. He is a member of Phi Kappa Phi (National Honorary), Pi Gamma Mu (National Social Science Honorary), the Western Political Science Association and the Western Social Science Association. He is the author of several books and numerous articles on American Hispanic politics, Mexican-American history and politics and New Mexico history and politics. His books include *Hispanics in American Politics: The Search for Political Power* (1987). *The Hispanics of New Mexico: Essays on History and Culture* (1986). *Chicano Politics: A Theoretical and Behavioral Analysis of Chicanos in American Politics* (1977). He has contributed chapters in the following books: *New Mexico Government* (University of New Mexico Press, 1982), *The Chicanos As We See Ourselves* (University of Arizona Press, 1979), and *Latinos in the Political System* (Notre Dame University Press, 1988).

Genaro M. Padilla was born in Albuquerque, Nuevo México—the Heart of Aztlán. He completed the Ph.D. at the University of Washington and teaches in the English department at the University of California, Berkeley. He has edited *The Stories of Fray Angélico Chávez* (U.N.M. Press, 1987), and is currently completing a book on the formation of Chicano autobiography. Among his publications on autobiography are "Self as Cultural Metaphor in Acosta's The Autobiography of a Brown Buffalo,"

The Journal of General Education (Winter 1984); "The Recovery of 19th Century Chicano Autobiography," *American Quarterly* (Fall 1988), "'Yo sola aprendí': Contra-Patriarchal Containment in Women's 19th Century Narrative" *Americas* (Fall-Winter 1988); "Imprisoned Narrative, or Lies, Secrets, and Silence in New Mexico Women's Autobiography" forthcoming in *Chicano Literary Criticism: New Essays Cultural Studies and Ideology* (José Saldívar and Hector Calderón, eds. Duke University Press.) And he has written occasional essays on "The Anti-Romantic City in Chicano Fiction," (*Puerto del Sol* 1987), "The Catholic Church and Chicano Literature," forthcoming in *Catholic Writers in the United States*, Daniel Tynan ed. Greenwood Press.

J. Jorge Klor de Alva, professor of anthropology at Princeton University, was born in Mexico City and studied at the University of California at Berkeley earning degrees in philosophy and law. His Ph.D. is in anthropology and history from the University of California at Santa Cruz, where he taught since 1975. He has also held appointments at San Jose State University, serving as chair of the Mexican American Graduate Studies Department, and was associate professor of anthropology and Latin American studies at the State University of New York at Albany, where he was the director of the Institute for Mesoamerican Studies. A former Fulbright scholar and 1987-88 John Simon Guggenheim Fellow, he is the author or editor of numerous articles and several books on Mexican, Mesoamerican, or Hispanic American ethnography, sociocultural history, and ethnohistory, including *The Work of Bernardino de Sahagún: Pioneer Ethnographer of Sixteenth-Century Aztec Mexico* (Texas, 1988), *Sociocultural and Service Issues in Working With Hispanic American Clients* (Rockefeller, 1985), "Chicana History and Historical Significance: Some Theoretical Considerations" (*Between Borders: Essays on Mexicana/ Chicana History* [Floricanto, 1989]), "Telling Hispanics Apart: Latino Sociocultural Diversity in the United States" (*The Hispanic Experience in the United States* [Praeger, 1988]), and "Language, Politics, and Translation: Colonial Discourse and Classical Nahuatl in New Spain" (*The Art of Translation: Voices from the Field* [Northeastern, 1989]). His forthcoming publications include an edition (with Miguel León-Portilla) of *Introduction to Nahua Culture: The Aztec Image of Self and Society* (Utah, 1990), *The*

Confession of the Other: Aztec Sins and the Birth of Anthropology, and *Devils in Disguise: Religious Discourse in the Conquest of Mexico*.

Ramón A. Gutiérrez is currently a Fellow at the Center for Advanced Study in the Behavioral Sciences in Stanford, California, and an Associate Professor of Latin American and Chicano History at the University of California, San Diego. He is the author of *When Padre Jesús Came, the Corn Mothers Went Away: Marriage, Sexuality and Power in New Mexico, 1500-1846* (Stanford University Press, forthcoming), and numerous articles on the history of the Southwest. He is currently undertaking research on New Mexico's genízaro population, on Indian slavery, and on the history of confession in colonial Latin America. Gutiérrez was born and raised in Albuquerque, where he attended St. Pius X High School and the University of New Mexico. He earned his doctoral degree in history from the University of Wisconsin, Madison in 1980.

Gloria E. Anzaldúa is a Chicana *tejana* lesbian-feminist poet and fiction writer living in Santa Cruz. She is co-editor of *This Bridge Called My Back: Writings by Radical Women of Color*, winner of the Before Columbus Foundation American Book Award. Her book *Borderlands/La Frontera: The New Mestiza*, (Spinsters/Aunt Lute July, 1987) was picked as one of the 38 Best Books of 1987 by the Library Journal. Gloria has taught Chicano Studies, Feminist Studies, and Creative Writing at the University of Texas, San Francisco State University, Vermont College of Norwich University, University of California at Santa Cruz and has conducted writing workshops around the country. She has been a contributing editor of *Sinister Wisdom* since 1984. Presently, Gloria is compiling and editing *Haciendo Caras/Making Faces, Making Soul: Constructing Colored Selves, A Reader of Creative and Critical Perspectives* (San Francisco: Spinsters/Aunt Lute, 1990) and *Entreguerras, Entremundos/Civil Wars Among the Worlds*, a book of autobiographical and fictitious narratives (also to be published by Spinsters/Aunt Lute, 1990).

Sergio D. Elizondo was born in El Fuerte, Sinaloa, México. He received his early education in his native country and a BA in social sciences from Findlay College in Ohio. His MA and PhD. in Spanish and French are from the University of North Carolina at Chapel Hill. He has held postdoctoral research fellowships in the Archivo de Indias in Spain and in anthropology in the Colegio de México, and he was awarded a National Endowment for the Arts Fellowship in 1981. In 1983 he established a Chicano studies collection in the University of Warsaw, Poland; he has consulted with the Czech and Slovakian Academies of Literary Sciences. Active in Chicano cultural affairs since 1957, he has lectured widely in this country, Europe, Mexico and Latin America. His work has appeared in *La palabra y el hombre, Plural, El cuento, El grito, La Palabra* and the *Revista Chicano-Riqueña*. His books include *Perros y antiperros* (poetry), *Libro para batos* (poetry), *Rosa, la flauta* (stories) and *Muerte en una estrella* (novel). He has taught at Western Washington University, San Bernardino State University and the University of Texas at Austin. He is presently professor of Spanish at New Mexico State University in Las Cruces, New Mexico.

Alurista is one of the most well known poets of the Chicano Movement. He has published six collections of poetry: *floricanto en aztlán, nationchild plumaroja, timespace huarcan, aunque, spik in glyph?* and *return*. He has edited various volumes as well as the journal *Maize*. He has read from his work at universities and communities throughout the United States as well as in Mexico, Germany, Holland and France. Alurista is currently an associate professor of Spanish at California Polytechnic University in San Luis, Obispo and at the University of California in Santa Barbara. He was born in Mexico City in 1947 and received his Ph.D. in Spanish literature from the University of San Diego in 1982. Alurista was involved with the Chicano Movement since its inception. He helped organize the first national Chicano Moratorium Against the Vietnam War, and he was a founding member of MECHA in San Diego. He helped establish the first Chicano Studies program in the country at San Diego State University. His work continues to be seminal in the evolution of Chicano literature. He was the author of *El Plan Espiritual de Aztlán*, and thus he has played a pivotal role in reintroducing the myth and reality of Aztlán to contemporary Chicano consciousness.

Francisco A. Lomelí, born in the state of Zacatecas, México, grew up in California and studied at San Diego State, Universidad de Concepción

(Concepción, Chile), Universidad Nacional de Cuyo (Mendoza, Argentina), and the University of New Mexico where he received his Ph.D. in 1978 in Romance Languages. He has held a position at the University of California at Santa Barbara in the Spanish & Portuguese and Chicano Studies Departments. His fields of study cover both Chicano and Latin American literatures, particularly in the area of fiction. He is a former Fulbright scholar in Argentina (1971-72), a Ford Foundation fellow in New Mexico (1986-87) and a Rockefeller Foundation fellow also in New Mexico (1989-90). He has served as editor of various journals such as *De Colores, Confluencia, Discurso Literario* and has published articles on a wide spectrum of subjects dealing with the border, feminist writings, literary generations and trends, varied thematics and specialized treatments on individual authors. One of his main areas of interest is literary history of New Mexico with such studies as "Eusebio Chacón: An Early Pioneer of the New Mexican Novel." His principal contributions have recently been in the area of reference works such as *Chicano Literature: A Reference Guide* (1985, with J. Martínez) and *Dictionary of Literary Biography* (1989, with C. Shirley).

Rudolfo A. Anaya is the author of *Bless Me Ultima, Heart of Aztlán* and *Tortuga*, a New Mexican trilogy. Other titles are: *The Silence of the Llano, Cuentos/Tales of the Hispanic Southwest, A Chicano in China, The Legend of La Llorona* and *Lord of the Dawn*. He was born in New Mexico and educated in the Santa Rosa and Albuquerque Public Schools. He teaches at the University of New Mexico. For Academia he has edited *Voces/An Anthology of Nuevo Mexicano Writers* and the Aztlán essays with Francisco Lomelí.